Management of
Chronic Schizophrenia

Management of Chronic Schizophrenia

CAROL L. M. CATON, Ph.D.

New York   Oxford
OXFORD UNIVERSITY PRESS
1984

Copyright © 1984 by Oxford University Press, Inc.

Library of Congress Cataloging in Publication Data

Caton, Carol.
    Management of chronic schizophrenia.

    Bibliography: p.
    Includes index.
    1. Chronically ill—Rehabilitation. 2. Mentally
ill—Rehabilitation. 3. Schizophrenics—Rehabilitation.
I. Title. [DNLM: 1. Mental disorders—Therapy. 2. Com-
munity psychiatry. 3. Chronic disease—Therapy. WM 30.6
C366M]
RC480.53.C38 1984   362.2   83-8347
ISBN 0-19-503346-9

Printing (last digit): 9 8 7 6 5 4 3 2 1

Printed in the United States of America

Foreword

Over the past two decades there has been a rising public outcry, particularly in larger American cities, over the daily confrontation with odd, disheveled and poorly dressed men and women who are recognized as the "deinstitutionalized" mentally ill. For about a century before middle- and upper-class America could comfortably ignore the unfortunate psychotics, they were nicely and often permanently committed through legal processing to large and distantly removed state, county, or federal institutions for the mentally ill. This neat social arrangement, made originally with good intentions both to provide humane care and to confine the sometimes violent and often idiosyncratic patients, began to break down in the face of the rapid medical, psychiatric, and technological advances of recent years and the intense revival of interest in civil rights in American life.

Community exposure of the seriously mentally ill in our time commenced in England shortly after World War I when a few courageous psychiatric superintendents of mental hospitals dared to open the doors of their institutions and allow many of their patients freedom of movement. They did so in the conviction that the vast majority of those confined therein were socially harmless and deserved the freedom of movement accorded others.

Then psychiatrists began to prescribe the newly discovered neuroleptic drugs which dramatically modified the grosser symptoms of psychotic behavior. Most new patient stays in the old institutions were drastically reduced by such medication and many chronic patients improved so much in their behavior that they were released as well. Early diagnosis and treatment in the community to prevent hospitalization, as well as aftercare services outside of mental hospitals, initiated the community mental health center drive. Hypotheses that psychopharmacology "cured" and that institutional care produced social incompetence were used then by federal and state planners to push for restriction of admission and more rapid discharge from the hospital. A myth appealing to state budget directors and legislators that community care was both better and cheaper and could be supported by federal funds generated another force toward deinstitutionalization. As had occurred many times since revolutionary days, the civil rights of the confined mentally ill and retarded persons became a matter of public concern. Legal assaults challenged bureaucratic restrictions of their liberties; legislators whittled away at statutes revising commitment procedures and much new legislation spelled out the rights of the mentally ill regarding education, housing, medical and psychiatric care, and special programming.

Community care arose as a slogan and deinstitutionalization moved forward in a rush borne by these forces. But with it came the obvious and ugly side. Clinical truths re-emerged. Lack of social skills and idiosyncratic behavior often are the product of the psychotic illness and not of submergence within institutional life. Nor are social skills magically acquired by treatment with neuroleptics, discharge into the larger society, modified legislation, invocation of civil rights, or management procedures devised by court decisions.

Carol Caton and her colleagues have brought together the written work of professionals who are attempting to correct the social deficiencies of psychotically mentally ill people to prepare them for independent living in the community or to help them live in sheltered groupings outside the large state institutions. Professor Caton particularly has been involved in assessing the effectiveness of various community care projects in New York City, working first within the academic framework of the Division of Community Psychiatry of the Departments of Psychiatry and Public Health of Columbia University, College of Physicians and Surgeons, and later with the Biometrics Laboratory and other related research services of the New York State Psychiatric Institute and the New York State Office of Mental Health. From her own investigations, she has evolved a broad perspective of the strengths and weaknesses of efforts to assist the seriously mentally ill to life outside protected institutional environments. Presented in this book is a timely and detailed description of recent and ongoing experiences, trials, and tests of community treatment of psychotic patients. The problems of such care are extraordinarily complex and range across a multitude of other social systems— general health, security, social services, transportation, and legal. The effects of deinstitutionalization upon these systems were not foreseen by the planners and administrators, yet all are strained by the vast shift which has taken place in care of the seriously mentally ill.

Many questions can be raised about the ongoing effort to carry out the various programs to assist mentally ill persons in the community. Which should be supported by administrators and under what organizational structure? Do the programs offer improvement in subjective life for those who come under treatment? What measures are to be taken to determine and firmly establish the effective therapeutic measures taking them beyond limited demonstration projects? Undoubtedly, social scientists, psychiatrists, educators, and administrators will find much in this book of interest and value with regard to these and other pressing questions.

LAWRENCE C. KOLB, M.D.

Preface

Deinstitutionalization has broadened the life options of chronic schizophrenics, many of whom would have been candidates for long-term institutional care in previous years. The creative efforts of clinicians and researchers to help these very sick people to live in the community have markedly advanced the "state of the art" in treatment and management of this disorder.

The idea for this book grew out of a series of studies of chronic schizophrenic patients initiated in the late 1970's in connection with New York State's Community Support System program. Findings from these investigations highlighting the experiences of patients in a variety of types of programs pointed to a need to synthesize the existing work on the care and treatment of chronic schizophrenia.

This book brings together the clinical research of the deinstitutionalization era bearing on diagnosis, treatment assessment, and the prescription of psychopharmacologic and psychosocial treatments. Principles of hospital treatment and community-based aftercare are described. Innovations in the treatment of families of schizophrenic patients and new therapies directed at improving a patient's social and coping skills are presented as attempts to maintain family and social ties and involvement in the life of society-at-large. Also discussed are housing and community residence programs and new modes of delivering psychiatric outpatient services that address a patient's needs for life support services and access to available treatments. Current information on the best uses of both institutional and community-based care is presented as a guide for mental health students and practitioners as well as policy makers, administrators and program planners.

New York   C.L.M.C.
June 1983

Contents

Management of
Chronic Schizophrenia

1. Mental Institutions and the Community: A Historical Perspective

Psychiatric professionals are taught to respect history early in their training. Just as history is important in individual patient care, a knowledge of the history of a social policy is crucial to an understanding of its present form. The issue of where the mentally ill should live and receive treatment has a past that sheds light on the current mental health policy of deinstitutionalization.

This policy, which de-emphasizes long-term treatment in public mental institutions in favor of management in a community setting (Bachrach 1976), was based on the hope that patients would suffer less disability and lead more meaningful lives outside the mental asylum. In the fifteen years since its inception, the successes and failures of deinstitutionalization have been revealed. More patients have spent a greater portion of their lives in the community, with the opportunity to struggle, like everyone else, for productivity and self-sufficiency. Some have taken up the challenge and have blended into the mainstream of society, but most tread lightly at its borders. The policy's shortcomings are reflected in those whose lives have not been improved by it. The homeless mentally ill who wander the streets of major cities recall the "Toms-o-Bedlam"[1,2] of Shakespeare's time and bring home the realization that modern industrial society has not yet fulfilled its obligations to helpless and dependent persons. Avoidance of long-term institutional care has neither done away with chronicity nor procured humane and appropriate care for the mentally ill to the satisfaction of patients, mental health professionals, and the community at large. Moreover, the need for mental hospitals has not been eliminated.

The proposal that a change in the locus of care would solve problems in dealing with the mentally ill is not new. Advocates of the large-scale expansion of mental institutions, a U.S. reform movement of the mid-nineteenth century, sought to end the deplorable treatment of the mentally ill living in the community by moving them to a new location. Although mental hospitals have provided a refuge for some patients disabled by serious mental disorder, the failures of institutionalization set the stage for deinstitutionalization. The poor care in many public mental hospitals was a stimulus to sending the mentally ill back to the community.

Returning the mentally ill to the community was not a radical proposal. Through the ages, those suffering from maladies of the mind have lived in the community. Mental institutions have existed in Western cultures for over 600 years, but at no time have they been used to permanently cloister the mentally ill from the larger society. The discharged patient has been in the community since institutions were founded. The asylum movement encountered bureaucratic and operational problems, which meant that many mentally ill persons remained in the community even though they qualified for admission to the new institutions. Since the American Revolution, the mentally ill in this country have been dispersed in mental asylums, in quasi-institutional community settings, and in kin living arrangements. The proportions in each setting have varied depending on alternatives available at different times.

Institutional and community-based care for the mentally ill have coexisted for nearly a century. Modern methods of community treatment paralleled the rise of institutionalization. The history of the relationship of the U.S. public mental institution to the community is a prologue to a critical appraisal of the locus of care as a factor in the treatment of mental illness.

The Mentally Ill Before the Establishment of Asylums

The manner of dealing with the mentally ill in the United States has been influenced by the traditions and practices of Europe. Families have always been charged with the first line of responsibility for caring for mentally ill kin (Deutsch 1937, Caplan 1969,

Grob 1973, Dain 1976). In colonial America, patients with affluent and supportive families or friends were cared for by them in their homes. If the caretaker had a medical view of the patient's affliction, available remedies or panaceas were applied by colonial doctors. Even with treatment, however, management problems existed. The mentally ill were without hesitation locked up or chained by family members in cellars, strong rooms, or outhouses if they were difficult to handle. Occasionally, the mild-mannered insane were hidden from public view in attics or other hideaways when it was thought they would disgrace their families (Deutsch 1937, p. 40).

The mentally ill without family support were permitted to wander freely as long as they were not violent or a public nuisance. Usually, the homeless wanderers were paupers. At best they were viewed with indifference, and at worst they were taunted and brutalized. The nonviolent mentally ill received the same treatment as the poor.

The mentally ill who committed crimes were treated like other criminals and held accountable for their crimes. Most often, the poor mentally ill who were violent were confined to jails, in the company of common criminals. In communities without jails, the whipping post and the gallows were used as substitutes.

The Beginnings of Public Support

A tendency for public authorities to assume limited responsibility for the mentally ill who caused public disturbances developed in medieval Europe. Public monies were given to families or other concerned persons to provide care for the mentally ill. The Elizabethan Poor Law Act of 1601, the model for poor relief in the American colonies, formalized this practice by placing support of the dependent mentally ill in the hands of the local community (Deutsch 1937, Grob 1973).

Whenever possible, communities avoided support of the poor by making it difficult for beggars, vagabonds, and other non-working persons to settle within their boundaries. The financial status of strangers was closely checked before they were allowed to settle in a community. A term of "quiet and undisturbed" residence in a locality, lasting for from three to twelve months, was required for legal residence, which carried with it the town's obligation for support in the event of need.

The reluctance of communities to welcome the poor was manifest when they were "warned out" from the town's borders. If a person dared to return to a locality after such an experience, he or she was frequently whipped before being driven out a second time. The dependent mentally ill were frequently spirited out of town in the dead of night and placed in or near a neighboring town in the hope that another community would assume responsibility for their care. As a consequence, a cadre of homeless wanderers emerged among the pauper lunatics in the American colonies (Deutsch 1937, pp. 39–54).

When public support was provided, it rarely included funds for medical treatment. However, Deutsch (1937, p. 48) cites a Massachusetts town that allowed a disturbed woman to stay with a series of physicians for more than a decade in the hope that she might be cured and thus be able to care for herself.

In most cases, however, families were the recipients of public monies for the care of their mentally ill relatives. It was not unusual for towns to bear the expense of boarding the dependent insane with parents, siblings, or spouses. In the late colonial era, laws were passed making it mandatory, under penalty of fine, for relatives within a certain degree of consanguinity to provide for mentally ill kin.

The Rise of Institutionalization

When towns were small, public support for the mentally ill and for other dependent persons was handled on an individual basis, the decision-making body being the town meeting. With the growth and concentration of populations in towns and cities, this mechanism was no longer workable, and the old methods were gradually replaced by institutional mechanisms.

Although hospitals for the mentally ill were well established in Europe more than a century before Columbus's journey, mental institutions were not created in the United States until the late eighteenth century. They were preceded by houses of correction, workhouses, and almshouses, which sprang up in the larger towns in the period from 1725 to 1750. One of the first was the

"Poor-House, Work-House, and House of Correction of New York City," established in 1736. Paupers and petty offenders were treated alike in the workhouse, and thus it served as a combination poorhouse and jail. The mildly to moderately mentally disturbed were put to work side by side with common paupers and criminals picking oakum, spinning wool and flax, knitting, and sewing. An equivalent of the workhouse in rural districts was the custom, which gradually evolved toward the end of the colonial era, of bidding for the insane at the auction block. The able-bodied insane, along with other dependent persons, were put to work on farms and given in return food, clothing, and shelter (Deutsch 1937, Ch. 5).

The disruptive behavior of the mentally ill, distracting to others in the workhouse, eventually led to their placement in almshouses, where they were kept separated from the common poor. Eighteenth-century almshouses were the precursors of hospitals specifically for the mentally ill.

Hospital treatment of the mentally ill in the United States accompanied the rise of psychiatry as a medical specialty. Hospitalization itself was not a medical advance but a necessary condition for the application of new approaches to treatment. The first U.S. hospital to provide care for the insane was the Pennsylvania Hospital, a general hospital founded in 1756, which had a psychiatric wing. Primitive treatments, such as purgatives and venesection, were applied, and physical control was common. Initially, patients were chained by the waist or ankle to the wall of a cell located in a below-ground level of the hospital. "Cell-keepers," or hospital attendants, guarded the insane to prevent escape, enforced strict rules, and used straitjackets and whippings as means of control.

Benjamin Rush, a physician connected with the Pennsylvania Hospital, and other early psychiatrists, such as Phillippe Pinel of France (Bockoven 1963, Grob 1973), were leaders in humanizing the care of the mentally ill. Key elements in "moral treatment" included the notion that hospitalization was beneficial and preferable to keeping the patient in his or her home environment. Patients had no visitors, were subject to a strict hospital routine, and were not permitted to return home until well recovered (Beck 1811, Rush 1962).

Other early private hospitals, such as New York City's Bloomingdale Asylum (1821) and Boston's McLean Asylum (1818), developed as psychiatric divisions of general hospitals. The first public hospital exclusively for the mentally ill was established in Williamsburg, Virginia, in 1773. Nine states sponsored mental hospitals during the early 1800's. Although hospital treatment represented a significant advance in the care of the mentally ill, private hospitals were able to accommodate only a small portion of those in need.

Most of the poor insane did not have access to these advances in psychiatric care and remained in jails, poorhouses, and almshouses under inadequate conditions. Although corporate hospitals accepted a small number of indigent persons, poor-law officials were reluctant, for economic reasons, to send their charges to these special institutions. The rates for pauper lunatics were as low as two dollars per week at New York's Bloomingdale Asylum, but the dependent insane were being cared for in almshouses and jails throughout the state at one quarter to one half that cost (Deutsch 1937). Admission of the poor to hospitals was made more difficult by the fact that institution administrators tended to give propertied patients preferential treatment over the poor in their admission practices.

The Era of the Mental Asylum

In 1825, the plight of pauper lunatics sparked a social movement. Successes reported by corporate hospitals gave thrust to large-scale expansion of state-sponsored mental institutions. Although the patient population of corporate hospitals was drawn primarily from the middle and upper classes and might have varied clinically from the population of immigrant and indigent persons not admitted to those facilities (Grob 1966, 1973), dramatic claims of success contributed to the perspective that a proportion of those suffering from mental disorders could be helped with new approaches to treatment. For example, between 1818 and 1830, the McLean Hospital discharged 666 patients. Of these, 247 were said to have recovered and 187 were considered improved. The Bloomingdale Asylum discharged 1762 patients between

1821 and 1844, claiming that 672 were cured and 422 improved (Grob 1973, p. 68).

In the early 1830's, the rise of public mental hospitals occurred simultaneously with the advocacy of an institutional approach to the management of an array of social ills, such as penal institutions for criminals, orphan asylums for homeless children, and reformatories for delinquents. This development in the care of society's deviant and dependent population, precipitated by urbanization, permitted the enforcement of a new social order based on conformity to the values of a burgeoning industrial economy (D. J. Rothman 1971).

Leaders in the movement to change the locus of care for the public psychiatric patient from the community to the state mental hospital were Horace Mann (1796–1856) and Dorothea Lynde Dix (1802–1887) (Deutsch 1937, Grob 1973). Mann pleaded to the Massachusetts legislature in 1828 that "the insane are the wards of the state." His advocacy for the insane poor began to bear fruit when Massachusetts opened the State Lunatic Hospital in Worcester in 1833. State mental hospitals were also established in New York, Tennessee, Maine, Vermont, Georgia, Ohio, and New Hampshire in the 1830's. Dix, a retired schoolteacher from Boston, was a militant crusader who, over a period of forty years, traveled across the country advocating the construction of mental hospitals. She is credited with founding thirty hospitals.

How Institutionalization Worked

Many of the new mental hospitals served their purpose well. When hospitals were small, well staffed, and able to control their own admission practices, there was relatively little discrepancy between the theory and the practice of moral treatment. The location of hospitals in rural isolation minimized outside influences and emphasized the importance of the hospital's internal atmosphere. Grob (1973, p. 176) has described the predictable daily routine characteristic of mental hospitals in the period before 1850, in which patients assumed a high level of responsibility for self-control and care of themselves and their environment. Productivity and constructive activities were encouraged, with men engaging in farming, carpentry, and maintenance of the hospital and its grounds and women working at domestic chores. The Utica (New York) Asylum even emphasized intellectual pursuits by sponsoring a literary journal, *The Opal*, edited by patients. Hospital superintendents had regular contact with patients through daily rounds and talks on such topics as diet, amusements, employment, and medication.

Efforts to create a constructive environment in the mental hospital all but ceased with the large-scale expansion of the state hospital system. A positive feature of the more widespread availability of institutional care was that no one was excluded on the basis of class, ethnicity, race, or clinical characteristics. By 1890, with the passage of New York's State Care Act (Deutsch 1937, Ch. 12), all types of mentally ill persons in need of public care in New York State could be admitted to a mental hospital owned, administered, and maintained by the state. In providing long-term care to severely disabled patients, including those who were violent or criminally insane, the state mental hospital became a necessary institution in U.S. society (Becker and Schulberg 1976, Morrissey et al. 1980). However, the larger size of the typical state mental institution and a wider range of clinical problems among its patient population, including incurable insanity and alcoholism, led to more frequent use of restraint (Grob 1973). Moreover, a vast increase in the number of patients from a lower-class immigrant background widened the social gap between doctors and patients, changing the doctor-patient relationship that existed with moral treatment.

A century after the state hospital movement was initiated, it was clear that public mental hospital care was not available for all who might need it. Hamilton's statistics show that in 1880 only 17.6 per cent of patients in need of care in a mental hospital actually received it; in 1941 the figure was 63 per cent (Hamilton, 1944, p. 86). When state institutions for the mentally ill were in the planning stage, it was thought that one institution per state would be sufficient, based on the expectation of a high cure rate (80 to 90 per cent), permitting rapid patient turnover. By the latter half of the nineteenth century, the expectation that mental illness was curable had been put to the test of experience (Earle 1887). Awareness was growing that many mental disorders were chronic and required long-term care and support. Although some patients recovered, Park's pioneering outcome studies of the Worcester (Massachusetts) State Hospital showed that, between 1833 and 1875, readmissions accounted for nearly one quarter of all admissions (Grob 1966, pp. 248–255). The large cadre of chronic patients, coupled with the increasing number of new cases of mental illness developing each year in an ever-increasing U.S. population (between 1840 and 1890 the population more than tripled), meant that state hospitals were always overcrowded.

Serious overcrowding after 1850 forced institutional authorities to set specific policies for admission and discharge. One view was that recent cases should be treated actively in hospitals but chronic cases required only custodial care and could be accommodated at a much lower cost in the community. Many untreated mentally ill remained in the community because there were not enough mental hospitals to handle the large numbers of people seeking admission. Acutely ill patients received preferential admission over the chronically ill and in time were the only patients admitted to state hospitals. The chronically ill, sometimes referred to as the "surplus insane," were confined to poorhouses and jails or were taken care of in the homes of friends or relatives. As a general principle, if a patient admitted for an acute illness did not recover within a stipulated period of time, she or he was discharged as "incurable."

The slow and steady expansion of state mental hospitals in the latter half of the nineteenth century eventually brought the chronic patient into the care system. In 1865, New York was the first state to establish a specific state institution for the *chronically* insane. This new facility, the Willard Asylum, marked the creation of two distinct types of state mental institutions: hospitals for the acutely ill and asylums providing less costly custodial care for the chronically ill.

The acutely and chronically insane were not placed in separate hospitals without professional controversy. In the Willard Asylum model, "chronically insane" was defined by inference. Those who were ill for less than a year were sent to the hospital for acutely ill patients. All others were admitted and maintained at Willard. John B. Gray, superintendent of the Utica State Asylum and editor-in-chief of the *American Journal of Insanity*, wrote in 1866 that the separation of the acutely and chronically insane was wrong in principle and led to abuses in practice (Deutsch 1937, pp. 238-239). Gray contended that it was often impossible for a physician to distinguish the curable from the incurable and that just because an illness is chronic does not mean that it is incurable. He contended that many chronic patients could benefit from treatment, even after many years of illness. By caring for acute and chronic patients in separate institutions, it would be difficult, if not impossible, to correct for errors in diagnosis. Moreover, assignment to an institution for the chronically insane would be grossly demoralizing to the patient and to family members.

The controversy concerning separation of the acutely and chronically insane interfered with the extension of the Willard Asylum model to other states. A compromise plan was the "colony" or "cottage" system imported from Europe, which allowed for segregation of patients by chronicity in various buildings on the grounds of a single institution. It was first implemented at the Friends Hospital in Pennsylvania and was later adopted by state institutions. Public mental hospitals tended to be large, often having the capacity to house thousands of patients (the 1930's Pilgrim State and Central Islip hospitals in New York State housed 8000 and 7000 patients, respectively; Deutsch 1937, p. 462).

Even with the provision of care for chronic patients in state hospitals, overcrowding remained a persistent problem (Grob 1966) and eventually led to the abandonment of all principles of therapy (Grob 1973). When the Willard Asylum opened in 1869 with a capacity of 1500 patients, it quickly became overcrowded. The asylum had to close its doors to new admissions, forcing the localities to continue coping with the ever-expanding number of mentally ill sheltered in local poorhouses and almshouses. In 1871, the New York state legislature acted to allow certain counties to provide care for the chronically mentally ill under local auspices (Deutsch 1937, pp. 252-253).

A similar crisis occurred in Iowa in 1878, when two state hospitals became so overcrowded that they were forced to refuse a large number of potential new admissions. In desperation, hospital authorities began to discharge harmless and incurable patients to their home communities. Large numbers of the chronically mentally ill were suddenly turned loose upon county poorhouses, which were ill prepared to handle them. Shifting the problem of caring for the dependent insane from the state hospital to the community led to the hasty construction of temporary shelters as adjuncts to poorhouses and often indistinguishable from them (Deutsch 1937, p. 263).

The extent to which overcrowding has been a permanent feature of public mental institutions in the United States is shown in a survey, "State Hospitals in the Depression," conducted by the National Committee for Mental Hygiene in 1934 (Deutsch 1937, p. 449). Of the 104 institutions included in the study, 77 reported overcrowding, 27 found it necessary to close their doors to new admissions, and 65 were receiving commitments in excess of budget capacity. In one state there was a waiting list of 2543 persons who had actually been legally committed to mental hospitals. In some states, many of the mentally ill were being jailed for long periods because there was no room for them in state hospitals.

At the end of 1934, there were 451 672 patients in mental hospitals in the United States. The vast majority of these patients (93.5 per cent) were in state or county mental hospitals. The average length of stay was three years.

One method for relieving overcrowded state institutions was the parole system. In 1935, more than 49 000 patients, or 10 per cent of the total mental hospital population in the United States, were on parole (Deutsch 1937, p. 451). The parole system was liberalized during the Great Depression as budget cuts and a halt to new hospital construction compounded the problem of overcrowding. At the same time, personal income was so reduced that families and friends were unable to take released patients back into their homes. Consequently, such patients were retained in poorhouses and jails, sometimes locked in cells or placed in chains.

The Rise of Community Care

The presence of discharged mental patients in the community stimulated the development of programs to help them. Placement of the mentally ill in families other than their own is a form of community care as old as the mental asylum. Foster-family care was started in Geel, Belgium, in the thirteenth century, about the time that the Hospital of St. Mary of Bethlehem was established in London. Geel was the site of a medieval religious shrine dedicated to St. Dymphna, an insane princess. The mentally ill from various parts of Europe traveled there to be cured, boarding with families of the town while attending ceremonies at the shrine. This system of foster-family care in Geel was brought under governmental regulation in the mid-1800's and was eventually affiliated with a mental hospital.

Family care spread to other parts of Europe and to the New World. A family-care program was set up in Massachusetts in 1885, and one was adopted by the New York state legislature in 1935. In the New York plan, family care was presented as a solution to overcrowding in state mental institutions (Pollock 1936). Programs remained small, and in 1940 there were only 902 patients in foster-family care, less than 0.2 per cent of the total number of patients on the books of U.S. mental hospitals (Hamilton 1944, p. 140).

The aftercare movement was first conceptualized at the Eberbach Asylum in Germany in 1829. Many prominent U.S. psychiatrists, neurologists, and social workers advocated the establishment of aftercare associations in the 1890's and early 1900's. Indeed, the readjustment of mental patients from state hospital to normal community life was a serious problem confronting the new discipline of social work. Proceedings of the National Conference of Social Work in the 1870's show concern for such environmental stressors in the readjustment phase as the stigma of having lost one's mind and requiring asylum care, strain in relationships with families and friends, and difficulty obtaining employment, all of which were seen as contributing factors to relapse or long-term dependence. In addition, it was noted that social problems, such as lack of financial support, unavailability of adequate living arrangements, and inability to work, delayed release from the hospital. When discharge finally occurred, it was often to a poorhouse to pursue a life as a public dependent (Deutsch 1937, p. 289).

The first outpatient psychiatric department was established at the Pennsylvania Hospital in 1885. Thereafter, outpatient clinics became an integral part of aftercare services. By the mid-1930's, nearly all state hospitals had at least one outpatient clinic and the more advanced systems had many.

Nineteenth-century British hostels were models for U.S. halfway houses. Massachusetts' Gould Farm, established in 1913, was the first U.S. halfway house, followed by Spring Lake Ranch in Vermont (1932) and Meadowlark Homestead in Kansas (1951). All were located in a rural setting and guided by the humanistic philosophy that a return to a simpler, more natural life was preferred. Rutland Corner House in Boston, the first modern urban halfway house, grew out of a shelter for distressed women set up in the 1870's. Its founding in 1954 was followed by the development of halfway houses across the country (Raush and Raush 1968, Glasscote et al. 1971b).

Day treatment, or partial hospitalization, was first developed as an alternative to inpatient treatment in Russia in the 1930's and spread to the United States via England and Canada. Whereas Russian day centers emphasized work and England's were social clubs, day hospitals in North America took a psychotherapeutic approach (Linn et al. 1979).

Finally, work "therapy" was part of the life experience of the mentally ill in U.S. poorhouses in the 1800's. Industrial therapy gained acceptance in England during the 1920's and 1930's (Black 1970), when simple bench assembly work was brought into hospitals on contract with local industries. Sheltered work programs of this nature, which enabled patients to work for pay while recovering in the hospital, have been slow to develop in the United States.

The Publicizing of Mental Care

The publicizing of social welfare services in the United States brought the issue of care of the mentally ill into the political arena. Early on, care of the mentally ill became a hotly debated issue in newspapers and periodicals. By the 1860's, a number of exposés on asylum life, some written by former patients, revealed the inadequacies of the best efforts of the time to improve the lot of the insane. In 1886, tales of abuse and neglect at New York City's Blackwell's Island were published in *Harper's Magazine*. A year later, newspaperwoman Nellie Bly had herself committed to the New York City Asylum in order to write a story, "Ten Days in a Mad-House," which was serialized in the *New York World* (Deutsch 1948).

The debate over quality of care in publicly funded mental institutions has continued to the present (*New York Times*, 1974, 1981). A common thread in both journalistic and scientific accounts of abuses in mental hospitals is that staff are unqualified and of inadequate numbers. Grob (1973, p. 212) reports that in 1843 there were physician complaints that keepers and attendants at the New York City Lunatic Asylum were recruited from among inmates of the penitentiary. Critics contended that the presence of criminals and vagrants on staff undermined control and discipline (Grob 1973, p. 213). In fact, staff were hard to recruit because of long hours and low wages. Staff turnover was high, as evidenced by an 1875 report that, at New York City's Wards Island, only two attendants held their jobs for at least one year. Sixty staff changes were reported in one-year, including thirty-eight dismissals for drinking, striking patients, and other infringements of the rules (New York City Asylum, 1975). More than a century later, Sheehan (1981) reported that staff shortages at New York City's Creedmoor Hospital had a marked effect on patient well-being and noted that staff theft of state-supplied food and equipment was widespread.

Social science studies conducted in the 1950's concluded that the custodial philosophy of public mental hospitals coupled with treatment by unskilled ward attendants has a negative impact on a patient's social identity and rehabilitation potential (Dunham and Weinberg 1960, Goffman 1961). Public hospitals have been plagued by understaffing and by difficulties in recruiting well-trained professionals (Talbott 1978a, 1978b, 1980). In addition to problems in attracting qualified nurses and ward attendants, the persistently poor employment conditions at state mental hospitals has drawn foreign medical graduates, many of whom move on to other jobs after their careers become established.

Studies of well-staffed private mental hospitals show how hidden conflict among staff could be acted out in the form of disturbed behavior among patients (Stanton and Schwartz 1954, Caudill 1958), emphasizing the skill and experience required to create an atmosphere beneficial to patients. Findings from these studies stimulated the development of "milieu therapy," in which the group and organizational dynamics of the institutional environment are viewed as an active treatment agent to facilitate insight and recovery (Jones 1953, Cumming and Cumming 1962). Such principles, basic to the creation of an atmosphere of reason and understanding, have barely permeated large state hospital systems (Klerman 1977).

Deinstitutionalization

The poor care in many state mental hospitals has contributed to the policy of deinstitutionalization. Beginning in the mid-1960's, deinstitutionalization became the most significant public mental health policy in most states. The goal of this policy has been the phasing out of the state mental hospital as the primary locus of care of the chronically mentally ill in favor of community-based treatment. Deinstitutionalization has been carried out by discharging long-term patients from state mental hospitals and controlling the admission of new patients more tightly. Its effect is reflected in a 70 per cent drop in the resident population in state and county mental hospitals, from 559 000 in 1955 to 150 000 today (DHHS Steering Committee, 1980). With the exception of California, large-scale closings of state mental hospitals have not taken place. Indeed, there has actually been an increase in the number of state and county mental hospitals across the nation during the period of deinstitutionalization. In 1955 there were 275 such hospitals; in 1975 there were 313 (Goldman et al. 1980).

That quality of care was the most important factor leading to deinstitutionalization is reflected in the fact that the policy has not spread to private mental hospitals, many of which still provide long-term care. As Borus (1981) has noted, private hospitals have escaped public outrage because, unlike state facilities, they have enough staff and resources to provide patients with adequate treatment.

Deinstitutionalization followed the psychopharmacologic revolution in psychiatry. The accidental discovery of the tranquilizing properties of phenothiazines by Henri Laborit, a French surgeon, in the 1940's radically changed the way the mentally ill were treated (Snyder 1974). The widespread use of these and other

drugs that control the florid symptoms of psychosis allowed
mental institutions to release many patients who might not otherwise have been discharged (Brill and Patten 1959). In addition,
innovative drug treatments have contributed to a decrease in the
length of inpatient stay from the pre-World War II average of
about three years to the current average of sixty days or less. In
general, the improved control of symptoms by drugs has drastically reduced the amount of time spent in the hospital over the
course of a chronic mental illness (Caffey et al. 1971, Glick et al.
1975, Herz et al. 1977).

Economic and political factors also contributed to the eclipse of
the state hospital, as new public funding initiatives presented
alternatives for both inpatient and outpatient care. The Community Mental Health Centers Act of 1963 allocated federal dollars
to the development of a new network of public mental health
services with heavy emphasis on brief hospitalization and outpatient programs based in local communities.

The mid-1960's also witnessed the Medicare (Title XVIII) and
Medicaid (Title XIX) legislation that now give the blind, elderly
disabled, and families with dependent children free choice of
health service providers. With guaranteed payment through health
insurance, voluntary and local public providers of mental health
care, particularly the general hospitals, have openly competed
with the state hospital systems for brief inpatient care of the
chronically mentally ill. As admissions to state and county mental
hospitals have decreased, psychiatric admissions to general hospitals have markedly increased (Bachrach 1981). In some locales,
general hospitals have become the major providers of emergency
and brief inpatient care to the chronically mentally ill.

With new funding options, the state hospital's function as a
provider of long-term care to those incapable of independent
living has been challenged by a variety of private nursing homes,
board-and-care facilities, and welfare hotels. Medicaid, Medicare,
and Supplemental Security Income (SSI) programs enable patients
to obtain life-support services in these settings with federal rather
than state dollars. This economic factor undoubtedly influenced
states to mandate the "mass release" of large numbers of long-stay
patients to sheltered care in the community.

How Deinstitutionalization Has Worked

It is difficult to date the beginnings of deinstitutionalization, as the utilization of state mental hospitals changed after the introduction of psychopharmacology in the late 1950's. However, directives to discharge large numbers of long-stay patients were issued in some states in the late 1960's (Cumming 1968).

Scherl and Macht (1979) noted that deinstitutionalization was not deliberately planned and that steps to implement it preceded consensus within the profession that it was the right thing to do. Moreover, deinstitutionalization moved ahead without adequate scientific evidence that community treatment was superior to institutional care for chronic patients (Arnhoff 1975, Klerman 1977). A number of unanticipated events—the social disturbance, the unmet needs of discharged patients in the community, "trans-institutionalization" of many long-stay patients to nursing homes, the "revolving-door" syndrome, and "falling between the cracks" —are all cited as evidence of the policy's failure.

Communities were ill prepared to cope with large numbers of discharge patients. Suddenly there appeared on city streets mentally disturbed people who "were dirty, who wore torn or inappropriate clothing, who hallucinated or shouted to others and who in general acted in a strange or bizarre way" (Talbott 1979). Patients were concentrated in welfare hotels and board-and-care homes in poor and deteriorating neighborhoods. The marginal quality of life in such "psychiatric ghettos" has been well documented (Lamb and Goertzel 1971, Wolpert et al. 1974). Patients were found to be living isolated, purposeless lives with minimal supervision and inadequate drug and aftercare treatment. The deplorable settings in which many former patients live have been called community "back wards" and equated with the worst of state hospital care.

Much of the decline in the resident population of state and county mental hospitals was due to the movement of seriously disabled patients, many of whom were elderly, to nursing homes. Kramer (1975) has pointed out that, during the period of aggressive deinstitutionalization, the percentage of the U.S. population living in institutions of all types has remained stable at about

1 per cent. From 1955 to 1970, the proportion of institutionalized persons residing in nursing homes rose from 19 to 44 per cent while the proportion in state mental hospitals fell from 39 to 20 per cent. The poor quality of life for public patients in some nursing homes has also produced scandals and exposés. Follow-up studies of elderly mentally ill patients transinstitutionalized from state hospitals to nursing homes document the "transfer trauma" of change in location, sometimes followed by death (Jasnau 1967, Markson and Cumming 1975, Gopelrud 1979).

An oft-cited indicator that deinstitutionalization had gone awry is the high rate of readmission to psychiatric inpatient facilities, a phenomenon referred to as the revolving-door syndrome. This is reflected in the increase in state and county mental hospital admissions (from 178 003 in 1955 to 375 156 in 1975) and discharges (from 126 498 in 1955 to 384 520 in 1975). Economic studies of the experiences of discharged chronic patients show that the revolving-door phenomenon is costly; rehospitalization episodes are the most expensive aspect of attempts to manage patients without long-term institutional care (Weisbrod et al. 1980, Muller and Caton 1983).

The revolving-door syndrome is frequently attributed to inadequate community support services and poor compliance with treatment. Many patients discharged from state hospitals were alleged to have "fallen between the cracks" between the state hospital system and community mental health centers (CMHCs), the other major public mental health care delivery system. While some CMHCs developed programs to help the chronically mentally ill obtain needed treatment and support services, most did not, preferring to focus their programs on the mildly or moderately ill (General Accounting Office 1977). Moreover, states "dumped" patients in the community with inadequate discharge planning and without arranging for receipt of whatever community services were available (General Accounting Office 1977, Group for the Advancement of Psychiatry 1978, Report to the President 1978).

Seriously disabled patients require help from many human services systems. They have economic needs and are eligible for public entitlements from the social welfare system (such as Aid to Dependent Children and SSI), they have medical needs, some require assistance with housing, and most require ongoing psychiatric aftercare. In many cases, these services have been badly coordinated. Noncompliance with prescribed treatment and outright refusal of treatment have proved to be serious problems in service delivery to chronic patients, particularly young adults (Caton 1981, Pepper et al. 1981, Schwartz and Goldfinger 1981) and the homeless (Mesnikoff 1982).

Before the late 1970's, mental health program planners were slow to recognize that many chronic patients need assistance with basic life-support services in addition to psychiatric care (Lamb 1981b). The plight of the homeless mentally ill (Hopper et al. 1982) dramatically underscores the failure of the mental health system to provide in the community what Bachrach (1976) has termed the "functional alternatives" to institutional care.

The Locus of Care for the Chronic Schizophrenic Patient

The most optimistic proponents of deinstitutionalization hoped that patients would lead more normal lives and blend into the mainstream of society if their illnesses were managed outside of hospitals. The experience of the past fifteen years has shown that chronicity is not merely an artefact of inadequate hospital treatment that will disappear if institutionalization is avoided (Kirk and Therrien 1975). The social disability thought to result from long-term hospitalization has been found among young chronic patients whose treatment has consisted of brief hospitalization and community-based aftercare (Caton 1981, Gruenberg 1982, Pepper et al. 1982). The lofty goals of deinstitutionalization have not been realized; some patients are doing better outside institution walls, but others are not (Klerman 1977).

This historical review of the relationship of the U.S. public mental institution to the community dispels the notion that locus of care is the critical factor in the outcome of mental illness. Schizophrenia, the most common diagnosis in state and county mental hospitals (Kramer 1975), is not a mythical entity (Szasz 1960, Rosenhann 1973) but a serious illness that causes immeasurable suffering to patients and to those close to them, regardless of where treatment is received. The most advanced treatments available have not been able to reverse the course of this intractable illness (Klerman 1977, Klein 1982), which has a pervasive effect on patients' day-to-day activities and sense of well-being.

Deinstitutionalization has stimulated the creative efforts of clinicians and researchers to help these very sick people to live in the community, markedly advancing the state of the art in the management of schizophrenia. In applying psychopharmacologic and psychosocial treatments, they have made good use of both institutional and community settings. Research findings have brought a growing awareness that only a small minority of long-term patients can achieve "normalization." A more realistic goal in the treatment of chronic mental illness is to enable patients to live lives of dignity with a reasonable amount of comfort (Lamb 1981b). The clinical research of the deinstitutionalization period, detailed in following chapters, defines quality of care in schizophrenia management and represents the best efforts to date to help patients remain maximally involved in life.

Notes

1. Patients discharged from London's Hospital of St. Mary of Bethlehem (founded in 1247), who roamed the countryside as homeless beggars (Deutsch 1937, Henry 1941).
2. "Poor Tom, that eats the swimming frog, the toad, the tadpole, the wall-newt and the water; that in the fury of his heart, when the foul fiend rages, eats cow-dung for sallets, swallows the old rat and the ditch-dog, drinks the green mantle of the standing pool; who is whipped from tithing to tithing, and stock-punished and imprisoned. . . ." (Shakespeare: *King Lear* III, 4)

2. Schizophrenic Patients in the 1980's

No discussion of the care of chronic schizophrenic patients would be complete without a picture of how patients are faring under current treatment policies. Deinstitutionalization was a natural experiment to determine how managing mental illness in a community setting would affect the social involvement of the patients. Depending on when psychiatric hospitalization was first required, deinstitutionalization has affected patients' lives differently. The typical long-stay patient first became ill when institutional treatment was in vogue and was released to the community after many years in a mental institution. Placement in the community, influenced by loss of family support and coping skills, was often in sheltered-care facilities. In contrast, patients who first became ill after deinstitutionalization went into effect in the late 1960's have had different careers. The "new chronic" patient, managed with brief hospitalization and outpatient care, has lived for longer periods in a natural community setting close to society's mainstream.

National statistics show that chronic mental patients are found in both institutional and noninstitutional settings (Minkoff 1978). The Department of Health and Human Services (DHHS 1980) has estimated that 800 000 chronic mental patients reside with families, in board-and-care homes, in single-room-occupancy hotels, and on the streets. A larger number, 900 000, are in such institutions as mental hospitals and nursing homes (Goldman et al. 1981).

Follow-up of chronic patients reveals that their living arrangements change frequently. Lamb's (1980) investigation of 101 patients, suffering mostly from psychosis, in a California board-and-care home revealed that, by six months, 32 had moved. Those who left returned to parental or conjugal living arrangements, obtained entry into a new board-and-care home, or moved on to independent living in about equal numbers. Patients who wandered from home to home were more often relative newcomers who had been hospitalized during the preceding year. Moreover, they tended to be younger than the stable board-and-care home population and were more often in search of a better life.

In a study of 119 lower-class chronic schizophrenic patients living with family or independently in New York City, Caton et al. (1983) found that 50 per cent changed living arrangements at least once in a one-year period. Housing changes were often precipitated by rehospitalization and were associated with interpersonal stress.

While frequent housing changes probably influence the fate of chronic mental patients, so do the settings in which they live. Patients' living arrangements vary considerably in the degree of independence offered, that is, the extent to which they can move about freely and assume responsibility for daily needs without control or supervision. Ideally, there should be a match between the abilities of the patient and the demands of the environment, but this is not always so. What is known about the lives of chronic mental patients in different types of living settings is described on the following pages.

Institutional Life-Styles

Sheltered-Care Facilities

"Sheltered care" is the term used to describe any type of living setting for disabled persons in which basic necessities and some degree of supervision are provided. Many nursing homes, such as skilled nursing facilities (SNF) and intermediate-care facilities (ICF), deliver nursing care on a daily (ICF) or twenty-four-hour (SNF) basis (Shadish and Bootzin 1981). California's "L" facilities, a type of SNF with locked doors, handle patients with serious psychiatric disorders. In general, however, nursing homes do not employ mental health professionals to provide specialized mental health care (Carling 1981).

The dramatic reduction in the resident population of state and county mental hospitals between 1955 and 1975 could not have been accomplished without the ready availability of alternative settings in the community. Indeed, the mass release of long-stay mental hospital residents affected the elderly more than any other group. Between 1969 and 1974, the number of hospitalized elderly psychiatric patients declined 56 per cent, from 135 322 to 59 685 (General Accounting Office 1977). A survey conducted by the National Center for Health Statistics over the same period showed a 48 per cent increase in the number of nursing home residents with mental disabilities (General Accounting Office 1977). An NIMH survey of elderly patients discharged from state and county mental hospitals revealed that 40 per cent went to nursing homes, more than to any other type of living arrangement (Redick 1974). The impact of deinstitutionalization on nursing homes is further illustrated by estimates of mental impairment among nursing home residents, which are as high as 80 per cent (General Accounting Office 1977). The importance of nursing homes as a locus of care for the mentally ill is reflected by the fact that 29.3 per cent of estimated direct-care costs for the mentally ill is expended in this type of setting. In contrast, state, county, and other public mental hospitals account for an estimated 22.8 per cent of direct-care costs (General Accounting Office 1977).

Deinstitutionalization has also stimulated the expansion of another type of sheltered-care facility, the board-and-care home. Food, shelter, and minimal supervision are provided to persons with various types of disabilities who are unable to live independently. Board-and-care homes range in size from small, homelike settings to large, hotel-like structures designed to accommodate several hundred people (Ch. 8). An advantage of board-and-care homes is that they allow patients to live in an open setting that is not restricted to the mentally ill. A study of sheltered-care residents in New York State in various settings revealed that only 29 per cent were former state hospital patients (New York State Welfare Research 1979).

Although Lamb (1979b) found that 95 per cent of 101 patients in a California board-and-care home regularly used restaurants and supermarkets, social integration of sheltered-care residents into the community at large tends to be minimal. Studies of residents of sheltered-care homes revealed high unemployment (Segal and Aviram 1978, Lamb 1979b) and isolation from family or kin (New York State Welfare Research 1979). The New York study showed that 51 per cent of former state hospital patients in adult homes had no contact with family or friends, in contrast to 21 per cent of other residents. Moreover, the low level of participation in psychiatric aftercare treatment by sheltered-care residents (Lamb 1979, New York State Welfare Research 1979) has stimulated the development of on-site mental health services (Prevost and Arnold 1978).

Studies of sheltered-care residents in California and New York have shown that high percentages are older persons (46 per cent were over age 50 in California, and 75 per cent were over age 65 in New York). Women predominated in the older age groups in both studies, but in the California study nearly one third of the men were between 18 and 33 years of age (Segal and Aviram 1978). While residence in sheltered-care facilities tends to be relatively stable (in the California study, 60 per cent had lived in their current facility for more than one year), young males are the most mobile subgroup. In the California study, 63 per cent had been in a facility for less than one year.

Some types of sheltered-care settings, particularly nursing homes, are overly restrictive for the typical adult mental patient (Carling 1981). However, the New York study (New York State Welfare Research Institute 1979) found that only 9 per cent of sheltered-care residents were capable of being placed in a more independent setting. The lack of skilled mental health workers in most sheltered-care settings renders these facilities less desirable for seriously disturbed patients.

The following description of a discharged schizophrenic patient residing in a New York City board-and-care home illustrates sheltered care life.

> Robert is a 51-year-old, single man who has lived for the past year at the Borough Manor, a motel converted to a private proprietary home for approximately 200 adults, located in a middle-class apartment house area of the Bronx. Residents of the home include the frail elderly and the medically disabled as well as the mentally ill. The home provides maid service and meals for $14 a day. Medication maintenance is prescribed by physicians under contract with the home and is administered by staff.

For fifteen years Robert lived in Manhattan with his stepuncle, his stepuncle's wife, and their children. Persistent bitter arguments, sometimes involving violence, preceded his rejection from the family home. Robert was evicted after he threw a door at the woman of the household, causing lacerations and a concussion. He now shares a room at the Borough Manor with a mentally retarded man who he describes as "very quiet." He denies having any close friends among fellow residents but has weekly telephone contact with his elderly mother. He works three hours a day at a local sheltered workshop. He rarely leaves the home on his own but does participate in group activities. On occasion he attends Broadway shows, sports events, and movies along with others from Borough Manor in connection with a publicly funded enrichment program for shut-ins.

Robert has been diagnosed at different times by different psychiatrists as a paranoid schizophrenic and as a manic depressive, manic type, during his nine stays at state hospitals in the New York City region. He has been suicidal and assaultive on numerous occasions, and long-term treatment with antipsychotic drugs has resulted in tardive dyskinesia.

He is well groomed and neatly dressed in second-hand clothing. His mood is frequently angry, and his language is often interspersed with numerous expletives, especially when discussing his relatives or his treatment with Haldol, which he blames for "t.d." He resents the fact that the proprietors of his adult home "force" him to continue to take Haldol even though he doesn't want it.

The State Hospital

Despite the reduction in the resident population of state and county mental hospitals, there remain about 150 000 chronic patients nationwide who cannot be discharged because there are no alternative facilities capable of handling the severity of their disabilities (DHHS Steering Committee 1980). Dorwart (1980) surveyed 137 state hospital patients in Massachusetts who could not be discharged in that state's aggressive deinstitutionalization effort because they required a high level of care, were acutely psychotic and dangerous to themselves or others, and lacked the ability to form social relationships. Nearly one third of Dorwart's subjects, evenly distributed by age between 20 and 70 years, had completed high school, and yet the majority had no job skills. Most were voluntary admissions and had a history of numerous hospitalizations. One third had been hospitalized for more than five consecutive years.

The following case of a long-term resident of a state hospital in New York is illustrative of the type of patient for whom the public mental hospital is home.

Audrey is a 50-year-old, single woman with a long history of hospitalizations "in practically every hospital in New York City" (quote from the hospital record) for chronic schizophrenia. She was voluntarily readmitted to the state hospital only three days after discharge from a six-week stay with complaints of restlessness, insomnia, depression, and a fear that people in her apartment building were going to attack her. She was not violent or suicidal. Drug and alcohol abuse have not been problems.

During the subsequent ten-month stay in the hospital, her paranoid and persecutory delusions, auditory hallucinations, intense anxiety in relation to people around her, and depression have persisted despite intensive therapy with antipsychotic drugs. Audrey describes herself as a "loner" who does not interact with fellow patients and relates poorly to the staff. However, she is cooperative on the ward and attends the self-care unit of the hospital to learn community coping skills.

Even though she was able to work at a night office-cleaning job for several years before her current hospitalization, severe isolation and an unbearable feeling of panic have repeatedly undermined her attempts to live independently in the community. Moreover, she is virtually without personal relationships or social support in the community.

Because of repeated failures at community living, Audrey was discharged only after a structured, protective setting in the community was found for her. She was placed in family care with a couple, their four children, and three other ex-patients, but she was readmitted to the hospital within months as a result of her inability to get along with the proprietor of the family-care home.

Jails and Prisons

The presence of large numbers of mental patients in communities has aroused concern about public safety. Unfortunately, studies comparing the relationship between mental disorder and the criminal justice system before and after the deinstitutionalization movement are rare. In fact, there is little empirical evidence that the psychiatric problems of criminals have changed. Steadman and Ribner (1980) examined the mental hospitalization histories of inmates from state prisons and local jails released to Albany County, New York, in 1968 (167 subjects) and again in 1975 (252 subjects). Sample subjects in the two years, mostly men in their late 20's and early 30's, did not differ significantly in history of prior psychiatric hospitalization. However, for those with histories, the average number of previous hospitalizations for the 1975 sample was twice that of the 1968 group.

Steadman and Ribner found that, in 1968, 19 per cent of offenders from state prisons had previous mental hospitalization, in contrast to only 13 per cent in 1975. In the subsample of subjects released from the county jail, 9 per cent had prior mental hospitalization in 1968 and 12 per cent had such histories in 1975. A similar study of inmates admitted to the Denver, Colorado, county jail revealed that 14 per cent had histories of psychiatric hospitalizations (Swank and Winer 1976). The extent to which county jail inmates have diagnosable mental illness was explored in a survey of 1084 jailed adults in five California counties. Nearly 7 per cent were psychotic, and another 9 per cent suffered from nonpsychotic disorders (Bolton 1976).

Lamb and Grant (1982) conducted an in-depth study of 102 male inmates in a California county jail, randomly selected from those referred by the jail staff for psychiatric evaluation. The racially mixed group of subjects had a median age of just under 30 years. Seventy-five per cent were given a DSM-III diagnosis of schizophrenia by the investigative team, and 22 per cent were classified as suffering from major affective disorder. Prior to their arrests, only 12 per cent were employed and the majority (56 per cent) were receiving SSI. The most common living arrangements were with relatives or friends (46 per cent); on the streets, at beaches, in cars, or in missions (25 per cent); and in cheap hotels or other solitary settings (20 per cent). More than half of those charged with misdemeanors had been living on the streets or in hotels when they were arrested.

Three quarters of the study subjects had histories of arrests for felonies and serious acts of physical violence against others. More than half of the arrests were for felonies, half of which were crimes of violence. Eighty per cent of the sample exhibited serious overt psychopathology on at least two out of three psychiatric assessment scales to measure delusions, hallucinations, and thought disorder. Psychiatric hospitalization was recommended for 76 per cent because they met the criteria for involuntary hospitalization. As such, they were deemed dangerous to themselves or others or were unable to provide for their own food, clothing, and shelter because of mental disturbance.

The following case of a young vagrant in New York City shows how the problems of the mentally ill affect both the mental health and the criminal justice system.

Eddie is a 27-year-old, unemployed man who was jailed briefly after he sexually assaulted a woman on an isolated street in lower Manhattan. This offense led to hospitalization at a state mental hospital on a criminal remand. After discharge he was placed on probation for five years, and he returned to the community to live in a single-room-occupancy hotel inhabited by ex-offenders, drug addicts, alcoholics, and the mentally ill.

Over the past two years, Eddie has been in a mental hospital five times. He has lived in seven different locations in the community, including the apartment of his brother, a YMCA, a public shelter, a supervised residence, and several cheap hotels. He was told to leave the supervised residence after assaulting a staff member, and he was evicted from a cheap hotel after exposing himself. At one point, penniless and homeless, he lived on the streets. In this down-and-out condition, he took an overdose of Prolixin, precipitating one of his numerous psychiatric inpatient episodes.

Eddie was born in New Orleans into a family with thirteen children. He did poorly in school and dropped out before finishing high school. His father beat him so severely that he ran away at age 17 to live with a brother in New York City. Within months of the move, he experienced his first psychiatric hospitalization for what was diagnosed as schizophrenia.

Relatively free of psychotic symptoms between episodes, Eddie has worked as a store clerk and messenger boy and at various other entry-level jobs obtained in connection with a transitional employment program sponsored by a social rehabilitation club. However, after attending the program for six years, he was not able to achieve independent employment and was asked to leave.

Eddie is currently supported by SSI. For the past six months, he has been attending an aftercare clinic program and studying three half days per week at an adult learning center in order to obtain his high school diploma. He takes no antipsychotic medication and has intermittent contact with an aunt, his mother, and his brother. He has no close friends but occasionally hangs out with fellow residents of his hotel. With them, he uses marijuana, cocaine, and alcohol.

Noninstitutional Life-Styles

Independent Living

A few patients with serious mental disabilities are able to sustain long-term independent living. In most cases the cost of an apartment or hotel room is underwritten by public entitlements, as very few patients are able to work steadily in income-producing jobs (Ch. 7). The following case example illustrates the rare schizophrenic patient who has been able to achieve a permanent independent life-style.

Betty is a 56-year-old woman who lives alone in an apartment. She manages all of her living expenses on earned income from her full-time job as a clerk for a state agency, a position she has held for twelve years. She has a modestly active social life involving family, friends, church, theatre, and movies. Divorced after a five-year childless marriage, she now has a male companion whom she sees frequently.

Betty moved to New York City from her native Arkansas at age 22. Her first psychotic episode occurred at age 40, and since then she has had five psychiatric hospitalizations for what has been diagnosed as schizophrenia. (Some clinicians might question the accuracy of this diagnosis since Betty's illness had a late onset.) Her last hospitalization, more than three years ago, was precipitated by intense anxiety, restlessness, sleeplessness, paranoid delusions, and confusion, which occurred after she had stopped taking prescribed antipsychotic drugs.

Adherence to drug therapy enables Betty to be free of painful symptoms. She takes Haldol only intermittently without apparent side effects and no longer participates in psychosocial therapies offered at her local aftercare clinics. Betty attributes her successful adjustment in the community to the support of her family, friends, and employer.

Family Settings

Deinstitutionalization has relied heavily on patients' families to provide shelter and support after discharge. Studies of chronic patients first treated in the era of brief hospitalization followed by community care reveal that family or kin living arrangements are most common (Lamb and Goertzel 1977, Caton 1981). In the 18-to-35 age group, nearly half are to be found with family (Pepper et al. 1982), often in a dependent relationship to the head of the household. Three-generation households, made up of the patient's parent or parents, the patient, and the patient's children, are not uncommon.

The following description of a schizophrenic patient discharged from a brief inpatient unit in New York City illustrates how patients live in family settings.

Tanya is a 40-year-old woman who lives with her mother and a 17-year-old son in a five-room apartment in upper Manhattan. Tanya and her mother have had a troubled relationship for years; arguments are frequent and intense. Her mother, critical and rejecting, has asked Tanya to find another home on numerous occasions. However, attempts to find an alternative living arrangement have never been successful. Tanya and her mother pool their entitlements (Tanya's SSI, her mother's Social Security, and Aid to Families with Dependent Children) for a total of $780 per month. They have no difficulty in meeting living expenses.

Unable to work, Tanya attends a day treatment program several times a week. At home, she occasionally reads or paints but does not assist in meal preparation or in the care of the household. She has no close friends or confidants, although she socializes with fellow patients in the aftercare program from time to time.

Tanya moved to the United States from Russia at age 4, along with her mother, a younger sister, an aunt, and her grandmother. She finished high school and was able to work as a secretary before her first hospitalization at age 20. This first episode, precipitated by a suicide attempt, occurred after two years of outpatient treatment. Numerous subsequent hospitalizations have resulted from suicide attempts.

Although Tanya never married, she became pregnant at the age of 22. From the fourth to the eighth month of her pregnancy, she was hospitalized at a state mental institution. When her child was born, she was able to work and care for him for about two years, with the help of her maternal grandmother, with whom she lived. After a recurrence of her illness, she moved back into her mother's home, where she and her son have lived since.

Tanya has a difficult relationship with her son, now 18 years old, shown by the fact that they do not speak to one another for long periods of time. Her son's school performance has been poor and he has no close friends of either sex.

Tanya is overweight and gives little attention to her appearance. Diagnosed as a schizophrenic, she is subject to mood swings. When she gets "high," her speech is rapid and she is hyperactive and tense. Her conversations ramble from memories of past events to fantasies, hallucinations, or happenings in the present. When she gets "low," she becomes morose, inactive, and suicidal. During a one-year period, she was rehospitalized twice as a result of suicide attempts. She is usually compliant with her medication, a combination of lithium and antipsychotic drugs.

Tanya frequently states that she would like to work. At one point, she painted greeting cards, intending to sell them. At another time, she became involved in campaigning for the cause of a Russian literary figure. Neither activity led to a satisfying job or avocation.

Homelessness

The number of mental patients who experience episodes of homelessness is at present unknown, but estimates of the history of mental illness among vagrants and street people range from about one fourth to one third. In a study of young vagrants in California, Segal et al. (1977) found that 22 per cent had histories of mental illness. Hopper et al. (1982) studied 85 homeless men under age 35 referred to a public shelter in New York City and discovered that 34 per cent had prior psychiatric hospitalizations. Estimates of mental disability among the homeless based on the use of mental status screening instruments are as high as 70 per cent (Hopper et al. 1982). In addition to mental disorder, drug and alcohol abuse are common in vagrant and homeless populations (Bahr 1973, Segal et al. 1977, Barrow 1980, New York State Department of Social Services 1980).

Homeless people sleep in abandoned buildings, public parks, doorways and lobbies of apartment houses, and bus depots and train stations (Baxter and Hopper 1981). Anecdotal sketches of life on the streets reveal that the homeless often sleep lightly in daytime, use public bathrooms, and frequent soup kitchens and publicly funded meal programs. Family ties have been broken for many, and connections with professional sources of support are loose if they exist at all (Chafetz and Terry 1981). A study of New York City "street people" with histories of mental illness, approached by an outreach team, showed that nearly two thirds refused referrals to mental health or health services (Barrow 1980).

The following is a description of a chronic schizophrenic patient whose nomadic life-style has included episodes of homelessness.

Sam is a 46-year-old, unemployed man who moves among single-room-occupancy hotels, a public shelter, and the streets of New York City. During a period of one year, Sam lived in at least six different welfare hotels. A major reason for this instability is his obstreperous behavior, which has led to numerous evictions. His assaultive outbursts have also resulted in exclusion from aftercare programs and church meetings.

Sam has not worked for many years and is currently supported by SSI. He frequently runs out of money before his next check is due and has to beg or borrow for food, subway fares, and cigarettes. Sam's days are spent wandering aimlessly about the city. He has no close friends or confidants. At Thanksgiving, he was seen on a local television news report eating a publicly funded dinner with other homeless men in the Bowery.

An artist who attended college, Sam married in his early 20's and was able to support his wife and baby daughter until his first psychotic episode. Repeated episodes, diagnosed as schizophrenia, interfered with his family, social, and work relationships. Now divorced, Sam still has intermittent contact with his former wife, but he is estranged from his daughter, who is now in her early 20's.

Sam's mental condition is marked by religious delusions and a persistent fear that he is suffering from cancer. He is often restless, agitated, sleepless, and angry.

He appears thin and malnourished, with personal hygiene so poor that he bears a strong and unpleasant body odor. His second-hand clothing is always ill fitting, in bad repair, and dirty. His bearded face is encrusted with dirt and marked with pimple-like lesions, as are his hands and arms. The index and middle fingers of his right hand are stained brown from tobacco, and his long fingernails are encrusted with dirt. His tongue rolls from cheek to cheek in an almost rhythmic fashion, a side effect of years of antipsychotic drug treatment. He seems unaware that his mouth is constantly in motion, even when he isn't talking.

He occasionally visits the outpatient clinic of a local general hospital spontaneously, without an appointment. However, he has persistently refused to take antipsychotic medications or comply with regularly prescribed aftercare treatment.

Managing the Schizophrenic Patient in the 1980's

Chronic disability has been observed in patients who have spent very little time, if any, in mental institutions (Gruenberg 1982, Pepper et al. 1982). The lives of chronic schizophrenic patients reflect the limits of current treatment technologies to prevent recurrences of psychosis, despite remarkable advances in the psychopharmacologic treatment of this disorder (Klein 1982). Hopefully, new therapies designed to minimize the breakdown of social competence and to preserve family and social relationships will moderate the idleness, loneliness, and demoralization that so often accompany chronic schizophrenia. Even so, settings that offer control and protection will still be required for patients whose behavior poses a danger to themselves or to others.

Indeed, a vital aspect of patient management is identification of the most appropriate treatment and level of supervision for patients displaying specific clinical and behavioral characteristics. While effective approaches can be applied in an array of settings, the decision of who among chronic schizophrenic patients can best be handled in sheltered-care facilities, hospitals, jails, family settings, or on their own is based on both the person and the environment. The best possible outcome of schizophrenia demands that patients' lives be carefully monitored, with active intervention when necessary to resolve crises, enhance social support, or control symptoms (Turner and Tenhoor 1978). The creative use of environment belongs in the skills armamentarium of mental health professionals.

Observers of the new chronic patients of the deinstitutionalization era, particularly young adults, have noted that resistance to treatment is a major problem (Caton 1981, Pepper et al. 1981,

Schwartz and Goldfinger 1981). The tendency of many mentally ill young adults to use psychiatric services on a crisis or sporadic basis and avoid long-term commitment to treatment seriously challenges the ability to control   schizophrenia and to prevent secondary disability. Although treatments are limited in their efficacy, too few of the seriously disturbed possess the necessary skills to forge a successful adaptation to life on their own (Pepper et al. 1982, Sheets et al. 1982). The problems of violent and suicidal behavior stretch the limits of management of schizophrenia under a policy of community care (Tsuang 1978, Caton 1981, Dunham and Pierce 1982) and emphasize the risks of allowing patients to decide alone whether or not they need treatment (Rachlin et al. 1975, Lamb and Grant 1982). Clearly, the development of strategies to involve patients in an ongoing dialogue with members of the mental health delivery system (Segal and Baumohl 1980, Bachrach 1982, Lamb and Grant 1982) is a high priority for the 1980's.

3. Diagnosis and Treatment of Chronic Schizophrenia: Current Concepts and Practice

MICHAEL SHEEHY, M.D.

Schizophrenic disorders account for the overwhelming majority of mental hospital admissions and readmissions. In the United States alone during 1971, there were more than 900 000 patient care episodes (inpatient and outpatient) involving patients carrying a diagnosis of schizophrenia (Kramer 1977). Estimates of the world-wide annual incidence of new cases run to over two million per year (World Health Organization 1973). In terms of disability, because schizophrenia is an illness of late adolescence and early adulthood, it exacts its greatest toll during what should be a productive time in life, that is, in those years when the goals of marriage, reproduction, and economic self-sufficiency are typically realized.

Optimal treatment of schizophrenia today depends on accurate diagnosis and judicious use of both drugs and environmental intervention, including hospital and alternative residential programs. Psychotherapy, behavior modification, and vocational and social rehabilitation must also be assessed and applied.

Any examination of modern treatment methods must be cast against a backdrop of the current social and political thought that shapes therapy options and to some degree defines their goals. The social goal of minimizing use of hospital inpatient services and legislation delineating patients' rights—for example, to refuse treatment—are two important influences. There is also an intense and increasing concern with cost containment that has kept staff salaries low in public mental hospitals and has shifted staff balance toward a system in which unskilled personnel provide the bulk of direct care (Greenblatt 1978). Cost consciousness has exalted the rapid discharge of patients to community living regardless of the individual's readiness or of the therapeutic and social adequacy of the placement (Greenblatt and Glazier 1975).

Diagnosis

During the past decade, psychiatric diagnosis has undergone a renaissance almost unimaginable twenty years ago. Before 1970, psychiatric diagnosis was widely attacked for its unreliability, limited utility for treatment, and lack of relevance to the complexities of psychiatric disorders (Spitzer and Fleiss 1974). Since then, however, the development of both specific criteria for diagnosis and more specific psychopharmacological drugs has greatly increased the reliability and usefulness of psychiatric diagnoses. There has emerged a whole new literature that examines specific treatments for specifically diagnosed conditions (Feighner et al. 1972, Spitzer et al. 1975), and the third edition of the *Diagnostic and Statistical Manual* (DSM III 1980) sets forth the most modern and clinically refined descriptions and criteria possible for the diagnosis of schizophrenia. These criteria are shown in Table 3-1.

Schizophrenia is now defined as a chronic illness of at least six months' duration. Its criteria explicitly exclude conditions that

TABLE 3-1   Diagnostic Criteria for a Schizophrenic Disorder

A. At least one of the following during a phase of the illness:

1. Bizarre delusions (content is patently absurd and has no possible basis in fact), such as delusions of being controlled, thought broadcasting, thought insertion, or thought withdrawal

2. Somatic, grandiose, religious, nihilistic, or other delusions without persecutory or jealous content

3. Delusions with persecutory or jealous content if accompanied by hallucinations of any type

4. Auditory hallucinations in which either a voice keeps up a running commentary on the individual's behavior or thoughts, or two or more voices converse with each other

5. Auditory hallucinations on several occasions with content of more than one or two words, having no apparent relation to depression or elation

6. Incoherence, marked loosening of associations, markedly illogical thinking, or marked poverty of content of speech if associated with at least one of the following:

(a) Blunted, flat, or inappropriate affect

(b) Delusions or hallucinations

(c) Catatonic or other grossly disorganized behavior

B. Deterioration from a previous level of functioning in such areas as work, social relations, and self-care

C. Duration: continuous signs of the illness for at least six months at some time during the person's life, with some signs of the illness at present. The six-month period must include an active phase during which there were symptoms from A, with or without a prodromal or residual phase, as defined below:

Prodromal phase: a clear deterioration in functioning before the active phase of the illness not due to a disturbance in mood or to a substance use disorder and involving at least *two* of the symptoms noted below

Residual phase: persistence, following the active phase of the illness, of at least *two* of the symptoms noted below, not due to a disturbance in mood or to a substance use disorder

Prodromal or Residual Symptoms

(1) Social isolation or withdrawal

(2) Marked impairment in role functioning as wage earner, student, or homemaker

(3) Markedly peculiar behavior (e.g., collecting garbage, talking to self in public, or hoarding food)

(4) Marked impairment in personal hygiene and grooming

(5) Blunted, flat, or inappropriate affect

(6) Digressive, vague, overelaborate, circumstantial, or metaphorical speech

(7) Odd or bizarre ideation or magical thinking, e.g., superstitiousness, clairvoyance, telepathy, "sixth sense," "others can feel my feelings," overvalued ideas, ideas of reference

(8) Unusual perceptual experiences, e.g., recurrent illusions, sensing the presence of a force or person not actually present

Examples: Six months of prodromal symptoms with one week of symptoms from A; no prodromal symptoms with six months of symptoms from A; no prodromal symptoms with two weeks of symptom from A and six months of residual symptoms; six months of symptoms from A, apparently followed by several years of complete remission, with one week of symptoms in A in current episode

D. The full depressive or manic syndrome (criteria A and B of major depressive or manic episode), if present, developed after any psychotic symptoms or was brief relative to the duration of the psychotic symptoms in A

E. Onset of prodromal or active phase of the illness before age 45

F. Not due to any organic mental disorder or mental retardation

Source: American Psychiatric Association, *Diagnostic and Statistical Manual of Mental Disorders*, 3rd ed. Washington, D.C.: AMA, 1980.

meet the criteria for a manic syndrome, an organic mental disorder, or mental retardation. By requiring that schizophrenia be accompanied at some time by a clearly psychotic picture (for example, hallucinations and/or delusions), the definition excludes these three other chronic and disabling personality disorders. Formerly, individuals suffering from manic syndrome, organic disorders, or mental retardation were often diagnosed as schizophrenic according to the comparatively loose descriptive language of DSM II (1968).

Mistakes are costly and harmful. When a diagnosis of schizophrenia is mistakenly applied to patients who closely fit the DSM III diagnostic criteria for a depressive illness or personality disorder, antipsychotic drugs are usually administered. Such treatment exposes the patient to all the risks of neuroleptic drugs but little or none of the benefits.

The impact of accurate, criterion-based diagnosis is not limited to drug treatment. The implications of a diagnosis of schizophrenia using DSM III criteria should influence such other aspects of treatment as vocational rehabilitation, duration of follow-up, and type, amount, and timing of psychotherapy. These issues are addressed in Chapters 5 through 8 of this text.

If the promise of improved treatment through improved diagnosis is to be realized, accurate diagnosis must be reasonably achievable in everyday clinical settings. There is evidence that, among the chronically mentally ill, it is not always easy to make an accurate diagnosis. In Caton's (1981) study of sixty chronically mentally ill patients, all of whom had been given a hospital diagnosis of schizophrenia, only forty-two could be diagnosed *at all* using criteria somewhat stricter than those of DSM III. The difficulties in formulating criterion-based diagnoses stemmed from two factors: the patients' poor history-telling abilities and the difficulty of determining the temporal relationship between the onset of psychotic symptoms and the use of street drugs.

Although these two factors were a major problem in Caton's research, they probably are not so influential in an office or emergency room setting, for the following reason. In diagnosing, clinicians typically apply rules of thumb that are not characteristic of the research interview. By being aware that any diagnosis is provisional, clinicians remind themselves that they may be wrong and are alerted to the possibility of treatment change. If the patient is hospitalized, they can also take advantage of a drug-free period to clarify any confusion between street drug psychosis and schizophrenia. Such a period also allows for a re-evaluation of the patient's history, a refinement not possible during a single interview.

Any practicing clinician knows that many schizophrenics *also* use drugs, have personality disorders, and avoid sustained involvement with mental health care providers except during crises. In sum, they are usually diagnosable, extremely dysfunctional, and not treatable with any consistency. Because these patients constitute a serious social tragedy, psychiatric planners and some clinicians diagnose by functional disability instead of by symptoms (Anthony 1977). Unfortunately, the thrust of functional disability diagnosis has traditionally been toward social planning rather than toward medical care.

Because of the severe social impairments associated with chronic mental illness in general and with schizophrenia in particular, any well-designed diagnostic scheme must establish a framework for dealing with interpersonal relationships and social functioning as well as with symptoms. Such a scheme takes into account the clinical observation that, in chronic mental illness, it is possible for social functioning to improve while symptoms remain unchanged. The converse is true as well.

Such a scheme has been in wide use for some years in the diagnosis of heart disease (Criteria Committee 1964). DSM III has adopted a similar approach by using a multiaxial classification in which axis V is restricted to a simple rating scale describing the highest level of adaptive functioning during the year preceding the diagnosis interview. Whether or not a global rating of adaptive functioning will prove valid and useful with schizophrenic patients remains to be seen. It may be necessary to separate interpersonal relationships from work functioning, as proposed by Strauss (1975).

Drug Treatment

In a comprehensive review of the efficacy of maintenance antipsychotic drugs in treating schizophrenia, Davis (1975) concluded that the probability of stated benefits resulting from chance alone was less than 10–80. To support this overwhelmingly positive stance on drug treatment, Davis reviewed twenty-four double-blind studies published over the last twenty years. Over 3000 patients participated in these studies in a variety of settings: private, state, VA, inpatient, and outpatient. Relapse was the criterion of failure. It is abundantly clear from this review that, for schizophrenic patients *who have achieved remission,* drug maintenance is unquestionably more effective in preventing relapse than is a placebo.

Thus, the questions of clinical importance are, what dose of antipsychotic drug should be used, for how long should it be used, and how can one anticipate and minimize the risks associated with these drugs? The choice of a particular drug for a particular patient and the limits of drug effectiveness are also questions of clinical significance. Finally, in comprehensive treatment planning for chronic schizophrenics, the special problems of the patient who does not respond to drugs and the interaction between anti-psychotic drugs and psychosocial therapies must be considered.

Antipsychotic drugs reduce all the well-described symptoms of schizophrenia. It is a common misconception to think that these drugs are more effective at the outset of illness in overactive, floridly psychotic schizophrenics than in withdrawn, retarded patients (Klein and Davis 1969). Numerous studies have shown that thought disorder, hostility, and delusions respond favorably, but so do blunted affect and indifference (Klein and Davis). The pertinent issue in chronic schizophrenia concerns maintenance treatment of the individual with reduced florid symptoms but established schizophrenic deficits. While any symptom of schizophrenia may be present, usually in an attenuated form, the majority of these individuals show blunted or inappropriate affect, social withdrawal, and eccentric behavior or some evidence of thought disorder (DSM III 1980). Many of these patients have a history of childhood asociality marked by limited social intelligence, fearfulness, and self-isolation. Klein and Davis (1969, p. 150) describes these individuals as "evasive, guarded and perplexed. . . . [C]ommunication with them is difficult."

Characteristically, these patients respond incompletely to drugs and remain socially impaired. Consequently, they tend to accumulate in state hospitals and, more recently, in board-and-care homes and welfare hotels. Florid psychotic symptoms in this group tend to be less prominent. In a recent study of a California board-and-care home for psychotic patients, 92 per cent of 101 residents were diagnosed as psychotic (probably, though not necessarily, schizophrenic), but only 32 per cent manifested overt florid symptoms (Lamb 1979b). Although Lamb did not address the issue specifically, it appears likely that many of the nonflorid patients were childhood asocial schizophrenics. Optimal drug management of this group requires an especially careful assessment of risks and benefits.

Drug Dosage

Using prevention of relapse as the criterion of success in maintenance therapy of chronic schizoprhenic patients, it has been possible to determine an optimal dosage range for antipsychotic drugs. This entails avoiding the risks of excessive dosage (oversedation, extrapyramidal effects, pigmentation of the skin and eyes, and obesity) as well as the risks of inadequate dosage (increased frequency of relapse). A range of 0.5 to 1 gram of chlorpromazine or its equivalent per day appears optimal for most patients (Clark et al. 1970). When patients known to require 500 milligrams daily had their medication withdrawn, the rate of relapse was very high: 60 per cent in one year. On the other hand, in cases where only 300 milligrams per day was sufficient, the rate of relapse over one year following drug withdrawal was only 23 per cent (Davis 1975).

Attempts to use very high doses either to relieve florid symptoms or to maintain chronic patients having reduced symptoms and living in the community have been disappointing. While it is possible that some patients metabolize antipsychotic drugs rapidly and thus benefit from high-dose regimens, the general value of high doses has not been demonstrated (Quitkin et al. 1975). On the contrary, such doses may worsen the condition, an effect characterized by a "zombie-like" appearance, perhaps attributable to severe extrapyramidal effects that are not responsive to the antiparkinson agents used to treat this condition. It is important to point out that the patients in the study by Quitkin et al. were not "good responders," even on their prestudy dose. More modest but still "megadose" drug treatments, for example, 4 grams of chlorpromazine or its equivalent, have also not proven better than standard doses in chronic patients (McGreadie and MacDonald 1977).

Thus, on balance it seems wise to treat patients on an individual basis, using continued symptom remission as the index of success. Although lower doses should be used if possible, 0.5 to 1 gram per day of chlorpromazine or its equivalent is likely the range needed for most patients.

There is evidence that response to drugs should not be judged until at least twelve weeks have passed (Quitkin et al. 1975). Agitated schizophrenic patients may require somewhat higher doses for a brief period at first, but doses can be reduced substantially as agitation diminishes, and a more typical maintenance range can be selected. If the patient takes the medicine as prescribed, relapse rates of 30 to 50 per cent can be expected over the first year for chronic schizophrenics. This compares favorably with cumulative relapse rates of 70 per cent over the first year for patients who take no medicine (Hogarty and Goldberg 1973).

In prescribing antipsychotic drugs, the clinician should keep in mind that different doses may be required at different stages of an illness. Just as higher-than-standard doses may be needed to control agitation in an acute psychotic episode, even during the course of a chronic illness, standard or less-than-standard doses may be adequate to prevent relapse over long periods. Some chronic patients without florid symptoms may benefit from no medicine at all, although there is no clear-cut way to identify such patients in advance (Davis 1975).

Since relapse rates in general decline substantially once a patient remains free of active psychosis for two years, dose reduction or elimination should always be kept in mind. No patient should be exposed to a rigid, unvarying, unreviewed dosage regimen month after month. The clinician should always attempt to use the lowest dose possible consonant with ongoing review of risks and benefits to the patient. Antipsychotic drugs are all long-acting and excreted only slowly from the body. If dosage is reduced in 20 per cent decrements, one to two weeks should be allowed for assessing the patient's psychiatric status before another change is made.

It is notable that 30 per cent of schizophrenics survive without relapse for one year after acute psychosis when treated with a placebo (Hogarty and Goldberg 1973). Maintenance antipsychotic drugs are perhaps twice as good as a placebo at forestalling relapse but are by no means perfect.

Choice of Drug, Duration of Treatment, and Management of Side Effects

Despite the introduction of numerous antipsychotic drugs over the past twenty years, there is no conclusive evidence that any are more effective than chlorpromazine. Choice of drug thus rests with an assessment of its side effects for a particular patient. It is in side effects that drugs show clinically important differences. The side effects that concern clinicians most in the maintenance treatment of schizophrenia are weight gain, extrapyramidal effects, and tardive dyskinesia.

Obesity is increasingly regarded as a significant long-term health hazard. Although this problem may seem relatively minor in the face of the immediate and long-term hazards of schizophrenia, obesity in this group should not be overlooked. Obesity in hospitalized schizophrenics is as high as 40 per cent, twice the prevalence in the general population (Gordon et al. 1960). While the relative inactivity of hospital life may contribute to this figure, nearly all antipsychotic drugs induce weight gain (Singh et al. 1970). When obesity is a major problem, molindone is the drug of choice (Gallant et al. 1968).

The management of extrapyramidal effects, including restlessness, rigidity, and akinesia, is a more immediate problem. Not only do these conditions affect appearance and motor performance, but they cause damaging psychological effects as well. Patients affected with motor restlessness often experience a sense of inescapable inner restlessness, a condition that has occasionally led to suicide. Patients with akinesia, a state characterized by deadened feelings and depression, feel and appear "zombie-like" (Rifkin et al. 1975). This, too, has been accompanied by suicide. These complications, which are frequently mistaken for parts of the schizophrenic disorder itself, can be avoided to a considerable degree by using antiparkinson drugs for a few months and then carefully evaluating the patient during withdrawal.

The prevention and treatment of tardive dyskinesia are more problematic. This condition is characterized by squirming movements of the tongue and lips, chewing movements, and cheek bulging. Blinking and grimacing are also common. In older patients, particularly those over 50, there may also be jerking and writhing movements of the trunk and limbs. Tapping of the feet while sitting is particularly noticeable. In the most severe cases, tardive dyskinesia can interfere with eating and breathing and even result in death.

Tardive dyskinesia is a frequent and lasting consequence of prolonged treatment with antipsychotic drugs. Among primarily chronic inpatients treated with antipsychotic drugs, the incidence is up to 56 per cent (Crane 1973), with a mean prevalence of 15 per cent (Baldessarini and Tarsey 1978). The prevalence among outpatients treated with antipsychotic drugs is less well documented. One study found a prevalence of 43.4 per cent (Asnis et al. 1977) but no significant correlation with age, sex, years of drug use, or organic brain disease. Such findings raise serious concerns for all patients receiving antipsychotic drugs.

Once well established, tardive dyskinesia is difficult to treat and disappears only slowly, if at all, when medication is stopped. Elimination of antipsychotic drugs over a ten-month period produced no improvement in 50 per cent of patients and varying degrees of improvement in the other half (Baldessarini and Tarsey 1978).

Certainly the best treatment for this condition is prevention. Careful diagnosis should be used to avoid giving maintenance antipsychotic drugs to nonschizophrenic patients except in unusual circumstances, such as in cases of lithium refractory manic or schizoaffective disorder patients. For nonschizophrenic but still psychotic patients, use of antipsychotic drugs should be as brief as possible. Even for chronic schizophrenics who require maintenance, the use of minimal effective doses and drug holidays seems wise. It must be remembered, however, that there is no clearly established evidence that such a regimen is effective in reducing tardive dyskinesia. Indeed, there is one troubling report that drug holidays may increase the likelihood of developing this condition (Jeste et al. 1979).

Active treatment of tardive dyskinesia with drugs is at present very unsatisfactory. A number of compounds have been used, including reserpine, lecithin, and deanol, but consistent evidence of their efficacy is scant. Increasing a patient's dose of anti-psychotic medication tends to suppress tardive dyskinesia but at the apparent risk of worsening the underlying disorder. Any attempt to raise the dose to suppress tardive dyskinesia must therefore be based on an overall assessment of risks and benefits. Clearly, there is a need for new, safe, antipsychotic agents that do not produce tardive dyskinesia.

Patients Who Do Not Respond to Drugs

For schizophrenic patients who show continued active symptoms despite a reasonable drug dosage, a few guidelines apply. If at all possible, such a patient should first receive a long-acting intra-muscular preparation to assure that the body accepts the drug. If this proves ineffective, it seems worthwhile to consider rehos-pitalization in order to withdraw the patient totally from drugs and re-evaluate the condition. Under these circumstances some patients will prove to have been misdiagnosed. They may be suffering a bipolar disorder instead of a schizophrenic disorder, they may have an organic mental disorder, or they may have been using, unbeknownst to the clinician, drugs that produce psy-chiatric symptoms. Deprived of these drugs in the hospital, some patients improve rapidly.

For those patients who fail to improve and who continue to be best diagnosed as schizophrenic, the clinician is left with psycho-social management as the only rational alternative. Whether this can be best accomplished in a hospital or in a sheltered setting in the community must be decided on a case-by-case basis. Some patients truly need indefinite hospitalization because they are unable to survive satisfactorily in any other setting. The clinician should not be afraid to make this recommendation when other alternatives prove ineffective.

The clinician's relationship with such patients and with their families may be damaged when treatment fails because such patients tend to become discouraged, to feel let down by the doctor, or to seek treatment elsewhere. Under these circumstances, considerable patience and humility are required on the part of the physician not to abandon the patient either overtly or indirectly.

Before a decision for indefinite hospitalization is made, it seems reasonable to attempt a systematic trial of other psychoactive medications, including lithium carbonate, both alone and in conjunction with antipsychotic drugs, keeping in mind that lithium may sensitize the patient to the neurotoxic effects of the antipsychotic drugs. Antidepressants may also be tried, particularly if the patient's symptoms are primarily apathy and withdrawal rather than hallucinations and delusions. Antidepressants may exacerbate hallucinations and delusions, but in some cases, which may constitute atypical depressions, such symptoms may be relieved by these medications. Though controversial, benzodiazepines or ECT may be tried as last resorts.

To some degree, a systematic experimental approach in treating patients who do not respond to drugs flouts current concepts of diagnosis and therapy. This approach seems justified, however, when the adverse consequences of chronic mental illness are considered. It may be wise under such circumstances to explain the plan in detail to patient and family and even to secure their written permission for such treatment.

Psychosocial Treatment

The relationship between modern psychiatric diagnosis and drug treatment is today becoming increasingly intimate. In contrast, however, a similar connection between diagnosis and psychosocial therapy is much more tenuous, primarily because of the limited evidence documenting the efficacy of psychosocial treatment with schizophrenic patients.

The publication of May's *Treatment of Schizophrenia* (1968) shook traditional notions about the role of psychotherapy in the treatment of schizophrenia. Although May's patient population consisted of 228 middle-prognosis, first-admission, hospitalized schizophrenics, his elaborately documented failure to find individual psychotherapy alone to be an effective treatment for this group raised some serious questions regarding the utility of psychotherapy for any schizophrenic patients. Following his lead, most subsequent research on psychotherapy with schizophrenic patients has focused on its interaction with drugs and has utilized an outpatient setting to study discharged schizophrenic patients over protracted periods of time.

There are no good modern studies that test the effects of traditional psychoanalytic psychotherapy with and without drugs on a group of chronic, hospitalized schizophrenic patients. The studies by Grinspoon et al. (1967, 1968, 1972, 1975) demonstrate much greater improvement in this population from antipsychotic drugs plus psychotherapy than from placebo plus psychotherapy, but such a finding is hardly unexpected today. In addition, the effects of combined treatment plateaued at twelve weeks, suggestive of the typical response to drugs alone. The effect of psychotherapy as opposed to drugs cannot be ascertained from these studies. Other modern studies with chronic, hospitalized schizophrenics assess the effects of various behavioral modification techniques with and without drugs (Chapters 6 and 8).

In a thorough review of studies completed prior to 1980, Mosher and Keith (1980) conclude that schizophrenic patients appear to profit most from treatments that involve extensive attention to the patient's social environment, such as nonhospital-based family therapy and various residential milieus. In particular, these authors emphasize the greater efficacy of nonhospital-based therapies and note the relative inefficacy of group and individual therapy. As with most studies in this area, the primary outcome measure was incidence of rehospitalization, certainly a very limited criterion given the complexity of schizophrenic illness.

Outpatient Treatment

It seems reasonable to conclude, from the dearth of studies on psychotherapy with hospitalized populations, that strong faith in its efficacy has faded. The same lack of interest, however, does not characterize studies on outpatients, from which sophisticated and useful findings have emerged.

Hogarty et al. (1974a, 1974b, 1977) in particular have addressed the role of psychotherapy in this group. The 374 patients admitted to their study had all been discharged with a diagnosis of schizophrenia from three Maryland state hospitals. All were between the ages of 18 and 55 and had most recently been hospitalized continuously for less than two years. They were not retarded, addicted to drugs or alcohol (manageable substance abuse was permitted), or homicidal/suicidal when off medication. To be accepted into the project, patients had to attend a study clinic within twenty-one days after discharge, provide a "significant other" for collateral ratings, and be either a wage earner or a homemaker (Hogarty et al. 1974b). The group was not exceptional in its motivation; only 14 of 527 eligible patients agreed to participate in the study while they were inpatients.

While participating in the two-year study, patients received one of four treatments: placebo alone, placebo plus major role therapy (MRT), antipsychotic drug alone, or antipsychotic drug plus MRT. MRT consisted of individual social work and vocational rehabilitation counseling at least once a month. The goals of MRT included resolution of personal and environmental problems affecting the patient's performance as wage earner or homemaker as well as improvement in interpersonal relationships, reduction of social isolation, and better self-care. Medication and money problems were discussed. MRT techniques included acceptance, clarification, support, and appropriate assurance. On the surface, not all clinicians may consider this treatment to be "psychotherapy" in the traditional sense. In fact, however, it operationally constitutes the supportive, reality-oriented psychotherapy customarily used by practicing clinicians in treating schizophrenic patients in an outpatient aftercare setting.

All patients in the study were randomly assigned to one of the four treatment groups and periodically evaluated six times in the two years. In addition to psychopathology, a broad range of other factors, including social behavior and community adjustment, were evaluated as well. Patients in the two drug groups received chlorpromazine in individually adjusted doses, but no medicated patient was given less than 100 mg per day.

At the end of the first year, relapse rates were 72.5 per cent for placebo alone, 62.6 per cent for placebo plus MRT, 32.6 per cent for durg alone, and 25.7 per cent for drug plus MRT. Drugs exerted the main effect. Comparison over the year between drug-alone and drug-plus-MRT groups showed no statistically significant differences. Over the second six months alone, the drug-plus-MRT group showed significantly less relapse than the drug-alone group. During the first six months, however, there was a trend favoring non-MRT for drug-treated patients.

Surprisingly, the effects of MRT on relapse prevention were the same with and without drugs. Thus, MRT did not appear to interact with drugs during the first year but had an additive effect. It should be kept in mind that the clinical (as opposed to statistical) significance of MRT on relapse prevention was small compared with the drug effect.

After the acute episode had been resolved, drugs proved purely prophylactic in forestalling relapse. They had no positive therapeutic effect on social adjustment during the first year. Female patients treated with drugs went longer without relapse than did males. Females also tended to benefit more from MRT than males (as measured by relapse rates), but this difference was not statistically significant. On placebo, both males and females relapsed at the same rate.

During the second year of the study, there emerged a number of important interactive effects between medication and MRT. These occurred for the first time at eighteen months and were even stronger at twenty-four months. For medicated patients, MRT helped social adjustment. For male patients on placebo, social adjustment was better if they did not receive MRT. Female patients on placebo still received some social adjustment benefit from MRT. However, MRT did not have any positive effects on symptoms during the second year. Finally, for patients who had poor prognostic signs at the start of the study, such as absence of a precipitating event, poor social history, or a rejecting family, MRT hastened relapse.

In using this work of Hogarty et al. to evaluate the role of psychotherapy in treating stabilized discharged schizophrenic patients, the issues of dosage and timing should be kept in mind. For too long, psychotherapy has been thought of in terms of "more is better." The implications of the Hogarty study are that more may be harmful—worsening social adjustment in unmedicated schizophrenic males and generally hastening relapse during the first six months of treatment.

It is also important to look beyond the relatively slight if statistically significant relapse prevention effects of psychotherapy to the more substantial effects on social adjustment, which did not appear until eighteen months into the study. For patients who comply with drug regimen, a useful psychotherapy model might be one in which session frequency and goals begin very modestly six to eight months after discharge and increase gradually over the next twelve months to the eighteen-month point, diminishing quickly if at any time it becomes clear that the patient has stopped taking medication. It remains to be seen whether MRT's beneficial effects on social adjustment begin abruptly if MRT is begun immediately or whether a long and perhaps risky induction phase is needed during the first eighteen months, as traditional psychotherapeutic ideology suggests.

Other Social Therapies

New intervention treatments for families of schizophrenics are described in Chapter 6. Innovative treatments such as the "psychoeducational" approach of Anderson et al. (1980) are not only rational and teachable but have also been carefully researched.

For a particular patient, the clinician can apply a few rules of thumb that are both consistent with research evidence and specific enough to allow individualized treatment. For acutely psychotic patients, the clinician should try to minimize social stress. Family members need to have the nature of the illness explained to them and their guilt alleviated. They should also be instructed on what to do if the patient becomes troublesome at home. Effort should be made to have the family accept the patient's idiosyncratic thinking and perception while at the same time maintaining limits on the patient's behavior. Because the family is usually distressed by the illness, considerable time should be devoted to listening to family members discuss their reactions to it.

Over the course of the therapy, the level of expectations placed on the patient must change as the illness changes. In general, expectations should be low to avoid exacerbation of symptoms.

Community-Based Alternatives

Transitional facilities, including day centers, halfway houses, and day hospitals, are an important part of psychosocial rehabilitation and serve both as alternatives to rehospitalization and as settings for structured psychosocial care. The dropout rate in such programs is typically high and is unfortunately associated with considerable symptom relapse. For patients who maintain contact with a transitional program, however, recidivism appears to be reduced (Anthony et al. 1972). In particular, the Training in Community Living (TCL) program of Stein and Test (1978) has been a subject of great interest in the field.

The TCL program aggressively attempts to avoid hospitalization by engaging the patient immediately in a full schedule of daily activities (in a day program setting) with pharmacotherapy when indicated. "Outreach" staff visit the patient at home to teach practical skills, maintain motivation, and help in finding employment. The patient's family is engaged as soon as possible. If it is determined that the relationship between patient and family is not a healthy one, a "constructive separation" is sought. Through liaison with community employers, the patient is placed in practical work as soon as possible. Staff of the program are on call twenty-four hours a day and fight dropout through constant outreach activities.

Patients in the TCL program were persons who had sought inpatient care at a mental health institute in Madison, Wisconsin, who were between the ages of 18 and 62, and who had a diagnosis other than severe organic brain syndrome or primary alcoholism. How many suffered from chronic schizophrenic remains unclear. Nonetheless, when compared with standard hospital treatment for chronically mentally ill patients in Madison, those patients who participated in the TCL program for one year made minimal use of the hospital and showed improved self-esteem and reduced symptoms. Employment status for the TCL group was also higher. Despite the inherently expensive nature of the program, a cost-benefit analysis showed it to be slightly less expensive than traditional treatment when the patient's earnings and the hypothetical costs of entanglement with the criminal justice system were taken into account.

Several caveats apply to the TCL program. First of all, its generalizability to places having greater racial and ethnic heterogeneity and fewer sympathetic employers is uncertain. Secondly, as noted, how the program applies specifically to the schizophrenic patient remains unclear. Thirdly, it would appear necessary to have competent and highly motivated staff to run such a program, a situation that does not exist in many large urban areas. Fourthly, the cost-benefit analysis, although favorable to the program, showed little differences in cost between TCL and brief hospitalization plus aftercare. Finally, Stein and Test acknowledge that the benefits of their program do not outlive the association between patient and program. Thus, there is no evidence of lasting benefit, and maintenance TCL seems needed. There can be little doubt, however, that, where the social and economic climates are "right" and motivated, trained personnel are available, the TCL program offers significant improvement in the quality of life for many mentally ill.

Determining the Need for Hospitalization

Stein and Test (1978) argue that, when a TCL program is available, the hospital need be used only (1) for protecting the patient or others where the patient is suicidal or homicidal and (2) as a refuge for patients whose psychosis is so severe that they require the structure and nursing that only a hospital can provide.

The author is not convinced that these criteria offer the optimal guide to treatment of the chronic schizophrenic patient. The social and economic popularity of avoiding the hospital can blind one to its advantages. With an extremely aggressive attempt to avoid hospitalization, it seems likely that many chronically mentally ill patients who are presumed to be schizophrenic may be being managed in the community in a fairly desultory manner. The opportunity for a drug-free period in the hospital to achieve the best therapeutic response consonant with modern medical science is passed by. The hospital can provide exclusion of street drugs, can monitor accurately a patient's use of therapeutic medication, and can attempt nonstandard drug trials as described above. Finally, a substantial number of schizophrenic patients will not maintain ongoing contact with any transitional or sheltered program. For these patients, the opportunity for chronic institutionalization may be both appropriate and humane.

4. Hospital Treatment

JERROLD S. MAXMEN, M.D.

> How sick we must be, ere we make men just!
> I think it frets the saints in heaven to see
> How many desolate creatures on the earth
> Have learnt the simple dues of fellowship
> And social comfort, in a hospital.
>
> ELIZABETH BARRETT BROWNING

To many, the psychiatric hospital symbolizes failure. To the patient, hospitalization is a concrete recognition of the inability to cope; in the family, it triggers feelings of blame, guilt, and despair; and to the therapist, it represents clinical defeat.

Instead of as an evil necessity, the psychiatric hospital should be viewed as a humane alternative to alleyways and park benches. Amid all the studies, statistics, and controversies, one should not overlook Browning's simple truth: to the lonely, the hospital may provide fellowship and comfort.

Yet the hospital can offer more than protection and camaraderie. It can afford patients a unique chance to "get their act together," especially when it becomes a critical link in a chain of rehabilitative resources. Without it, no system of care for the chronically ill is complete. So when we consider the role of the hospital in the context of deinstitutionalization, the issue is not how quickly we can eliminate it but rather how it can be used most effectively. Of all the treatment settings for chronic psychiatric patients, only the hospital allows for round-the-clock interaction, assessment, and treatment. It is a total environment that can exert greater influence, for good or ill, than any other rehabilitative setting.

This chapter addresses four questions:

1. What are the different inpatient services potentially available to chronic patients?
2. What is the comparative effectiveness of each?
3. How can the chronically ill be best served by hospitalization?
4. What is the role of hospitalization in the deinstitutionalization process?

The chapter emphasizes unitwide programs, that is, how the hospital's overall structure influences therapeutic change. (Specific psychological, social, and drug therapies are discussed in other chapters.) Because the hospital is the most frequently used total environment in the care of the chronically ill, its role is unique and important. Because unitwide programs are expensive, they deserve closer attention.

Types of Hospitals

Hospitals can be classified by many criteria: government-sponsored versus private, length of stay, primary treatment method, staff-to-patient ratio, open- versus closed-door, and so forth. In this chapter they are classified according to length of stay and type of unitwide program.

Length of Stay

Whether a length of stay is viewed as long-term or short-term varies historically. In the 1950's, an eight-month hospitalization was typical for chronic patients and often referred to as short-term, whereas today it would be called long-term. The following definitions reflect current realities:

A *short-term* unit has a median length of stay of less than thirty days.

An *intermediate-term* unit has a median length of stay of between thirty days and six months.

A *long-term* unit has a median length of stay of longer than six months.

Types of Unitwide Programs

Although every inpatient service uses a variety of treatments, each also has an overriding unitwide program that derives from a specific theory about effecting change. For example, token economies are based on behavioral theories and therapeutic communities on interpersonal theories. Nevertheless, a strong argument could be made that interpersonal theories account for the benefits afforded by token economies and, vice versa, that behavioral principles do the same for therapeutic communities. Assuming that it is unknown whether the theoretical underpinnings ascribed to a unitwide program validly explain why change occurs, this chapter classifies units by descriptive, not theoretical, criteria.

In categorizing unitwide programs, one should pay more attention to what actually happens in the hospital than to any official label. For example, a custodial program may be called a "therapeutic community" merely because it has a weekly community meeting. Moreover, there is disagreement among hospital psychiatrists as to definitions and parameters. There is no consensus, for instance, on the distinction between "milieu therapy" and "therapeutic community." Despite these limitations, it is hoped that the following definitions will provide a common vocabulary and be of heuristic value.

Crisis intervention units (CI) are often attributed to the theories of Lindemann (1944) and G. Caplan (1964). By definition, these units are short-term and focus on the immediate crisis only. The staff quickly tries to identify and rectify the psychological, social, and biological changes triggering the crisis. By restricting assessment and intervention to acute changes, treatment purposely avoids other issues, such as daily living skills, character traits, and family problems. To qualify for admission, the patient usually must exhibit acutely changed behavior or symptoms. Hence it would be inappropriate to admit gradually deteriorating patients to a CI unit. On the other hand, chronic patients who suddenly decompensate, especially under clearly identifiable stresses and with readily available social supports, might be quite suitable for admission (Maxmen and Tucker, 1973).

The concept of a *therapeutic community* (TC) was initiated by Main (1957) and first applied in psychiatry by Jones (1953). After

Wilmer (1958) and Detre et al. (1961) set up TCs in San Francisco and New Haven, respectively, they blossomed throughout the United States and became so popular that, during the mid-1960's, no self-respecting hospital psychiatrist would confess to not having a TC. In the process, the TC became an "institutional Rorschach," meaning many different things to many different professionals. Any unit that encouraged patient decision making, provided homelike furnishings, practiced democracy, or held community meetings was deemed a TC. As Pinsker (1966) noted, any collection of staff and patients constitutes a community and staff will ever say that their program is less than "therapeutic." What's more, the terms "therapeutic community" and "milieu treatment" were often used interchangeably. This chapter easily resolves this confusion: it completely ignores the meaningless phrase "milieu treatment."

A therapeutic community is defined here as a unitwide treatment that not only attempts to employ the full therapeutic resources of the entire staff but, most characteristically, has the patients serve as the major agents of change. Activities are arranged so that patients being therapeutic to one another usually takes precedence over all other treatment efforts (Maxmen et al. 1974). For example, Tompkins I, the New Haven unit developed by Detre et al. (1961), restricted individual psychotherapy to one hour a week. If a greater amount of individual therapy was provided, the rationale went, patients would look primarily to therapists and not to other patients as their principal therapeutic resource. To serve effectively as agents of change, patients know all relevant psychiatric data about one another and have substantial, albeit not unlimited, authority to grant privileges to other patients. Accountable for their own as well as every other patient's actions, those hospitalized on a TC are expected to help their mates resolve personal problems. At Tompkins I, for example, if some patients persisted in keeping secrets from the group, all patients were taken to task. To encourage patients to act as agents of change, systematic rewards and punishments are frequently used, although they are not a necessary ingredient of a TC.

In identifying the essence of a TC, principles have been confused with methods. Patient voting, community meetings, staff egalitarianism, and so forth are not crucial to a TC. Often used as window-dressing, these virtues frequently obscure what distinguishes the TC—namely, its primary focus on having patients serve as agents of change and on fashioning an environment for this to occur.

A *token economy unit* (TE) applies the principles of operant learning. In theory, a TE strengthens the patient's desirable behaviors and weakens maladaptive ones by using tokens, which are tangible, convenient, and serviceable intermediaries between the patient's desirable activities and the available positive reinforcers. For example, a withdrawn patient may receive tokens for socializing with other patients; she or he can then exchange the tokens for privileges or commodities. In theory at least, and probably in fact, social reinforcers (e.g., people being nice to the patient) increasingly substitute for tokens in this model.

Although TEs have many of the characteristics of TCs, the latter rely more on group pressure, especially from patients, whereas the former emphasize response-contingent consequences as the basis for rewards, which come from the staff. Because the TE is a child of experimental psychology, there is a greater focus on measurable behavior and a tendency to ignore such intrapsychic phenomena as feelings, memories, and dreams. As evidenced by the pioneering work of Ayllon and Azrin (1968) and Atthowe and Krasner (1968), rigorous standards have generally been applied in determining the effectiveness of TE programs.

Painfully, I must now resort to a neologism—*individualized eclecticism unit* (IEU). These units are without an overriding program for all patients; if there is any unitwide philosophy, it is that treatments are used selectively, depending solely on the specific needs and problems of each patient. The phrase "individualized eclecticism unit" encompasses those services in which the major clinical investment is in specific biological and psychological therapies or both.

Finally, a *custodial care unit* (CC), which is usually found in state hospitals, primarily seeks to keep the patient alive and safe from physical and medical harm. Unlike the previous four types of units, CC wards do not attempt therapeutic change; this is a descriptive statement, not a value judgment. Few clinicians or administrators will admit to running a CC unit because to do so is politically unwise and an implicit admission of "giving up" on the patient. What role these units should play, if any, is discussed later in this chapter.

CI units are by definition short-term services, but TCs, TEs, ICUs, and even CCs can be of short, intermediate, or long-term duration.

Comparison of Unitwide Programs for Chronic Patients

At present, it is impossible to show that one type of unitwide program is better than another. Comparative outcome measures are difficult to obtain. Besides the usual methodologic problems (Bachrach 1980, Braun et al. 1981), outcome studies rarely examine all the relevant variables. Also, as Bachrach emphasizes, there is a crucial difference between model experimental programs and their use in complex mental health systems. As she says, "Model programs are best seen as experimental efforts, not as solutions" (p. 1023). Thus, the following conclusions are tentative.

Although the utility of CI units is theoretically and fiscally appealing, data regarding their use for chronic patients are scarce. Yale's Emergency Treatment Unit (Weisman et al. 1969) provided a maximum three-day hospitalization for acutely decompensated patients plus a thirty-day outpatient follow-up by the same inpatient team. Although the ETU staff claimed that most of the patients had "marked chronic psychopathology," only 39 per cent had been hospitalized before and only 38 per cent had a psychotic diagnosis. Thus, in examining their outcome measures, it is hard to tease out the ETU's specific impact on chronic patients. Overall, 18 per cent of patients were transferred from the ETU directly to longer-term facilities, and an additional 19 per cent were rehospitalized within one year of discharge. However, of those patients who had three or more prior hospitalizations, 73 per cent were rehospitalized within a year. No further outcome measures were obtained, nor was there a matched control group (Weisman et al.). This study suggests that three-day CI units provide immediate assistance for chronic patients but little else. Perhaps a more significant issue is whether these brief hospitalizations are as effective for chronic patients as those of longer duration.

Length of Stay Comparisons

There have been four major studies comparing the effectiveness of various lengths of stay in what I have called individualized eclecticism units. Caffey et al. (1971) studied 201 newly admitted schizophrenic men in 14 different VA hospitals. These patients were randomly assigned to three groups: (1) standard, intermediate-term hospital care with the usual VA referral for aftercare; (2) standard, intermediate-term hospital care with one-year outpatient follow-up by the same inpatient staff; and (3) "accelerated discharge" after short-term care with one-year follow-up by the same staff. The average length of stay for the standard and accelerated groups was eighty-three and twenty-nine days, respectively. No differences in outcome were found between these groups.

Glick et al. (1977) obtained substantial data on 119 schizophrenic subjects assigned randomly to either a short-term (21 to 28 days) or intermediate-term (90 to 120 days) unit. No continuity of care was provided, although arrangements for subsequent therapy were made. Global outcome measures showed that patients with relatively good preadmission functioning did better with intermediate-term than with short-term hospitalization. Those with relatively poor prehospital functioning did as well, if not better, two years after a short-term than after an intermediate-term hospitalization. Both these trends were greater in women. Assuming that patients with relatively poor preadmission functioning are more representative of a chronic patient population, then short-term hospitalization seems preferable.

Yet these findings may be more related to the nature of the postdischarge treatment than to the length of hospital stay. Regardless of preadmission functioning, intermediate-term patients in Glick's study received more medication than did short-term patients. Among the intermediate-term patients, those with poor preadmission functioning received greater amounts of antipsychotic drugs. For the good-preadmission-functioning patients, those discharged from the intermediate-term units received more follow-up psychotherapy than did their short-term counterparts. For the poor-prehospital-functioning patients, however, the short-term group and the intermediate-term group received the same amount of follow-up psychotherapy. Thus, chronic patients in the intermediate-term group received more medication than chronic patients in the short-term group plus an equal amount of psychotherapy during the two-year follow-up. Collectively, these findings suggest that, two years following discharge, chronic schizophrenic patients discharged from short-term units do as well as, if not slightly better than, those treated on intermediate-term units (Glick et al. 1977, Hargreaves et al. 1977).

A third major set of studies was conducted by Herz et al. (1977, 1979) and Endicott et al. (1979) on 175 patients newly admitted to the Washington Heights Community Service (WHCS), a psychiatric inpatient service in New York City. All patients had a functional illness, and 63 per cent were schizophrenic. Patients were randomly assigned to one of three groups: (1) intermediate-term (sixty days) with discharge to the WHCS aftercare clinic; (2) "short-day," in which an average eleven-day inpatient stay was followed by day care on the same ward followed by a referral to the WHCS aftercare program; and (3) "short-out," in which an average eleven-day inpatient stay was followed by aftercare in the WHCS clinic. If patients were readmitted during the two-year follow-up, they returned to their initial inpatient assignment. The average number of days spent in inpatient care throughout the two-year study was 115 days in the intermediate-term group, 27 days in the short-day group, and 47 days in the short-out group. Unlike in Glick's study, there was no statistical difference here among the three groups in terms of prognostic parameters. The only exception was that there were fewer married patients in the short-out group.

In general, at two years, the short-day group showed the least psychopathology and impaired social and occupational functioning and the intermediate-term group showed the most. The patients from both short-term groups were also less of a psychological and financial burden on their families (Herz et al. 1979). This finding contradicts the belief that brief inpatient stays merely shift the burden away from the staff and onto the family. These results are of further interest because, at the outset, the staff favored longer-term treatment, believing that short-term inpatient care would eventually lead to more psychopathology and rehospitalization.

That support for short-term hospitalization of chronic patients is less equivocal in Herz and Endicott's study than in Glick's may be partially accounted for by the fact that continuity of care was not automically available to the latter group. In Herz and Endicott's research, number of days in the community decreased as number of readmissions increased for those in the intermediate-term unit but not for those on either of the short-term units. Consequently, this research contradicts the conventional clinical wisdom that "revolving-door patients" should be given a longer period of inpatient care early on to prevent future regression and rehospitalization. In a separate study, Kuldau and Dirks (1977) reached a similar conclusion; they found no differences in the number of days spent in the community between two groups of patients, one group released from a unit emphasizing rapid discharge and the other from a unit providing inpatient care, a day hospital, community housing, and sheltered work.

A fourth study, that by Caton (1982) of 119 chronic schizophrenics, showed that short-term (21 days) and intermediate-term (70 days) admissions bore no relationship to subsequent treatment compliance, clinical status, social functioning, or rehospitalization rate. The intensity of treatment on the short-term units being greater than on the intermediate-term units might account for the same outcome being achieved by briefer hospitalization. This speculation is bolstered by Rosen et al. (1976), whose data show that, by itself, the presence of group therapy on a short-term unit could largely account for the superiority of short-term over intermediate-term treatment.

Because these studies report overall results, it is possible that some chronic patients might do better on intermediate-term and long-term units. Yet so far, there are no data to support or refute this contention.

In summary, at least for IEUs, research suggests that, for chronic patients, short-term hospitalization is as good as, and probably better than, longer-term hospitalization. Patients on short-term units generally spend less time in the hospital, have fewer readmissions, exhibit superior occupational and social functioning, and are less of an economic and emotional burden on their families. In addition, the costs of short-term hospitalization are less (Endicott 1978, Caton 1980). Whether these results hold up for other types of hospitals remains unknown.

Therapeutic Communities Versus Custodial Care Units

Most of the reports that compare TC and CC units are uncontrolled and anecdotal. Even among these, it is unclear whether it was the TC or some other specific activity on the unit that was principally responsible for the outcome. For example, Spadoni and Smith (1969) describe the failure of a chaotic TC in treating schizophrenic patients. On this unit, the staff—with the best of intentions—deliberately and persistently avoided responding to the manifest content of a patient's speech but instead focused exclusively on covert messages. If a patient said, "I hear my mother's voice," a staff member might reply, "Why are you afraid of me?" Patients had the good sense to resent this type of response, accusing the staff of "double talk" and "trying to read minds." (Of course, clinicians do try to "read minds"; in a way, that is what we are paid for.) As the authors point out, continually responding to latent content may have further confused these already disorganized patients. Therefore, the failure of this program may rest less with the use of a TC and more with the staff's interpretive idiosyncrasies.

Beyond the semantic obstacle of making overall statements about the efficacy of TCs, a review of the literature strongly suggests that four factors account for whatever benefits TCs might offer: *clarity, structure, genuine opportunity, and restraint.* By this I mean

1. That effective units are relatively well-structured*
2. That this structure is made clear to patients
3. That, within this structure, patients are able to make constructive changes in their own (and perhaps others') actions
4. That the staff clearly shows patients (and their families) how to make these changes
5. That communication between staff and patients is straight-

---

*As discussed later, the study by Stoffelmayr et al. (1973) study showed significantly more social interaction among patients in a highly structured TC than in a less structured one.

forward, emphasizing what patients can do while pointing out what is realistically outside their control

6. That the staff and the ward structure encourage some emotional restraint in the pace and intensity of the hospital program and in the family's contact with the patient.

Mosher and Keith's (1980) review of various psychosocial treatments for schizophrenics confirms these conclusions. Anderson et al. (1980) obtained strikingly favorable results using a "psycho-educational approach" that included teaching families of schizophrenics about the illness and how to create an atmosphere of low expressed emotion, which dramatically improved the patient's postdischarge course. Furthermore, Van Putten (1973) has pointed out that the high level of activity usually occurring in many TCs may be psychonoxious to schizophrenics, who are frequently vulnerable to overstimulation.

Although no adequately controlled studies have proved the value of TCs for chronic patients, many reports suggest that these units reduce symptoms, enhance social interaction, and promote the patients' sense of responsibility, at least while residing in the hospital. Many authors note that the positive effects developed when the TC approach was introduced into a CC service (Martin 1950, Miller and Clancy 1952, Barrett et al. 1957, Rashkis and Smarr 1957). Others have described higher discharge rates (Miller 1954, Ellsworth et al. 1958, Ellsworth and Stokes 1963, Brooks 1960, Wing 1965, May 1968, Myers and Clark 1972). Whitely (1970) demonstrated that an intermediate-term TC for "psychopaths" effected a 40 per cent decrease in convictions and psychiatric admissions two years after discharge. He emphasized that psychologically mature psychopaths benefited from the program but egocentric, acting-out, impulsive ones did not.

Similarly (potentially), better-functioning schizophrenics seem more equipped to capitalize on the benefits of a TC. For instance, Wing (1965) showed that patients with higher rehabilitative potential profited from a TC. (Yet this might occur on any unit-wide program.) Van Putten (1973) felt that chronic schizophrenics could readily decompensate in an active TC. He cites many studies supporting this contention, including the finding of Letemendia et al. (1967) that the introduction of a TC had no therapeutic benefit in a five-year follow-up of seventy-seven discharged chronic male schizophrenics. Letemendia studied all schizophrenics in the hospital, including many apathetic, withdrawn, and hebephrenic patients.

In contrast, Myers and Clark (1972) evaluated a long-term (4.7-year) TC with chronic patients who were "still struggling with their fate and reacting against their institutional environment" (p. 56). In comparison to a CC group, their TC patients showed fewer symptoms, interacted more with staff and other patients, and were more likely to be released directly into the community. However, because no follow-up was performed and because the nurses preferred the TC, one might conclude only that dedicated staff get better results.

The value of a TC also depends on whether one looks at discharge rates or at long-term outcomes. For example, Galioni et al. (1953) showed that the discharge rate for "back ward" chronic patients from a long-term TC was 2.5 times that of a comparable CC group. Nevertheless, eighteen months after discharge, no difference between the groups was discernible. Galioni's TC focused more on intense staff involvement than on patients serving as agents of change, and thus it is unclear whether it was a TC at all, at least according to the definition advanced here.

Another study using similar patients revealed that moderate in-hospital improvement disappeared on five-year follow-up (C. L. Bennett 1966). Findings by Sanders et al. (1967) were almost identical. Still, to assess the effectiveness of a TC, or of any inpatient hospitalization, based on what occurs five years after discharge is absurd. The effects of any therapy are likely to be short-term, not long-term, especially for the treatment of chronic patients, who almost by definition are frequently rehospitalized.

Therefore it is not surprising that, for example, Ellsworth (1964) found that among 142 male "functional psychotics" who had been incarcerated for at least five consecutive years, those subsequently assigned to a TC had a 59 per cent release rate and those remaining in a CC unit had a 25 per cent release rate. One-year follow-up revealed that only 13 per cent of the TC patients were rehospitalized versus 23 per cent of the CC patients. It is likely, however, that both these relatively low readmission figures resulted not from the effects of a TC but because more than two thirds of the patients were released to sheltered-care facilities.

In summary, though nearly thirty years have passed since the introduction of the TC concept, proof of its utility for chronic patients remains elusive. If well structured and not overly stimulating, a TC is clearly better than custodial care on humanitarian grounds. Clinically, most reports suggest that in-hospital behavior improves in a TC. Whether this improvement is maintained in the community is doubtful but still unknown. Only nominal data show that a TC by itself significantly prolongs adaptive behavior in discharged chronic patients. Although many TCs have been evaluated, it is not clear how many of them emphasized the use of patients as agents of change. Indeed, it is still an open question whether results might have been different if they had.

Token Economies Versus Custodial Care Units

Despite the extensive application of behavioral techniques to the treatment of specific symptoms in chronic hospitalized patients, few studies have assessed the impact of unitwide TEs. In general, the handful of well-designed investigations restrict their focus to the in-hospital behavior of severely impaired patients in long-term settings.

Given these limits, these studies had uniformly favorable results. Atthowe and Krasner (1968) demonstrated that geriatric and brain-damaged patients displayed significantly more adaptive social behavior in a TE than in a CC facility. Although their program did not view discharge as a principal objective, their release rate was twice that of the preceding baseline year with the same staff. Using an intermediate-term TE, Schaefer and Martin (1966) showed that twenty chronic patients exhibited less apathy, more social interaction, and greater self-care than a control group of CC residents. Several noncontrolled investigations of long-term TEs have demonstrated similar improvements with severely impaired patient (Gericke 1965, Steffy et al. 1966, Lloyd and Abel 1970, Fullerton et al. 1978).

The average discharge rate of chronic patients treated by eight different TE units is 40 per cent (Atthowe and Krasner 1968, Heap et al. 1970, Lloyd and Abel 1970, Birky et al. 1971, Shean and Zeidberg 1971, McReynolds and Coleman 1972, Rybolt 1975, Fullerton et al. 1978). Fullerton et al. reported the highest discharge rate—72 per cent. This is an impressive figure since these patients had spent an average of ten years in the hospital. This 72 per cent, however, reflects only those who completed the program; only 29 per cent of those who did not finish eventually joined the community. Three-year follow-up showed that patients most likely to benefit from a TE were those who were hospitalized for under ten years and had a "functional" diagnosis and an IQ above 80.

Among chronic patients who were discharged from five different TEs and spent from six months to three years in the community, 46.4 per cent were employed, though many were in sheltered workshops (Isaacs and LaFave 1964, Anthony et al. 1972, Fakhruddin et al. 1972, Hollingsworth and Fareyt 1975, Fullerton et al. 1978). Nevertheless, the results are encouraging, given the severity of illness among these individuals.

Thus, the ability of TEs to help chronic patients in a hospital is well documented. As with TCs, the questions of whether TEs by themselves generate persistent postdischarge improvements or even facilitate community living are unknown. Yet some clues exist.

Therapeutic Communities Versus Token Economies

The few well-designed studies comparing TEs and TCs in the treatment of chronic patients clearly favor TEs. In my view, Paul and Lentz (1977) deserve credit for implementing the most well-designed and thorough investigation comparing long-term CC, TE, and TC units. Their patients were severely impaired and had been hospitalized for a long time. The thoroughness of their findings, the sophistication of their methods, and the practical problems that arose during their project make it difficult to summarize all the valuable information in their report.

Overall, they found that a TE was more effective than a TC, which in turn was better than a CC. At the outset of the four-year in-hospital phase of the program, a high level of interaction between staff and patients in both the TC and the TE quickly generated positive results. Soon afterwards, however, the two programs yielded different findings. For instance, although in the TC quality of self-care doubled by eight weeks, it then remained at this level throughout the rest of the program. By contrast, self-care among TE patients continued to improve even after eight weeks, reaching four times the baseline level after thirty months. A more striking difference was noted with socialization. At eight weeks, both groups showed better interpersonal behavior. Yet by twenty-eight months, the TE group had improved ten times over baseline, while even at thirty-seven months the TC patients had improved only two times over baseline. When the TC procedures were temporarily stopped (by design), these patients returned to baseline levels and did not improve even when the program was begun again. In comparison, when the TE procedures were temporarily terminated, there was a slight decline which immediately reversed once the program was restarted.

Similar patterns were observed when enhanced instrumental role performance and diminished bizarre behavior were assessed. The TC was particularly ineffective at reducing violence, whereas the TE eliminated violence in 75 per cent of the patients and kept it at a tolerable level in the others. Although administrative red tape confounded assessment of posthospital functioning, clear differences still emerged. Eighteen months after the four-year in-hospital phase, 90, 70, and 50 per cent of the patients from the TE, TC, and CC units, respectively, were living in the community. In short, the TE outclassed the TC and CC units in resocialization, instrumental role functioning, behavior, release rates, duration of community living, and cost-effectiveness.

Showing similar results in a one-year Scottish study, Stoffelmayr et al. (1973) described severely withdrawn males who, after being hospitalized for over twenty years, were taken from open wards and placed in either (1) a traditional CC unit, (2) a slightly structured TC, (3) a highly structured TC, or (4) a TE. The TE consistently surpassed the other three units in self-care, increased activity, and diminished apathy. As with the Paul and Lentz study, Stoffelmayr's team found initial improvements in all these areas with the TC but the gains were lost over time. By the end of the year, except for seclusiveness, neither TC demonstrated any advantages over the traditional CC unit. Decreased seclusiveness was equal in the TE and in both TCs. Level of social interaction increased most in the TE; the highly structured TC patients displayed considerably higher levels of social interaction than did the remaining two groups. Bizarre behavior was not significantly affected by any of the programs, though slight improvement persisted in the TE. The TCs initially reduced bizarre behavior, but as the year progressed, these gains faded. Stoffelmayr's findings conform to those of Paul and Lentz.

Deciding on meaningful outcome criteria is always problematic. Quite reasonably, these two studies use criteria that are readily measurable since such criteria are easier to deal with. Yet in evaluating patients, factors that are difficult to quantify, such as self-esteem, hopelessness, love, and futility, are also important. As part of the human condition, they should not be overlooked simply because they are difficult to measure. It is more than possible, but far from proven, that TCs give poorer results than TEs partially because these "intangibles" are not examined and partially because the staffs of TCs place greater emphasis on them than do the staffs of TEs.

Consider Hofmeister et al.'s (1979) behaviorist approach, which suggests the superiority of a TE over a TC. Although this study did not directly compare the two programs, it is noteworthy for several reasons. Hoffmeister's TE was at the Fort Logan Mental Health Center, a facility long committed to the TC concept. Moreover, this study describes an *intermediate-term* TE for chronic patients who did not benefit from a TC.

During the first nine months of the TE program, 75 per cent of the 105 patients were discharged. Of these, 59 per cent went to their own home, family, or apartment; 24 per cent went to nursing homes; and 6 per cent went to boarding homes. The remaining 11 per cent were transferred to another hospital or signed out against medical advice. Excluding one patient who died from a pre-existing heart condition, 80 per cent of those discharged were living in the community one year later.

Especially intriguing about this TE is that, in an *average of only fifty-eight days*, 68 per cent of a group of chronic schizo-phrenics were discharged; these patients had not been helped by a TC and had previously spent an average of 3.3 years in the hospital. Thus, the utility of intermediate-term TEs for the treatment of the chronically ill deserves much more attention.

Length of Stay and Unitwide Programs

The question is often raised as to whether short-term hospitalization, which is quite popular nowadays, is conducive to or compatible with either a TC or a TE. By streamlining procedures in both TCs and TEs, units with short-term stays have produced positive results. Hersen et al. (1972) did so with a thirty-day TE, and so did the Bronx Municipal Hospital Center (BMHC) with a twenty-one-day TC (unpublished). Yet in both cases, half the patients were acute. When Hersen stopped behavioral intervention, the acute patients began to model the chronic ones by becoming withdrawn, isolated, and so forth.

Approximately 80 per cent of the chronic patients in the BMHC TC were discharged to the community within twenty-one days. (This information is, however, anecdotal and unpublished.) Although the ready availability of aftercare facilities helped, this impressive result was also possible because the TC was tightly structured, used the better-functioning patients to mobilize chronic ones, and employed a trimmed-down version of the Tompkins I TC described by Maxmen (1974).

It is doubtful that a short-term TC with only chronic patients could exert the desired effect. Indeed, with too much stimulation, a TC might be harmful. Reading between the lines, I believe the study by Hersen et al. (1972) study suggests that a short-term TE with only chronic patients would be an equally questionable enterprise.

Implications of Unitwide Programs

Investigators invariably state that further studies are merited. After all, if one devotes years to studying a topic, one is hardly about to say it is no longer important. Yet, in evaluating unitwide programs, this conclusion is deserved. Considering the time, effort, and money involved in the hospital treatment of the chronically ill, it is imperative to know whether these programs make a difference. Meanwhile, clinicians must care for these patients. They must do something, for even doing "nothing" is "doing" something. So until more solid data emerge, four tentative conclusions can be advanced.

First of all, IEU, TC, and TE units are more efficacious than CC services.

Second, for chronic patients on IEUs, short-term hospitalization is preferable to intermediate-term, which in turn is preferable to long-term (Braun et al. 1981). Studies do not show that longer and earlier hospitalizations are prophylactic for chronic patients.

Third, research indicates that a truly comprehensive system of care for the chronically ill should include a TE. This conclusion may be premature and overstated. With its fetish for fads, the mental health field is notorious for adopting and then disposing of treatments (Maxmen et al. 1974). Enthusiasm for TEs may fade as it did for TCs in the 1970's. Nevertheless, hospital psychiatrists should follow, if not create, the most promising paths.

IEUs and TCs derive from a medical tradition; TEs stem from an experimental psychology heritage. Being less familiar with the latter approach, psychiatrists (as physicians) may be reluctant to consider a TE a necessary component of a comprehensive system of care for the chronically ill. Because to me TCs are fun and TEs are dull, I regret the more favorable outcomes of TEs, but the data force us to realize that what we like and what is best for our patients are not always the same thing. Such recognition is especially germane when selecting treatment and hospitals for chronic patients. Given how frustrated many staff feel working with such patients, all professionals are prone to "forget" that the aim of therapy is to care for the patient and not for the caretaker. In order to keep the patient's well-being as the primary goal, however, methods for reinforcing positive staff behavior are crucial. Indeed, motivating staff to care for chronic patients may be one of the most vital, but least researched, areas.

Thus, if chronic patients are refractory to short-term IEUs, then, after reassessing the patient and the kind and quality of treatment received, appropriate adjustments should be made. If that fails, decisions about longer hospitals stays, especially in a TE, deserve serious consideration. If a TE is not available, then this is a moot point—though the consideration of establishing one is not. It is at times bewildering how many hospitals (especially state facilities) that treat the chronically ill have scores of inpatient services with identical unitwide programs. If there was greater diversity, these hospitals could attract more staff, increase the morale of existing personnel, and afford more therapeutic alternatives for patients.

Fourth, given the vast array of inpatient and outpatient specific treatments—psychological, social, and biological—and the repeated evidence that any types of active unitwide program is superior to custodial care, there is no appropriate indication, from a *strictly clinical* perspective, for prolonged custodial care. This apparently dogmatic and potentially controversial assertion deserves clarification.

By "custodial care," I mean exclusively the provision of safe shelter, adequate nutrition, and enough staff to cope with psychological and medical emergencies; no active treatment or rehabilitation is intended. Custodial care may occur wherever hired workers are responsible for the patients' supervision, be it in a hospital, nursing home, or any other type of sheltered facility.

Temporary placement in a CC residence can be clinically justified under two circumstances. One, it could be used, if absolutely necessary, as a holding station until an active treatment program is found. Two, although scientific documentation is lacking, a few patients seem to benefit from a "cooling off" period, either because they have been overstimulated by active treatment or because they can stop acting out and start cooperating in an active treatment only after spending time in a CC facility.

Because of the many treatments, unitwide programs, and therapists that can potentially help chronic patients, the issue of choosing protracted, perhaps lifelong, CC units is never a clinical question, but one of ethics, administration, economics, and politics. Even with such stiff competition for scarce dollars from overburdened taxpayers, there is much that can be done in a mental health system, as discussed elsewhere in this book, to employ funds more efficiently and therefore more humanely. Patients would be better served if we focused more on the money we do have and can control, rather than automically excusing our inadequacies for lack of funds. The clinician may not find a decent facility because none exists or because he or she has not looked hard enough. Even here, the choice of long-term custodial care is not clinically justified. Neither in public nor in private should we ever pretend otherwise.

The Hospital as Toxin:
The Irony of Deinstitutionalization

Ask most people who know (or care) about deinstitutionalization and they will say, "It tries to quickly discharge patients from gloomy hospitals to more humane and cost-effective community settings. To accomplish this, those who operate mental health care systems should redistribute funds and staff into the community and away from the hospital, since in properly conducted deinstitutionalization the 'action' is in the community and not in the hospital."

This notion has reinforced the idea among mental health professionals that hospital treatment is somehow less important if not downright harmful. In other words, it is as if the hospital is a toxin and the less exposure patients (and perhaps staff) have to this institutional poison, the better it will be for all concerned. The buzz words and programs of deinstitutionalization, bolstered by conventional interpretations of research data and by "Cuckoo's Nest" portrayals in the media, all reinforce this view.

Yet at times hospitalization *is* necessary. Unless this view of the hospital as toxin changes, inpatient staff will continue to be demoralized. Better clinicians will shun hospitals and prefer clinic jobs even though chronic patients are usually at their worst in the hospital and it is there that they deserves the best possible care.

This brings us full circle. At the outset, I indicated that hospitals are often perceived as concrete signs of failure by patients, families, and professionals. Overtly or covertly, deinstitutionalization may augment this view; lower inpatient staff morale; misguide clinical, administrative, and government policy makers; and escalate tensions between hospital and clinic workers so as to undermine the very continuity of care that is the hallmark of deinstitutionalization. Paradoxically, we are discovering that we cannot take the institution out of deinstitutionalization and that the hospital requires not less, but more, attention.

5. Delivery of Aftercare Services

Inpatient care is only one part of a whole network of modern psychiatric services that address the needs of the chronic schizophrenic patient. The importance of aftercare, another critical part of this network, has been heightened by today's greater emphasis on short hospital stays. While the resident population of state and county mental hospitals was declining between 1955 and 1975, the proportion of patients treated as outpatients jumped from 23 per cent to 65 per cent (Bassuk and Gerson 1978). These changes in care patterns were accompanied by a change in attitude among mental health professionals; for the typical patient, long-term care was increasingly viewed as more effective and economical when done outside the hospital (Glick and Hargreaves 1979).

Maintenance doses of antipsychotic drugs are the cornerstone of aftercare therapy for the chronic schizophrenic patient, based on the well-established fact that such medication decreases symptoms of psychosis and helps patients remain out of the hospital longer (Chapter 3). That antipsychotic drugs are widely used is abundantly clear; a study of a New York State mental hospital showed that 88 per cent of schizophrenics were being treated with antipsychotic medication (Laska et al. 1973).

Psychosocial treatments are also frequently prescribed to supplement drug therapy. Their efficacy in forestalling relapse or in moderating the effects of secondary social handicaps has not yet been adequately demonstrated, but important work is currently under way (Chapters 6 and 7). There are many kinds of psychosocial programs used in aftercare. Data on care patterns are not available, but the mix of drug and psychosocial therapies in a typical mental health care delivery system is usually tailored to the individual.

Aftercare Compliance

Despite the growth of outpatient programs and the consensus among professionals on the importance of aftercare, gross deficiencies in aftercare services for the chronically mentally ill have been noted (Fox and Potter 1973, Gunderson and Mosher 1975, May 1975, General Accounting Office 1977). One problem is that many patients do not make use of available programs. Patients' refusal of treatment has been identified as the major source of discontinuity of care in one community mental health center (Bass and Windle 1973), and some studies report a general resistance to aftercare on the part of the schizophrenic patients, with dropout rates as high as 75 per cent (Labreche et al. 1969, T. Rothman 1970, Serban and Thomas 1974). In addition, it has been estimated that from 24 to 63 per cent of schizophrenic outpatients take less than the prescribed amount of antipsychotic drugs (Van Putten 1974). Among chronic schizophrenics, failure to comply with prescribed drug schedule is the most common reason for hospital readmission (Davis 1975, Reilly et al. 1976, Van Putten 1978, Amdur 1979, O'Brian 1979) and a major factor in aftercare program dropout rates (Hogarty and Goldberg 1973, Linn et al. 1979, Barrow et al. 1979). Compliance is the extent to which behavior, such as taking medication or keeping appointments, coincides with medical advice (Haynes 1979). In an extensive review of the compliance literature, Haynes concluded that disease features are not an important determinant of compliance except with psychiatric patients, particularly those with schizophrenia. It has been suggested that schizophrenic patients may be particularly prone to noncompliance because they are unable to comprehend instructions or to cooperate (Blackwell 1972, 1979).

There is a sizable literature on patient factors associated with rejection of aftercare treatment (Baekeland and Lundwall 1975). In studies focused specifically on schizophrenic patients, noncompliance has been associated with severity of psychiatric impairment (Labreche et al. 1969), presence of paranoid delusions (Wilson and Enoch 1967), lack of insight into the illness (Serban and Gidynski 1974), objection to being told what to do (Richards

1964), and lower social class (Labreche et al. 1969). In a two-year survey of the drug-taking behavior of 85 chronic schizophrenics, 46 per cent took lower-than-prescribed amounts of antipsychotic drugs. The reluctance to take antipsychotic medication was significantly associated with extrapyramidal symptoms, particularly a subtle akathisia (Van Putten 1974). Studies have revealed that some patients adjust their phenothiazine dosage downward according to need (McClellan and Cowan 1970) and that patients are less likely to comply with a complex medication regimen (Blackwell 1972).

Klein and Davis (1969) emphasize the importance of enlisting the patient's cooperation when prescribing psychotropic drugs. Patients who recognize that they are ill are more amenable to long-term drug therapy. In a study of discharge planning, Caton et al. (1983) found that more adequate discharge planning, which included education in compliance, was associated with a more positive attitude toward aftercare treatment, greater familiarity with the aftercare treatment plan, and improved compliance after discharge. Compliance has also been associated with residential stability (Barrow et al. 1979) and social support in the home (Wilcox 1965, Renton 1968), suggesting that manipulating the patient's social environment may improve compliance. It is likely that characteristics of outpatient facilities, such as staff training and commitment, how easy (or difficult) the clinic is to get to, and attention to patients' cultural background, are also important.

Discharge Planning

Linking the patient to community-based treatment and support has become an important aspect of hospital care, regardless of the type of unitwide program. Efforts to ensure that a patient will comply with prescribed treatment and is returning to an adequate living environment begin in the hospital with discharge planning. Several states, including Massachusetts, Rhode Island, and New York, have discharge planning laws designed to expedite linking patients to community services. The laws mandate that comprehensive community care tailored to individual needs—including psychiatric aftercare services, a place to live, economic support, and social and vocational rehabilitation—be arranged prior to release. An essential part of this program is careful assessment of the patient's needs. Specifically, the following issues are addressed in discharge planning:

1. *Medication management*   Most often, it is antipsychotic drugs that are prescribed for schizophrenic patients, alone or in combination with other medication (Ch. 3). Good discharge planning includes educating the patient about the effects of the drugs prescribed and about the importance of consistent follow-through. Frequently, family or others are asked to remind the patient to take the prescribed medication.

2. *Psychosocial treatments*   involve the patient alone, a patient group, and/or family members and focus on such areas as vocational rehabilitation, communication and social skills, interpersonal relationships, and life enrichment. The inpatient staff should transfer to the outpatient staff the patient's history and hospital treatment experience, so that the latter can prescribe therapy. Good discharge planning involves familiarizing the patient with the outpatient clinic and its staff and with the nature and intent of the prescribed therapy. Before leaving the hospital, the patient should be informed of the time and date of the first aftercare clinic appointment.

3. *Life support needs*   are essential considerations in discharge planning. The safety, cleanliness, and social support potential of a housing placement deserve investigation before arrangements are made for a patient to live there. Moreover, the patient's source of income after discharge must be assured. In some cases, discharge planning involves arranging for public entitlements. Attention to community survival skills, such as the ability to manage money or to attend to personal hygiene needs, will determine the degree of independence appropriate for each patient.

4. *Daily activities*   other than employment or treatment should be evaluated. Concern for how patients fill their day is especially important for those who are not working. Too often, patients are left with nothing to do but watch television or spend time alone.

Community Service Needs

Because of its dependence on community treatment programs, gaps in community services have been revealed through study of discharge planning. Critics of deinstitutionalization have pointed out that, in mnany locales, needed services for the chronically mentally ill have not been available (General Accounting Office 1977, Group for the Advancement of Psychiatry 1978) and this has sometimes resulted in delayed discharge. Using a new instrument to assess clinical readiness for discharge, the Discharge Readiness Inventory, Hogarty (1968, 1972) found that hospital differences in discharge rates were closely tied to availabililty to outpatient services and residential placements rather than to the patient's clinical condition.

A study of discharge planning for 119 chronic schizophrenics in New York City revealed no shortage of aftercare treatment services (Caton et al. 1983). Nearly all (97 per cent) were referred for clinic-based drug maintenance treatment and were offered an array of psychosocial treatments, such as individual and group therapy, day hospital care, and social and vocational rehabilitation. Of the patients in the study, 55 per cent were deemed in need of vocational rehabilitation. However, services were arranged for only one third of those in need, largely because of patient refusal, poor motivation, and severe emotional impairment.

Although there were many community-based psychiatric treatment programs available, there was a serious shortage of alternative living arrangements (halfway houses, shared apartments, and other supervised living settings) in the Caton et al. study. Discharge planners judged that a different living arrangement was advisable in 39 per cent of cases, but an alternative was available for only 13 per cent of those. The majority of patients in this study were poor and relied heavily on "natural" (as opposed to alternative) living arrangements, such as family settings, welfare hotels, or their own apartment.

A staff's efforts at discharge planning were reflected in the patient's understanding and knowledge of the treatment plan. Patients who received better discharge planning had a more positive attitude toward aftercare and were more familiar with the drug and aftercare treatment plan, such as the location of the clinic, the name of the therapist, and the date and time of the first aftercare visit.

Institutional Factors

In an analysis of hospital records from thirty VA facilities, Ullman and Gurel (1964) found that higher staff-to-patient ratios and smaller hospital size were related to more discharges and longer stays in the community. Caton et al. (1983) found significant differences in the adequacy of aftercare planning among staff on six administratively distinct inpatient units in New York City, attributed to communication and coordination between hospital and outpatient service networks, staff-to-patient ratios, and staff effort and commitment. The two units with the worst discharge planning were integral parts of the state mental hospital, where the staff-to-patient ratio was 1:55. Better discharge planning was found in units with a staff-to-patient ratio of 1:5. However, excellent planning was found on one well-coordinated unit with a staff-to-patient ratio of 1:55.

Discharge planning is often carried out by a team, with one professional coordinating. In Caton et al.'s study, social workers (53 per cent) and psychiatrists (39 per cent) were most often responsible for discharge planning, but psychologists, nurses, and mental health therapy aides also participated. There was no correlation between adequacy of discharge planning and professional background of the planner. Discharge planning is a skill known to all competent mental health professionals, regardless of professional degree.

Length of stay on inpatient units studied by Caton et al. varied from an average of twenty-one days on "brief" units to an average of seventy days at the state mental hospital. There was no correlation between adequacy of discharge planning and length of stay.

Outcome

Good discharge planning helps patients to remain out of the hospital. In 1968, Zolik et al. reported that patients with prerelease plans had lower readmission rates than patients without plans. In a more recent investigation, Caton et al. (1983) found that inadequacy of discharge planning contributes to early relapse.

In the Caton et al. study, the springboard for studying discharge planning outcome was the observation that there were patterns of "good" and "poor" discharge planning in the facilities studied. The research procedure rated the adequacy of staff efforts to plan effectively for the community care of the 119 chronic schizophrenics before their release. Only 29.4 per cent of patients received adequate overall discharge planning. While nearly half obtained planning rated fair, 21 per cent received poor or grossly inadequate planning. There were variations in adequacy in specific areas as well, such as aftercare, living arrangements, and patient's economic situation. Thus, there was a "natural" experimental situation for studying discharge planning outcome. Although discharge planning was not controlled, no biases in adequacy of planning were found to be related to the sociodemographic, clinical, or prognostic characteristics of the study subjects.

Patients were interviewed at discharge and at quarterly intervals for one year. The adequacy of discharge planning for aftercare treatment significantly influenced both treatment compliance at three months and early rehospitalization (within fourteen weeks of discharge). Because effective discharge planning successfully connected patients to community treatment services, there was greater adherence to treatment and longer periods of clinical remission for patients receiving good planning. Poor discharge planning resulted in inadequate linkage to community services, with consequences which include early rehospitalization. Although patients with a poor prognosis were more likely to be rehospitalized early on than those with a good prognosis, multiple regression analysis revealed that, when prognosis was controlled, more than half of the explained variance (18.7 per cent of a total explained variance of 34.9 per cent) in early rehospitalization was attributable to discharge planning. Although planning for aftercare treatment is the most critical area of discharge planning, the fact that living arrangements and economic factors contributed substantially to explained variance in early rehospitalization suggests the importance of including these points in planning.

Three months after discharge, the adequacy of discharge planning for patients' daily activities and economic situation had *no* impact on daily activities, role functioning, ability to manage money, or community coping skills. Moreover, the adequacy of discharge planning for living arangements had *no* appreciable impact on aspects of the patient's social environment. This may be because assessment of a patient's community coping skills and environment was not a high priority in the service systems studied. However, systematic monitoring of patients' social environment and coping skills can be included in discharge planning and then continued by outpatient clinic staff. Model programs, such as the one developed by Stein and Test (1978), have shown that attention to these issues has considerable impact on patients' lives.

Because the goal of discharge planning is to connect patients to community programs rather than to treat them, its effects are not longlasting. Caton and her colleagues found that the effects of discharge planning, most apparent in the first fourteen weeks after release, totally disappeared by the end of one year. In another analysis focused exclusively on rehospitalization, Caton et al. (1983) found that long-term outcome depends not only on discharge planning but on interpersonal stress and social support in the patient's environment and on compliance with community treatment. Indeed, the longer the patient is in the community, the more influential are environmental factors and community treatment and the less influential is discharge planning. However, because discharge planning is a cost-effective intervention with immediate and short-term effects in controlling rehospitalization, it deserves a prominent role in contemporary psychiatric hospital treatment.

Clinic-Based Aftercare

Most outpatient care across all medical specialties is rendered in clinics and offices. Mental health services are no exception to this standard, regardless of whether services are organized under medical or nonmedical auspices. Modern aftercare clinics usually offer a potpourri of programs ranging from psychotherapy by appointment to informal "coffee groups." Many programs are organized so that patients can easily move into and out of the various aspects of aftercare.

Psychosocial Rehabilitation Centers

The psychosocial rehabilitation center has provided a model for aftercare (Glasscote et al. 1917a, Beard 1978). New York City's Fountain House, founded by a group of discharged state hospital patients in the late 1940's, was one of the first day centers of this kind. It provides a clubhouse environment where patients can socialize informally, participate in vocational training, or use time productively when there is little interest in joining the labor force. For example, members shop for food and prepare and serve the noonday meal to fellow members. They also publish a daily newspaper; conduct tours of the house for visitors; operate the switchboard, a snack bar, and a thrift shop; and assist in the maintenance of house-sponsored satellite apartments. A transitional employment program helps patients work their way into jobs. Although there is a satellite apartment program, Fountain House is not a community residence. Most patients make their own living arrangements and have their medication therapy monitored by outside clinics and therapists. House staff, who have training in psychology, social work, and rehabilitation counseling, focus on the patients' social and vocational needs.

Although rigorous evaluations of psychosocial rehabilitation centers are lacking, it is known that those who consistently attend programs such as Fountain House have a low rehospitalization rate (Beard 1978). A serious problem, however, is an extremely high "no-show" rate. Beard's ten-year study of 4575 applicants to Fountain House revealed that 28 per cent of referred patients failed to keep even the first appointment. Also, there are many dropouts, that is, patients who leave the program before staff feel they are ready to. In the Fountain House study, 19 per cent failed to make more than five visits to the clubhouse.

Day Treatment Centers

Day treatment, or partial hospitalization, includes many of the programs of psychosocial rehabilitation centers in addition to such traditional treatment as drug maintenance and psychotherapy. First developed as an alternative to inpatient treatment, day treatment is now mandated at more than 500 community mental health centers and has been set up as a adjunct to state hospital programs. On the basis of size alone, day-treatment programs deserve to be taken seriously.

Most day-treatment aftercare programs offer a smorgasbord of therapies and activities designed to help the patient improve interpersonal relations and vocational performance. Open for at least six hours a day, five days a week, day-treatment centers provide a place to socialize and engage in productive activities, with enough shelter from real-life stress to enable patients to live outside a hospital. The day-treatment program studied by Meltzoff and Blumenthal (1966) consisted of regularly scheduled group activities, informal and spontaneous group activities, and individual activities, such as courses in music appreciation, art, dramatics, and current events. Vocational rehabilitation included prevocational assessment, industrial assignment, and paid work. Linn et al. (1979) studied ten day-treatment programs operated by VA hospitals and found marked differences in emphasis. Some centers focused on group therapy, whereas others emphasized vocational rehabilitation.

Most day-treatment studies have compared day treatment with inpatient care (Kris 1961, Wilder et al. 1966, Herz et al. 1971, Michaux et al. 1973, Washburn et al. 1976). The three key studies contrasting day treatment with outpatient care (Meltzoff and Blumenthal 1966, Guy et al. 1969, Linn et al. 1979) looked at the effect of the total day-treatment package (Table 5-1). Meltzoff and Blumenthal found day treatment more effective than usual outpatient care. Their sample comprised eighty primarily schizophrenic men, all of whom were unemployed when randomly assigned to treatment and control groups at discharge from inpatient care. More day-treatment patients than controls (30 versus 14 per cent) had found employment by the end of the eighteenth-month follow-up period. Moreover, only 30 per cent of the day-treatment patients had been rehospitalized, in contrast to 64 per cent of the control patients. Unfortunately, antipsychotic drug treatment was not controlled.

Guy et al. compared a day-treatment program with both inpatient and outpatient care and found day treatment more effective than either. All patients were on antipsychotic medication, but

TABLE 5-1. Comparison of day-treatment and outpatient programs

Investigators	Day-treatment program	Outpatient Control group	Random assignment	Diagnosis	Sample size	Sex	Rehospitalization	Functioning
Guy et al. (1969)	One center having drug treatment, group therapy, rehabilitation, recreational therapies	State outpatient clinic	Not consistent	Mixed	92	Mixed	No differences, but day-treatment patients were hospitalized for shorter periods	Day treatment superior for schizophrenics with emotional withdrawal, suspiciousness, unusual thought content, hostility
Meltzoff and Blumenthal (1966)	One center having group activities, special events, vocational rehabilitation, patient government, individual activities	Conventional outpatient treatment (drug therapy not controlled)	Yes	91% schizophrenic	80	Males only	Fewer rehospitalizations in day-treatment group (30% vs. 64%)	More job starts in day-treatment group (30% vs. 14%)
Linn et al. (1979)	10 centers at VA hospitals, varying in program emphasis plus drug treatment	Drugs alone	Yes	100% schizophrenic	162	Males only	No differences in days in the community or in hospital Six good-result centers significantly delayed relapse	All 10 centers improved patients' social functioning

random assignment was not uniformly applied to those meeting the study criteria.

The most sophisticated evaluation of day treatment, a study by Linn et al. (1979) of ten VA day-treatment aftercare centers, used careful diagnostic measures in sample selection, control of antipsychotic drugs, and random assignment to treatment and control groups as well as baseline assessments and a longitudinal prospective schedule of outcome assessment for two years after discharge. In this study, 162 schizophrenic men on maintenance levels of antipsychotic drugs were randomly assigned at discharge to day treatment or to drugs alone. An effort was made to ensure diagnostic homogeneity by having the project psychiatrist confirm the hospital diagnosis shown in the discharge summary.

Patients in the day-treatment program attended an average of sixty-five days during each six-month period. For 88 per cent of the patients, participation was on a full-day basis. Seventy-two per cent received social and recreational therapy, 64 per cent received group therapy, and 48 per cent received individual counseling. Also, 32 per cent received occupational therapy and 20 per cent received work training. Ten per cent of the sample had a very low attendance record (fewer than three days per month) and were dropped from the analysis.

Drug maintenance, the sole therapy for the control group, was the same for experimental and control groups. Medication was monitored by a psychiatrist who saw the patients every six weeks and also rendered limited supportive contact. About one fourth of the patients in both the experimental group and the control group did not comply with their drug regimen.

Patients were studied prior to discharge and at six, twelve, eighteen, and twenty-four months. Criterion ratings were repeated when a patient was readmitted to hospital. A relapse was defined as readmission plus the presence of symptoms, as assessed with the Brief Psychiatric Rating Scale. Patients readmitted to the study were returned to the group to which they had been randomly assigned at discharge. Project social workers used the twenty-one items of the Social Dysfunction Rating Scale to evaluate patients' interaction with their personal and social environment. A variety of other dependent measures based on professional raters, patient self-reports, reports from relatives, and data from medical records were also assessed.

There were no significant differences either in days in the community or in number of hospital days between the day-treatment group and the drugs-alone group. However, social dysfunction ratings showed significant change in favor of day treatment when baseline scores were compared with scores at twenty-four months. There were no significant differences in the cost of the two treatments, even though day treatment is more staff-intensive.

Important differences existed among the ten day-treatment centers studied. Based on two-year relapse rates, six received an overall rating of good and four were rated poor. The six significantly delayed relapse (average relapse rate of 50 per cent at the end of two years versus 67 per cent at poor-result centers). The four poor-result centers had longer professional staff hours, more group therapy, and higher patient turnover. Good-result centers offered more occupational therapy and a sustained nonthreatening environment. In terms of patient mix, centers specializing in the treatment of schizophrenia more often did better. Cost of care at poor-result centers was higher, at $7170 per patient, than at good-result centers ($4662).

It is of interest that the effects of day treatment were most pronounced twenty-four months after discharge. The delayed effect of day treatment, similar to the effect of major role therapy (Hogarty et al. 1974b), suggests that a long time is required for sociotherapies to change patients' social life.

Differences in therapeutic approach in good-result and poor-result centers support the contention that certain treatment environments are toxic for the schizophrenic. Patients with symptoms of motor retardation, emotional withdrawal, and anxiety, identified by Goldberg et al. (1977) as critical residual symptoms, were at particularly high risk of relapse in day treatment, especially in the first six to twelve months. As with major role therapy, patients who responded poorly to day treatment were those who were anxious, intropunitive, and hyperactive, had motor retardation, or showed little insight. Thus, treatment appear to have different effects on patients with different levels of vulnerability.

According to the interference hypothesis of Venables and Wing (1962), process schizophrenics who have poor premorbid histories cannot distinguish among and filter out vast amounts of irrelevant stimuli. If stimulated too much, such patients may attempt to reduce the noxious stimuli by restricting their cognitive field to a manageable size. Venables and Wing contend that hyperarousal is related to withdrawal in chronic schizophrenia. Brown et al. (1972) noted that, when patients cannot withdraw, latent thought disorders manifest themselves in delusions and odd behavior. Thus, when attempts to rehabilitation are too aggressive, relapse can result. May et al. (1976) found that some of the psychotherapies derived from neurotics, such as insight and milieu therapies, can be toxic to schizophrenics. Less-personal treatments, with limited social and vocational goals, produce better results. The challenge in devising treatment for the schizophrenic, then, is to strike a balance between too much stimulation and too little. Future studies of day treatment should examine the effects of specific care elements on specific types of patients.

Noncompliance was a problem in the day-treatment programs studied. Meltzoff and Blumenthal (1966) found that a caseload of 100 yielded an average daily attendance of 50, with a range of 35 to 70. Although daily attendance is not always required in a day-treatment program, patients are usually encouraged to attend three to five days per week. In the Linn et al. (1979) study, patients attended an average of sixty-five days during each six-month period, or two to three days per week. As noted previously, about 25 per cent of the patients in both experimental and control groups did not comply with their drug regimen.

"On-Site" Aftercare

The high rate of noncompliance with drug and aftercare schedules has inspired some clinicians to abandon clinic-based service and bring treatment to the patient's home.

The first "on-site" programs contrasted home care with hospital care in the management of patients sick enough to require hospitalization under ordinary circumstances. Pasamanick et al. (1967) conducted a study of home care of 152 acutely disturbed schizophrenics who were not suicidal or homicidal and had family support in the community (Table 5-2). Patients were randomly assigned to one of three groups: antipsychotic drugs and home care (fifty-seven patients), placebo and home care (forty-one), and a hospital control group (fifty-four). Patients in both home-care groups were seen primarily by a public health nurse, who visited weekly for the first three months, distributed medication or placebo, and discussed any problems encountered in the family. A psychiatrist, psychologist, and social worker were also available as needed and for evaluation. The psychiatrist saw the patient at least once every three months. After each visit the nurse submitted a written report to the psychiatrist, who then reviewed the patient's progress. In the fourth, fifth, and sixth months, the nurse visited every other week. After six months, visits were once a month. All patients were followed for from six to thirty months.

The readmission rate for home-care drug patients was only 23 per cent, but it was 46 per cent for the controls. The mental status of patients improved significantly in all groups, with no significant differences between them. Social functioning in both groups was quite low. A follow-up five years after treatment had stopped, conducted by Davis et al. (1974), revealed that differences between home treatment and hospital care disappeared over time, with many patients from both groups requiring rehospitalization. Such findings suggest that, to maintain any gains, aggressive treatment must be ongoing rather than time-limited.

Another example of home-based aftercare is Weinman and Kleiner's (1978) "enabler" program (Table 5-2). Members of the community, typically women with no more than a high school education, were trained to work with chronic patients. These women, most of whom had school-age or grown children, were interested in working with patients primarily because they had spare time and a desire to be useful. Trained and supervised by mental health professionals, these enablers focused on teaching patients basic daily living skills.

Enabler services were tested in a study that also explored the most effective use of backup professional intervention. Two chief aspects of home treatment were distinguished: the *patient-centered* condition and the *enabler-centered* condition. Patients in both conditions were assigned enablers, but backup professional intervention was offered in two ways. In the patient-centered condition,

TABLE 5-2.   Random assignment studies of community-treatment

Investigators	Program	Control group	Sample size	Diagnosis	Exclusion criteria
Pasamanick et al. (1967)	Drugs or placebo plus home care	Hospital treatment (long-term)	152 Drugs plus home care = 57 Placebo plus home care = 41 Hospital = 34	Hospital diagnosis of schizophrenia	Suicidal, homicidal, no family support
Weinman and Kleiner (1978)	Community care: patient-centered plus enabler-centered	4 comparison groups (see text)	263	90% had hospital diagnosis of schizophrenia	Family placement
Stein and Test (1978, 1980)	TCL	Brief hospital treatment plus usual aftercare	130	Functional psychosis	No organicity or alcoholism

professional counselors worked directly with the patients. In the enabler-centered condition, trained enablers worked with the patients.

In order to identify the living situation in which the enabler would be most successful, two types were designed: the *live-in enabler* condition, in which the patient lived in the enabler's home, usually with other patients, and the *visiting enabler* condition, in which the patient lived in an apartment with other patients and was visited daily for two hours, five days a week, by an enabler.

programs with "on-site" delivery of services

Duration of follow-up	Read-mission	Symptoms	Social functioning	Economic cost	Social cost
6 to 30 months and 5 years	E group 23%, C group 46%, no difference in long-term follow-up	Improved for both groups	Low for both groups	—	—
2 years	Visiting 23%, live-in 4%; live-in enabler is better	Less in enabler-centered; visiting enabler better	Visiting enabler better	—	—
1 year and 2 years	E = 12 of 65, C = 58 of 65 after one year; no difference after program terminated	TCL less sympto-matic dur-ing test; no difference after program terminated	TCL more time in competitive employ-ment; results per-sisted after program terminated	TCL slightly higher direct costs but greater benefits in terms of patient produc-tivity	No dif-ference

Patients were 263 functionally psychotic men and women, 90 per cent of whom had been diagnosed schizophrenic and could not be placed with families. Patients, whose average age was 49 years, had spent an average of thirteen years in the hospital.

A twelve-week orientation program prepared patients for the program while they were still inpatients. They were then randomly assigned to one of four conditions:

1. Patient-centered focus in a live-in enabler setting
2. Patient-centered focus in a visiting enabler setting

3. Enabler-centered focus in a live-in enabler setting
4. Enabler-centered focus in a visiting enabler setting

After discharge, patients received counselor and enabler services for about twelve months. The first eight months were spent in the program. The remaining four months were devoted to transition to a more independent living situation. Some patients relocated to new quarters and started full-time or part-time competitive jobs. Others took assignments at sheltered workshops or vocational training centers. At the end of the twelve months, the enabler project was discontinued. Although left to their own devices, most patients received routine aftercare at their local community mental health center.

Weinman and Kleiner's study had several methodological drawbacks: diagnosis and drug treatment were not carefully controlled, and little is known about the routine aftercare received by patients following termination of the program. A two-year follow-up revealed no differences in readmission rates for the patient-centered and enabler-centered conditions. However, patients in the enabler-centered condition showed significantly less psychiatric disability as treatment ended than did their counterparts in the patient-centered condition.

The rehospitalization rate two years after treatment was significantly greater for the visiting enabler condition (22 per cent) than for the live-in enabler condition (4 per cent). In contrast, outcome data on psychiatric status and role performance show that the visiting enabler condition is superior.

In summary, living in the home of an enabler proved better for patients' community tenure and self-esteem. Living independently and having a visiting enabler was better for patients' psychiatric status and instrumental performance. Although the personality and social characteristics of the enablers were not studied in detail, conflict expressed by the least experienced enablers (those in the patient-centered condition) was associated with poorer patient instrumental performance and lower patient self-esteem. The effect of staff characteristics on patients' adjustment deserves further study.

Stein and Test (1978) have devised a community-based treatment program, Training in Community Living (TCL), designed to manage patients both in an acutely psychotic state and afterwards, when florid symptoms are in remission (Table 5-2). The TCL program is staffed by a typical mental hospital ward staff (psychiatrist, psychologist, social worker, occupational therapist, nurses, and aides; about ten in all) retrained to carry out the TCL program. Staff spend their time working with patients in their homes, in the workplace, in supermarkets, and in community recreational facilities and occasionally consulting with police, landlords, and employers. A rented house is the headquarters of the program and is the meeting place for staff, who gather twice daily to share information about patients and plan future steps in patient care. They work in two shifts, from 7:00 AM to 11:00 PM, seven days a week, and a clinician takes calls during the night so that coverage is around the clock.

The goal of the TCL program is the creation of a support system that ensures adequate material resources, such as food, clothing, shelter, and medical care. "In vivo" teaching of community coping skills is an important aspect of TCL. In the beginning, patient-staff contact may be daily or even hourly, but this is gradually diminished as patients progress. Detailed knowledge of patients and awareness of their assets and liabilities enable the staff to know when to intervene and when to withdraw.

Careful assessment of family relationships is another important aspect of TCL. When it is determined that pathological family ties significantly contribute to the patient's problems, "constructive separation" is advocated (Stein and Test 1980). In such cases, patients are discouraged from living with or receiving any support from family and guidelines are set up to regulate family visits, telephone calls, and letters. Contact with family is resumed when the patient has gained sufficient independence to relate in a more mature fashion.

Stein and Test evaluated their TCL program against brief hospitalization (seventeen days) in a public facility plus unspecified routine aftercare. Unfortunately, neither drug treatment nor diagnosis was controlled. The 130 subjects in the study were young adult chronic patients who sought inpatient admission to the Mendota Mental Health Institute and who had a diagnosis other than alcoholism or severe organic brain syndrome. Patients were assessed on clinical and social variables before random assignment to treatment and then every four months for twenty-eight months.

At the end of twelve months, only twelve of the sixty-five

patients in the TCL program were hospitalized, whereas fifty-eight of sixty-five control subjects required inpatient treatment. In addition, those hospitalized in the TCL group spent significantly less time in hospital than control patients requiring hospitalization. TCL subjects spent significantly less time unemployed and significantly more time in sheltered employment or full-time, competitive employment.

Although there were no differences between TCL and control subjects on leisure activities and quality of community environment, TCL patients had significantly more contact with close friends and were more involved in social groups. In addition, TCL patients expressed greater satisfaction with life, as assessed with the scale of Fairweather et al. (1969). TCL patients also fared better than controls on some symptoms, probably because they were more compliant with treatment than control patients (Stein and Test 1980).

Longer-term follow-up carried out after the TCL program had been discontinued, revealed that performance for TCL patients deteriorated once the program was stopped: hospital use rose sharply, symptoms increased, and compliance with treatment schedules dropped. Employment was the only area in which gains did not deteriorate after the program was terminated.

Evaluation of family burden, using the Family Burden Scale devised by Grad and Sainsbury (1963)—which measures household disruption precipitated by the patient in terms of days missed from work or school, difficulties with neighbors, and disruptions in social and leisure activities—revealed that TCL imposed no greater burden than the control approach (Stein and Test 1980). Community burden—based on an analysis of frequency of patient arrests, number of suicidal gestures requiring medical attention, and frequency of emergency room use—was no greater for TCL patients than for controls.

When the TCL program was devised and evaluated in Madison, Wisconsin, during the mid-1970's, costs were greater than $7200 per patient per year regardless of the type of program (Weisbrod et al. 1980). The TCL had higher direct treatment costs (the hospital-based program was 10 per cent cheaper) but lower indirect costs, such as law enforcement costs and dollar cost to families. With the TCL program, patients' work productivity doubled. Thus, while the TCL program had slightly higher direct costs, benefits were also greater.

Case Management: Linking Clinic to Community

On-site aftercare programs, while effective in controlling patients' compliance with treatment, have not yet achieved widespread popularity in public mental health care delivery systems. Moving from the office to the patient in a home environment has not come easily to mental health professionals in the United States. A compromise has been the development of the "case manager," a member of the mental health care team who links clinic-based care with the patient's home and the larger community.

Community support system guidelines (Lourie 1978, Prevost and Arnold 1978, Turner and Tenhoor 1978, Lamb 1980b) propose case managers to oversee the planning and delivery of community services for chronic patients on an individual basis. Although there is considerable variation in job definition, most case managers do not function as primary therapists. Routine case management activities include making clinic appointments and introducing patients to clinic staff; visiting patients in their homes, community residences, aftercare programs, or sheltered workshops; and relaying information about the patient to the clinic staff (Baker et al. 1980). Case managers are responsible for anywhere from twenty-five to fifty-five patients (Baker et al. 1980), with differences in caseload size reflecting differences in job definitions and program philosophies.

The lack of consensus on the function of case managers is reflected in the wide variation in their educational background and experience. Baker et al. found that nearly two thirds had a bachelor's (62.5 per cent) or master's (4.7 per cent) degree and at least one year of experience in human services. About one fifth had a high school diploma as the highest degree, and 12.5 per cent had at least two years of college. There is at present little information about how case managers work with other members of the mental health care team and with patients and their families.

There have been no well-designed evaluations of case manager programs. One quasi-experimental study of forty case-managed and thirty-two non-case-managed chronic patients has been reported (Muller 1981). This study, in which each patient served as her or his own control, revealed that the presence of a case manager significantly helped patients obtain services in housing, mental health, medical and dental care, socialization, and community living skills. Differences in levels of environmental support and in severity of symptoms were also found.

Carefully controlled studies of case management should specify further how this mental health care role affects treatment compliance, rehospitalization, and cost of aftercare services. Such studies would provide an ideal opportunity for identifying characteristic differences between patients who use clinic-based services well and those who require outreach into the home. Identification of effective methods of delivering aftercare services to specific groups of chronic schizophrenic patients is one of the most pressing issues facing contemporary public psychiatry.

6. The Schizophrenic Patient and The Family

The family has always played a critical role in the care of the mentally ill. Today's increased emphasis on placing patients in community settings means relying on families more than ever for long-term care and support. This, however, has aroused controversy over how such prolonged dependent relationships affect both young adult patients and their parents. In addition, the question has been raised as to whether young adult patients who are themselves parents can meet their children's material and emotional needs.

Because its onset is in late adolescence or young adulthood, schizophrenia interferes with the usual progression toward self-sufficiency taking place at this point in the life cycle. Some schizophrenics never achieve independence from their families. Others, successful in establishing lives of their own, must interrupt family responsibilities when psychosis recurs. Therapeutic intervention to maximize the support potential of the family or to assist patients in fulfilling their family obligations has been slow to develop for two reasons. First, there has been considerable confusion over the family's role in producing mental disturbance in one of its members, with the family frequently being blamed for causing schizophrenia. Second, the relationship of family life to illness course in schizophrenia has until recently been poorly understood. It is now apparent that families involved in the long-term care of the chronic schizophrenic often become overburdened with the illness. Their hostility, criticism, and overinvolvement, unmodified by treatment, are known contributors to relapse.

It has not been unusual for clinicians to encourage young schizophrenics to become independent of their parents, just as healthy people their age do. Social rehabilitation programs such as Fountain House and Thresholds (Fairweather et al. 1969) deliberately discourage family contact on the premise that destructive intrusions by family members can undermine successful rehabilitation. A similar posture has been taken by Mosher et al. (1975), who urged young adult patients in an experimental psychosocial treatment program to live independently. Likewise, Stein and Test (1978) noted that some of the chronic patients in their model program were pathologically dependent on their families and felt that these ties must be broken through "constructive separation."

Isolation of patient from family may be necessary in individual cases under certain conditions. However, a general policy of separation does not follow from the current evidence on the family's role in schizophrenia onset or on its influence on illness course.

Genetic studies have established that the lifetime risk for developing schizophrenia is higher among biologic relatives of schizophrenic patients than in the general population (Gottesman 1978). When a schizophrenic man marries a normal woman, the risk that their offspring will develop schizophrenia is about 1.8 per cent. Risk rises to 10 to 16 per cent when the affected parent is the mother (Garmezy 1980). In cases where both parents are psychotic, the risk of schizophrenia is from 25 to 46 per cent (Kringlen 1978). The concordance rate for schizophrenia among identical twins is about three times the rate for fraternal twins (45 per cent versus 15 per cent).

Despite such genetic evidence, many still believe that the family plays a role in the onset of schizophrenia. Lidz and his colleagues (1958, 1965, 1978) presented the view that parents of schizophrenics show more conflict and disharmony than parents of other psychiatric patients. In their studies on the families of schizophrenics, they cited two chief characteristics of troubled parenting: schism and skew. *Schismatic* behavior engages the child in persistent family conflicts. The child internalizes the conflict between two irreconcilable parents, in which each parent undercuts the worth of the other. This interferes with the ability of the same-sex parent to serve as a role model. *Skewed* parental behavior fails to establish boundaries (psychological or generational) between parent and child and uses the child to serve the parent's psychological needs. A mother behaving skewedly is not sensitive to the child's needs and feelings as a separate individual, thus interfering with the child's ability to devote attention to its own development.

Studies spanning nearly two decades have led Singer et al. (1978) to conclude that inability to communicate is a distinguishing feature of families with young adult schizophrenics. Using Rorschach procedures, Singer et al. found that communication in families of schizophrenics is disturbed even before the patient becomes ill. Problems in focusing attention and in sharing the focus of attention are revealed by hard-to-follow and ambiguous remarks, unstable perceptions, and illogical and idiosyncratic thinking. These findings were not replicated by Hirsch and Leff (1975), who made a deliberate effort to duplicate Singer's method. In a five-year follow-up of fifty-two disturbed adolescents and their families, Rodnick et al. (1983) found that those children whose parents had trouble communicating developed schizophrenic disorders in young adulthood more often than those whose parents could communicate.

The Family and Illness Course

In an early study on the relationship between types of community living arrangements and outcome, Brown (1959) found that patients who lived with spouses and parents showed higher readmission rates than those living with siblings or more-distant kin or in separate lodgings. This finding was not supported by Brown's later work (Brown et al. 1966). Indeed, there is little evidence that patients who live with their families fare any better or worse than patients living in other settings.

A study of living arrangements of discharged state hospital patients in New York conducted by Blumenthal et al. (1982) revealed no differences in rehospitalization rates between patients who returned to families and those who returned to other settings. Goldstein and Caton (1983) compared the community experiences of 119 chronic schizophrenics living with their families, in single-room-occupancy hotels, or in their own apartments. No differences in rehospitalization rates or clinical or social functioning were found among patients in the various settings.

An obvious difficulty in comparing patients living in family settings with those living in nonfamily settings is that living arrangements involve choice, not random assignment, and thus are affected by opportunity, material assets, and good fortune. Patients who continue to live with their families have probably negotiated reasonably satisfactory relationships with family members. Patients who cannot get along with their families are often forced to find shelter elsewhere. In their study, Goldstein and Caton examined patients' commitment to their living arrangements. Patients did not prefer either family or nonfamily settings, but other characteristics were important. Patients valued settings that provided social support and settings with adequate space, cleanliness, and safety. No significant relationship was found between commitment to the living arrangement and interpersonal stress.

Because our contemporary mental health care delivery system depends heavily on the families of the mentally ill for meeting patients' material and social needs, loss of family ties is of compelling significance. To be sure, natural living environments can be unstable, particularly for lower-income patients. In one of the few studies on housing changes among the chronically mentally ill, Caton and Goldstein (1983) found that 50 per cent of 119 lower-class chronic schizophrenics in New York City had changed their living arrangements at least once in one year and 21 per cent had changed two or more times. Housing change was related to the revolving-door phenomenon: the greater the number of rehospitalizations, the greater the number of housing changes. Although patients gave many reasons for changing housing, those in high-stress environments were more likely to change than those in low-stress environments.

Studies of the reaction of a family to the mental illness of one of its members predate deinstitutionalization. The first such studies, in the 1950's, were conducted before the practice of educating patients and families about the more serious mental illnesses came into vogue. Yarrow and his colleagues (1955a, 1955b) described how the wives of thirty-three mental patients responded to the illness. Each woman was interviewed soon after her husband was hospitalized and again six months and one year after discharge, permitting intensive study of the phases the wives went through in coming to terms with the illness. The investigators found that the wives were often naive about psychiatric symptoms. Interpretations of the meaning of symptoms frequently shifted, and outright denial was common. Wives often minimized the deviance of their husbands' behavior by pointing out that lesser forms of the symptoms were found in "normal" people. During the early phases of illness, problems with the husbands were most frequently attributed to environmental stress, physical ailments, or character weaknesses. Fewer than one quarter of the wives had a psychological explanation early on; those who did felt that something was seriously wrong when the symptoms were first noted.

Hollingshead and Redlich (1958) found that families of lower-class patients showed a marked tendency to rely on heredity, somatic theories, or folk myths to explain deviant behavior. In contrast, upper-class families had more detailed information about their relatives' illness and explained the deviance on the basis of nerve strain, overwork, or fatigue. Freeman (1961) found that better-educated and younger relatives had a more positive attitude toward the patient and that a belief that the illness was caused by environmental rather than biological factors was linked with the view that the patient could recover and was not to blame for being ill.

In general, families tend to share the negative views of mental illness held by the public (Rabkin 1972). Resentment, fear, shame, and guilt are common reactions (Hollingshead and Redlich 1958, Myers and Roberts 1959). Using a measure of social distance devised by Whatley (1958), Swanson and Spitzer (1970) studied 670 patients and their families at different points in the patients' career. They found that family members were less rejecting of the mentally ill than the patients themselves. In a study of the families of 132 schizophrenics in New Haven, Schwartz et al. (1974) found that families felt more stigmatized when the patient's behavior was markedly deviant or bizarre.

Family members tend to conceal the patient's plight in the early phases of illness but not once it has become chronic. Clausen and Yarrow (1955) uncovered a pattern of concealment in one third of their sample, marked by avoidance of certain friendships or moving to another part of town. While shame motivated relatives to avoid friends in studies conducted by Rose (1959) and by Freeman and Simmons (1963), the more chronic the patient and the longer the hospitalization history, the more open and communicative were families with friends and relatives about the patient's condition.

Family members are more likely to be close to a person suffering from a mental disorder when florid symptoms have subsided and when there is no deviant or embarrassing behavior. However, Vaughn and Leff (1976) found that family members complain most not about florid positive symptoms but about persistent unpleasant character traits and social incompetence. Sampson et al. (1962) studied seventeen schizophrenic women and their husbands during and after the wife's first hospitalization. They found that some marriages were characterized by mutual withdrawal and others by the wife's intense involvement with her mother. In an intensive study of male patients and their families two to five years after discharge, Waters and Northover (1965) found that wives were often frightened of their schizophrenic husbands and experienced long periods of tension.

There is considerable evidence that rejection, estrangement, and abandonment by the family increases as the patient's illness becomes more chronic. Rose (1959) found that reluctance to take the patient home increased with number of years spent in the hospital. Myers and Bean (1968), interviewing 387 of 1563 relatives of patients in the original Hollingshead and Redlich study, discovered that, with each successive hospitalization, many more lower-class families cut ties with the patient than upper-class families. In fact, hospital discharge rates over time decreased more in the lower classes than in the upper and middle classes. In a study of the families of 300 chronic schizophrenics in Greece, Alivisatos and Lyketsos (1964) found that 88 per cent wanted the patient to remain in the hospital and felt no obligation for care. Half the families in this study wanted total cure as a condition for the patient's return to the family. Grad and Sainsbury (1963) found that families who had problems dealing with the patient were more likely to reject: 81 per cent of rejecting families had problems in contrast to 63 per cent of accepting families.

Family contact in institutionalized populations is inversely related to length of stay. Sommer (1959) studied 1600 mental hospital patients and found that only 12 per cent were visited at least once during a three-week study. In a later two-week period, only

10 per cent either sent or received a letter (Sommer 1958). Sommer found that mothers were the most frequent visitors and that patients were visited more often by parents than by spouses. Myers and Roberts (1959) and Myers and Bean (1968) reported that lower-class families visit mentally ill relatives less than middle-class and upper-class families do.

Community studies have shown that family ties are also lost by patients treated outside of institutions. In Caton's study (1981), 39 per cent of 119 community-resident, chronic schizophrenics had severely limited contact with kin. As Grad and Sainsbury (1963) demonstrated, a community-treatment approach increases the burden on families. Of 179 families who had lived continuously with a former patient for at least four years, 56 per cent were rated by social workers to be operating under objective burden (Hoenig and Hamilton 1969). These investigators found the parental home to be less burdened than the conjugal home.

One indicator of the long-term impact of mental illness is changes in family structure. Fewer schizophrenics marry (only 25 to 50 per cent), and, among those who do, the divorce/separation rate is higher than for the population at large (Kreisman and Joy 1974). Brown et al. (1966) found a divorce/separation rate in a sample of British schizophrenics three times the national average. In the group of lower-class chronic patients studied by Caton (1981) in the late 1970's in New York City, 52.5 per cent of those who had been married were divorced or separated.

Intrafamily Stress as a Factor in Relapse

The level of stress between family members is the only family factor that shows a relationship to the outcome or course of schizophrenia. A series of studies conducted at the Medical Research Council Social Psychiatry Unit in London by Brown et al. (1958, 1962, 1972) and Vaughn and Leff (1976) showed that patients living with relatives who are either highly critical or emotionally overinvolved (high expressed emotion, EE) are much more likely to experience relapse than those living with relatives who have less negative feelings toward them (low EE). The relationship between high EE and relapse is found in both conjugal and parental homes. Vulnerability to relapse is increased when the patient has continuous close contact with a relative(s) with whom he or she does not get along. Because adherence to a prescribed treatment can help a patient to deal with interpersonal stress, noncompliance increases the chances of relapse in a problem family setting.

Brown et al. (1962) rated the feelings expressed by the key relative (the most closely related female, usually a wife or mother) in a sample of 128 schizophrenic men. A joint interview with both patient and relative conducted in the home two weeks after discharge was the basis for the ratings. Relatives were scored on expression of uncontrolled emotion and hostility, taking into account the content of speech, tone of voice, and gestures during the interview as well as their description of how they behaved toward the patient outside the interview. Follow-up revealed that 56 per cent of patients from high-EE homes relapsed, in contrast to 21 per cent in low-EE homes. Those who had moderate to severe symptoms at discharge and who returned to high-EE homes did better if they had minimal contact, defined as fewer than thirty-five hours per week, with the key relative.

Brown et al. (1972) replicated this study in a sample of 101 schizophrenics, refining the measurement technique and including patients of both sexes. Family attitudes were rated in two interviews with the spouse or parents while the patient was still hospitalized (parents were interviewed separately). After the patient's discharge, a joint interview with patient and family was conducted. The following areas were evaluated in a detailed assessment called the Camberwell Family Interview.

Critical comments, the most crucial aspect of expressed emotion, were counted in units of conversation that ended with a change of topic or a question from the interviewer. Ratings were determined by tone of voice and context. Defined as critical comments were unambiguous statements of resentment, disapproval, or dislike. However, remarks were rated as critical based on tone alone. Berkowitz et al. (1981), who used the Camberwell Family Interview to rate EE, give the following examples of critical comments:

> Moan, moan all the time, and you think, if only he'd be consistent, but he never is, and that's how bad it is.

> They're going to give her £28 a week now. She gets £24 a week, and she goes through it like anything. (p. 30)

Hostility, rarer than critical comments, was rated as present or absent and defined as rejection of the patient, usually based on a character trait rather than on behavior. Hostility was usually expressed in extreme criticism. Examples of hostility from Berkowitz et al. are

> I get bloody angry, and at times I wish he'd die.
>
> She's so bent on destroying everything, torpedo-ing her mother's prospects, jealous of her mother's clothes. She'd go out and buy the same dress, you know, this kind of thing. It's such a disease with her. (p. 31)

Dissatisfaction with the patient or his or her situation was noted regardless of whether it was expressed with warmth and understanding or in a critical and hostile manner. In other words, a family member could be dissatisfied with something concerning the patient without being critical or hostile.

Warmth and positive remarks were rated on the tone of voice used when talking about the patient. Stereotyped endearments were ignored, but positive comments of sympathy, concern, or interest were included. One example from Berkowitz et al. is

> It's a relief they've [voices] left him alone for awhile. (p. 32)

Emotional overinvolvement, a more complex parameter, was defined as unusual concern about the patient, as indicated by feelings expressed in the interview (including crying) or reports of behavior taking place outside the interview. Overinvolved relatives tended to dramatize events, evidencing a symbiotic relationship with constant anxiety and an overprotective attitude about the patient's activities. A Berkowitz et al. example of overinvolvement is

> Everything was put onto me; therefore, she couldn't go out with other people. And the strain sometimes; she pinpointed everything at me. It was a lot to take. (p. 31)

Hostility correlated positively with critical comments, and warmth correlated negatively with both. Emotional overinvolvement correlated positively with warmth, but only half of the over-involved relatives were also warm.

In this study, patients were followed up for nine months. Twice as many men relapsed as women, and the unmarried were greater risks for relapse than the married. The nine-month relapse rate among patients living with high-EE relatives was 58 per cent, whereas only 16 per cent of patients living with low-EE relatives experienced relapse. Two thirds of the patients in this study took one of the major tranquilizing drugs for a large part of the follow-up period or until they experienced relapse. More patients in high-EE homes were noncompliant than patients in low-EE homes. The relapse rate for those in high-EE homes was 66 per cent for those who did not take medication and 46 per cent for those who adhered to the medication regimen. Medication compliance did not appear to be as critical in low-EE homes, as evidenced by comparable (15 and 14 per cent) relapse rates for those who complied and those who did not. It was again found that contact for more than thirty-five hours per week with key high-EE relatives was associated with greater risk of relapse. Seventy-nine per cent of patients having much face-to-face contact with high-EE relatives relapsed, in contrast to 29 per cent of patients who had less contact with such relatives. These results supported those of Brown et al. (1962, 1972).

Nine-month relapse rates for the 128 schizophrenics (Figure 6-1) illustrate the relationship between high expressed emotion, greater contact with high-EE relatives, and antipsychotic drug treatment. Patients returning to high-EE families where there is much contact who do not comply with their drug regimen are at the highest risk of relapse (92 per cent). Low contact with high-EE relatives and adherence to a drug regimen reduces the risk of relapse. Only 15 per cent of patients in this situation experienced relapse, a figure comparable to that for patients returning to low-EE homes.

Thus, while the influence of the family on the onset of schizophrenia is yet to be identified, the important work of the Maudsley group (Brown et al. 1962, 1972; Vaughn and Leff 1976; Berkowitz et al. 1981) has uncovered socioenvironmental determinants of the course of illness. Their method of assessing expressed emotion has inspired other investigators to devise briefer measures of

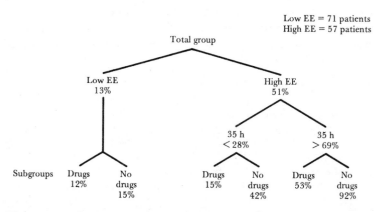

Figure 6.1   Nine-month relapse rates of total group of 128 schizophrenic patient (Vaugh and Leff 1976).

criticism and hostility, leading to the wide use of techniques that assess the quality of the family setting. For example, Kreisman et al. (1979) have devised a rejection scale that predicts relapse.

Self-help Groups for Families of the Mentally Ill

Traditional psychotherapies tend to overlook the needs of caretakers in the patient's environment. Research conducted over the past two decades on families of schizophrenics has led to new treatment methods to help families cope better with mentally ill relatives.

The vicissitudes of life with a schizophrenic relative have drawn some families together into self-help groups. Organizations such as Schizophrenia Associated of Greater Washington have cropped up in many cities to bring together those seeking a support group with whom to share the experiences of living with the chronically mentally ill. Hatfield (1979) surveyed eighty-nine members of a voluntary self-help organization to find out how families cope with a relative's long-term illness. It is notable that 71 per cent of the patients were men, most were single, and half were in their 20's. Of the relatives, 85 per cent were parents and the rest were spouses, siblings, or other close kin. All had above-average incomes and college degrees and resided in suburbs. Through trial and error, the families had developed a wealth of information on how to live with and manage the chronic patient. They reported four central needs:

1. Knowledge about the illness
2. Advice about handling problems
3. Someone to talk to
4. Some form of collaboration with staff treating the patient

Hatfield also found that burden is not shared equally by all family members; mothers frequently bear the greatest burden.

In Richmond, Virginia, Shenoy et al. (1981) have set up "Schiz-Anon" groups in which families are urged to be the primary caretakers for ambulatory schizophrenics whose clinical course has been marked by multiple hospitalizations and repeated failure to follow through with aftercare treatment. A variation of multiple-family therapy, Schiz-Anon groups are led by psychiatric nurses and social workers but rely heavily on the mutual support of family members, who are encouraged to share practical tips on behavior management as well as their feelings about having a mentally ill relative.

All patients placed on injectable phenothiazines participate in the triweekly family sessions, which include education about the nature and treatment of schizophrenia, medication use, and side effects. Preliminary findings in eleven families indicate that patients participating in Schiz-Anon spent fewer days in the hospital than they did before joining the program.

Treatment Innovations

Interest in family treatment methods has stemmed primarily from the work of Wynne and his associates (1958) on communication deviance in families of schizophrenics and from Brown (et al.'s (1962, 1972) studies on the role of intrafamily stress in precipitating relapse in schizophrenics residing with their families. Together with findings from earlier studies on families of the mentally ill, this research provides the backbone of five new intervention programs for families of schizophrenics developed within the past five years. Although there are some critical distinctions between the programs of Goldstein and Kopeikin (1981) at UCLA, Snyder and Liberman (1981) at UCLA-Camarillo, Falloon et al. (1981, 1982) at the University of Southern California, Berkowitz et al. (1981) of the Maudsley Hospital in London, and Anderson et al. (1981, 1982) at the University of Pittsburgh, all of these new programs are based on the same body of research.

Educating Patients and Families About Schizophrenia

Each program has an educational component designed to reduce the guilt, overresponsibility, confusion, and helplessness of family members and enable them to be less judgmental and critical of the patient. Patients are encouraged to come to terms with their illness, thus reducing denial and encouraging a reasonable hope for modest improvements based on fact rather than fantasy.

Goldstein et al. and Anderson et al. begin their family therapy programs by allowing each participant to describe events before and during the patient's psychotic break. Goldstein notes that mental health professionals rarely ask patients or relatives about their subjective experiences during the breakdown. Consequently, there is a tendency for important feelings to be sealed over and for families to feel shame about the patient's illness. Anderson feels that family members must express their pain, frustration, embarrassment, and anger early in family therapy.

In the Berkowitz program, four short talks in two separate sessions cover diagnosis, symptoms, etiology, course, and prognosis of the illness. There is a similar component in the other programs.

All programs go over the rationale for long-term medication and effective stress management. Drug effects are discussed, and the importance of drug compliance in forestalling relapse is emphasized. Prodromal warning signals of impending relapse are defined to facilitate early intervention. Drug side effects are described, including tardive dyskinesia, and the need for antiparkinsonian drugs is outlined. The negative effects of street drugs are emphasized, and patients are encouraged to avoid amphetamines, hallucinogenic drugs, alcohol, and marijuana.

Finally, patients and relatives are informed that full recovery of social functioning may take at least six months. Premature efforts

TABLE 6-1. New Interventions for families or schizophrenics

Investigators	Level of chronicity of patient group	Participants in family therapy sessions	Frequency of interventions	Duration of treatment
Goldstein and Kopeikin, UCLA (1981)	First (69%) and second admission	Patient and family	At discharge, then every 2 weeks	6 weeks
Leff et al., Maudsley (1982)	Multiple admission	Patient in joint interview with own family Multiple-family group, relatives only	Every 2 weeks	9 months
Synder and Liberman, UCLA, Camarillo (1981)	Multiple admission	Multiple-family groups (3 patients and families in each)	Weekly	9 weeks
Falloon et al., USC (1981)	Multiple admission	One family, including patient	First 3 months, weekly; second 3 months, biweekly; last 18 months, monthly	2 years (40 sessions)
Anderson et al., University of Pittsburgh (1980, 1981)	Multiple admission	Individual family with-out patient Multiple-family group Patient with family	Every 2 or 3 weeks	At least 1 year

to push patients beyond their functional capacity are discouraged. While patients and relatives are usually relieved when the pressure to make rapid improvement is decreased, some are reluctant to acknowledge that they might have difficulty in returning to work or school just then. Goldstein notes the importance of emphasizing that even slight progress is an antidote to hopelessness.

Stress Identification and Control

A second distinctive feature of these new family therapy programs is their focus on improving the family's ability to identify and deal with stressful situations involving the patient. In this way, criticism and overinvolvement, both critical components of stress, are reduced.

The five programs use different techniques to accomplish this goal, depending on the extent to which the patient is involved, on the duration of treatment, and on whether the intervention is focused on a single family or on several families. Goldstein's six-week program, focused on a single family, offers a highly systematic approach to stress. Indeed, an initial objective is to identify situations stressful to the patient by querying all members of the family. An initial list of general complaints about the patient is whittled down to the two or three problems that pose the greatest threat to the patient's future. For example, a father argues frequently with his patient son about the son's lack of plans to return to work. Through probing, the therapist discovers that arguments are most likely to occur when the father is coming home or going to work and observes his son drinking beer and watching television (Goldstein and Kopeikin 1981, p. 8). Although family members may identify specific symptoms, such as hallucinations or excessive sleeping, as a source of conflict, therapists focus not on the symptoms themselves but rather on the interpersonal consequences.

Identification of stressful situations provides the basis for the second therapy objective: development of stress avoidance and coping mechanisms. Each precisely defined stressful situation is discussed by the therapist and the family and a plan is developed for avoiding it. Because stress prevention and coping strategies are sometimes unfamiliar even to those in therapy, the therapist must encourage families to work on the objectives, often through modeling or direct suggestion of specific coping strategies. Even so, stressful situations sometimes arise and thus secondary strategies, such as avoidance, are discussed. By engaging the family in joint planning to cope with stress, consensus within the family is maximized. Participants are instructed to implement prevention and coping plans, report on their effectiveness, and note any difficulties encountered.

The final treatment objective in Goldstein's program is anticipatory planning: preparing patient and family for future stress that might occur after therapy ends.

The nine-week (nine-session) program of Snyder and Liberman uses a slightly different approach. Specific communication skills, such as listening actively and reflectively, expressing strong emotions, and coping with unexpected anger, are the focus of sessions for groups of three patients and their families. One skill is addressed in each meeting, and topics covered include the purpose of the targeted skill, step-by-step instruction in how to develop the skill, role-playing demonstrations, and homework assignments on practicing the skill. Skills taught in previous sessions are reviewed, and written material delineating each skill is provided.

Berkowitz et al.'s nine-month program and Anderson et al.'s year-long intervention geared to multiple-family groups are less structured in teaching communication and coping skills. Family members are encouraged to express themselves freely, share experiences, and learn from one another. Although Berkowitz et al. use role-playing to teach skills such as empathy, both programs use traditional family therapy methods (Minuchin 1974). Parents of patients are encouraged to work together to find solutions to problems, go out together, and separate as a unit from the patient. Anderson emphasizes the need for delineating generational boundaries so as to increase the structure within the family and allow each member increased personal space. Berkowitz concentrates on devising ways of reducing contact between patient and family, based on the notion that less time together is better. Although independence is encouraged, it is difficult to reduce dependency in relationships, and too vigorous an effort may lock emotionally overinvolved families even more firmly together.

Anderson et al. stress the need for clarity and simplicity in communication by addressing four issues:

1. Avoiding excessive details, abstractions, or verbiage, thus keeping discussion at a moderate level of specificity
2. Differentiating description from evaluation (giving a precise account of some event without interjecting feelings)
3. Accepting responsibility for one's own statements and allowing others to do the same
4. Making and acknowledging positive messages and supportive comments

The Falloon et al. program is distinguished from the others by its length (two years) and its focus on a single family. Strengths and weaknesses of individual members and of the group as a whole are obtained in detailed behavioral assessments conducted in the clinic and in the home. Individual and group problems are identified, and communication skills and coping behavior are taught. Family interaction is studied so that the history of the patient's problems can be viewed in relation to the responses of other family members. Falloon et al. note that the sick person often becomes the focus of much of the family interaction. Excessive attention to the patient can unintentionally reduce motivation to recover, as recovery would mean loss of special status within the family. In addition, when families focus too much attention on the patient, they diminish their ability to resolve other family problems.

For the first three months of the Falloon program, sessions are held weekly. Biweekly sessions are held for the next six months, followed by monthly sessions during the last fifteen months. For the first nine months, sessions are held in the home to encourage full family participation. Therapists are available around the clock to make home visits or to provide telephone consultation in crisis situations. The following six factors represent the highlights of the program.

1. *Positive reinforcement* Praise, attention, and interest are used by the therapist to build a supportive family milieu for problem resolution and fruitful communication.
2. *Shaping* The therapist selectively reinforces changes that improved family relationships. Family members are rewarded for even small signs of change.
3. *Extinction* At the other extreme, minimum reinforcement

through lack of attention, interest, or acknowledgment is given to inappropriate, undesirable behavior.

4. *Modeling* In order to help the family learn more adaptive interpersonal skills, the therapist models such behavior as active listening, expression of negative feelings, and positive requests for behavior change. The behavior of the therapist gives the family a new model to emulate.

5. *Rehearsal* In every session, interpersonal situations are repeatedly acted out with accompanying constructive feedback from the therapist. In this way, families can go over past problem situations and learn alternative responses.

6. *Homework*   Practice assignments on the behavior dealt with in the session are given to each member at the conclusion of each session.

Falloon's program, like Goldstein's, is designed to help families master difficult problems through structured problem-solving. After a problem has been identified, the family lists possible solutions without prejudging any of them. The pros and cons of each solution are discussed. A solution is chosen by the group and a plan developed to implement it. Frequently, rehearsals are used to assist the family in preparing to implement the solution. Finally, the efficacy of the solution is reviewed after the family has had an opportunity to try it out. Review enables the family to learn from their efforts, gradually improving their choices of best solutions and facilitating greater independence from the therapist. Structured problem-solving allows the family to focus its resources on a specific task that might arouse intense negative feeling under other conditions. Falloon contends that mobilization of the family's energies on problem resolution reduces tension. Some of the solutions involve "contracts" among family members ("I'll do this for you if you do that for me") and set limits on unacceptable behavior.

Efficacy of New Family Interventions

Because these interventions are new, their efficacy has not yet been proved. Goldstein's six-week intervention was studied with 104 primarily young (mean age 23 years), white (79 per cent), single (62 per cent), prechronic schizophrenics (69 per cent were first admission) and their families chosen from a brief-stay in-patient unit at a California community mental health center. Schizophrenia was diagnosed through two brief diagnostic rating scales plus independent clinical assessments by the project psy-chiatrist and psychologist. Patients meetings the criteria for schizophrenia were divided into good and poor premorbid groups before random assignment to one of four treatment groups: moderate dose of phenothiazine plus family therapy, low dose plus family therapy, moderate dose with no family therapy, and low dose with no family therapy.

Goldstein and his coworkers found that at six weeks (termina-tion of the intervention) there were no relapses in the moderate dose, family therapy group. In contrast, 24 per cent of those in the low dose, no therapy group relapsed. Relapse rates in the moderate dose, no therapy and the low dose, therapy groups were about the same (9 to 10 per cent). Similar trends were ap-parent at six-month follow-up, with no relapses in the moderate dose, therapy group and 48 per cent relapse in the low dose, no therapy group. Good premorbid males had a consistently low relapse rate regardless of therapy assignment. In contrast, good premorbid females did better when assigned to family therapy intervention. Poor premorbids showed marked sensitivity to drug therapy, as evidenced by a high relapse rate among poor pre-morbids assigned to the two low dose groups. Patients assigned to therapy showed less withdrawal, anxiety, depression, and schizo-phrenic thought at six weeks (intervention termination) and at six-month follow-up.

Because long-term follow-up was obtained for only 58 per cent of the sample, the finding that relapse at three years was unrelated to any of the four treatment combinations is tenuous.

Leff et al. (1982) ran a controlled trial of the family intervention program of Berkowitz et al. (1981). Twenty-four patients and their families were selected for the study after the patients had received a diagnosis of schizophrenia based on the Present State Examination (Wing et al. 1974) and had spent at least thirty-five hours per week in face-to-face contact with one or more relatives in the three months prior to hospital admission. A further re-quirement for selection was high expressed emotion in the parent or spouse, determined with a modified form of the Camberwell Family Interviews (Vaughn and Leff 1976).

Half of the families were randomly assigned to the new family intervention, and the other half received routine outpatient care. All patients were maintained on neuroleptic drugs. The mean age of patients was in the 30's, and only one third were first-admission cases. Relapse rates, defined as a recurrence of schizophrenic symptoms as detected by the Present State Examination, were 9 per cent in the experimental group and 50 per cent in the control group nine months after discharge. However, the goals of the intervention were achieved in only about three quarters of the experimental families. There were no relapses where the intervention was adequately implemented. Follow-up scores on level of expressed emotion showed a significant drop in number of critical comments in experimental families.

Falloon et al. (1982) contrasted their home-based family therapy intervention with clinic-based patient-only supportive care in thirty-six patients taking maintenance medication. Both types of treatment were administered by the research team (who hopefully did not favor family therapy!). Schizophrenia was diagnosed with the Present State Examination (Wing et al. 1974), and most patients were living in households with close daily contact with one or both parents. Moreover, most patients came from households with high ratings on expressed emotion, based on interviews with the parents using the Camberwell Family Interview. Patients were mostly in their mid-20's, and most had been in a psychiatric hospital before. Exacerbation of symptoms was determined with the Present State Examination at follow-up.

At the end of nine months, only one family-treated patient (6 per cent of all patients) had had a clinical relapse, whereas eight patients (44 per cent) treated individually experienced relapse. Family-treated patients also averaged less time in the hospital than patients in individualized treatment (0.88 days versus 8.39 days) and had significantly less severe psychotic symptoms. Moreover, family-treated patients were more compliant about their medication than controls, suggesting that a home-care approach involving families may help in long-term drug management.

Long-term controlled studies of neuroleptic drug treatment of schizophrenia have shown that symptomatic relapse is not prevented by drugs alone, and so the efficacy of family treatment cannot be explained by drugs alone. Findings suggest that control of the patient's environmental support system may be an important aspect of community rehabilitation in schizophrenia.

The Patient as Parent

The parenting behavior of schizophrenic patients has received little study. Yet even when long-term hospitalization of the mentally ill was in vogue, many of those diagnosed as schizophrenic managed to marry and have children. In Bleuler's Swiss sample (1974), half of 208 schizophrenic patients married and produced a total of 184 children. The women, who married earlier and developed mental illness later than the men, had nearly twice as many offspring as the men.

The effect of community care on marriage and childbirth rates for schizophrenics remains unclear. However, the impact of early discharge on the health of other members of the patient's family, particularly children, has aroused concern. Wing et al. (1964) found that 57 per cent of 113 schizophrenics discharged from eight London hospitals exhibited moderate symptoms at discharge and another 17 per cent had severe symptoms. Over half of these patients deteriorated in the year after discharge, and 43 per cent were rehospitalized. In a similar study in New Haven, 25 per cent of 132 patients had psychotic symptoms (Astrachan et al. 1974). In a New York City study, 36 per cent of 119 schizophrenic patients had at least one psychotic symptom when interviewed at quarterly intervals for one year (Caton 1981), and 58 per cent were rehospitalized during that period. In the Wing et al. study, social relationships in the patient's family became disturbed in three out of five cases and an acute social crisis involving the patient, neighbors, the police, or the general public occurred after severe family distress in two out of five cases.

Such statistics have motivated Rutter (1966) and others (Rodnick and Goldstein 1974, Garmezy 1980) to wonder whether there is any risk that the children of a schizophrenic parent residing in the community might development a psychiatric disorder. As pointed out earlier, children of schizophrenics carry a 10 to 16 per cent genetic risk of developing schizophrenia. How parental psychosis could increase this risk through disturbed parent-child relations and inadequate rearing has been given little attention.

In his classic study of the children of sick parents, Rutter showed how parental deviance may be related to disturbances in children. Of 737 disturbed children selected for study from among those using the service system of an English hospital over a two-year period, 137 had one or both parents suffering from mental illness. Of those 137, 20.4 per cent had two sick parents, 52.6 per cent had a sick mother only, and 27 per cent had a sick father only. Psychiatric illness occurred more often in the child when the mother was mentally ill. When both parents were sick, or when a healthy parent was either absent or unable to take over from the sick parent, children suffered more.

In Rutter's study, psychiatrically ill children were more often boys than girls (61.8 versus 38.2 per cent). Neither the diagnosis nor the severity of the parent's illness was an important determinant of disorder in the child. Few parents diagnosed as schizophrenic had disturbed children. Rather, what emerged as important was the extent to which symptoms in the parent directly involved or influenced the child. Some children were victims of aggressive or hostile behavior in the parent, and others were abused sexually or neglected or were targets of delusion. Harmful consequences for the child increased when the illness in the parent was chronic. However, long-standing personality abnormalities in the parent were not likely to be associated with behavioral disturbances in the child.

Garmezy (1974) has pointed out that today the children of psychiatric patients are not separated from the sick parent for long. Yet very little is known about how children react to mental illness in a parent.

Bleuler's (1974) twenty-year follow-up study revealed that only 46 per cent of the 184 children of schizophrenics in his sample ever lived with the schizophrenic parent for a significant amount of time before age 20. Those who lived with the schizophrenic parent did so for only an average of seven years before age 20. Children who lived with a schizophrenic parent were not more likely to develop schizophrenia than those who did not. Bleuler noted, however, that living conditions were stable for only half of the children he studied. The living conditions of children of male schizophrenics were more stable than those of children of female patients. Bleuler estimated that the suffering of children of schizophrenics was extreme. Shame of mental illness in the family, social ridicule, and bad experiences in foster homes were only a few of the problems encountered by the children.

Mothering has been targeted as particularly critical to the fate of offspring of schizophrenics. Early studies of schizophrenic mothers and their offspring, although they suffer from methodological flaws, such as small sample size and unreliable measurement of behavior in both mother and child, indicated that many schizophrenics were "good" mothers. Baker et al. (1961) studied puerperal schizophrenic mothers and their babies on a psychiatric inpatient ward in England. Overt hostility to the child was rarely observed, and most mothers were able to look after their babies throughout the hospital stay. Follow-up after discharge revealed that mothers showed considerable affection to their very young children despite problems in other social relationships and that younger children appeared well adjusted. However, schizophrenic mothers had more difficulty in coping with older children.

Similarly, Sussex (1963) and Sussex et al. (1963), who studied psychotic mothers treated at home, found that many could meet the emotional needs of their children regardless of how much illness had disrupted other areas of their lives. In the patient group studied by Sussex, other adults substituted for the schizophrenic mother when her parenting capacities were impaired.

In contrast, in a study by Sobel (1961) of four infants cared for by a schizophrenic or depressed mother, three were somber and irritable, lacked spontaneity, and were retarded in motor skills at 18 months of age. The schizophrenic mothers played very little with their infants and appeared to lack positive feelings for them.

Using a sophisticated research design, Rodnick and Goldstein (1974) studied the mothering behavior of twenty-seven first-admission, acute schizophrenic women treated briefly (median stay, ten days) in a community mental health center before returning home to their husbands and children. The women in this group, which included eight poor premorbid and nineteen good premorbid patients, were interviewed along with their husbands. Home observations were made at one month, six months, and one year following discharge. The mean age was 21 years for poor premorbid mothers and 28 years for good premorbid mothers. Consequently, the children of poor premorbid mothers were considerably younger than the children of good premorbid mothers when their mothers became ill (mean age of children of poor premorbid mothers: 0.63 year for youngest child, 1.75 years for oldest child; mean age of children of good premorbid mothers: 3.47 years for youngest child, 7.47 years for oldest child). In this study group, therefore, illness in the poor premorbid mother was of particular consequence for her younger family, who did not have the advantage of the fairly normal mothering throughout infancy and toddlerhood experienced by children of good premorbid mothers. Moreover, using the mothers' capacities for warmth, affection, and enjoyment versus apathy, indifference, and unresponsiveness, Rodnick and Goldstein found that it took the good premorbid mothers six months to return to an adequate level of caretaking. In contrast, poor premorbid mothers required one year.

Mednick et al. (1975) noted three characteristics of schizophrenic women that were associated with subsequent schizophrenia in their children. First, mothers of children who became schizophrenic developed their own illness at an earlier age than the child. Second, such mothers were separated from their children when the children were quite young. Third, such mothers experienced more difficulties during the birth of the child. Talovic et al. (1983) found that two maternal characteristics—having a psychotic episode within six months of childbirth (usually that of a sibling of the schizophrenic offspring) and a history of unstable relationships with men—accounted for 38 per cent of the variance related to onset of schizophrenia in the offspring.

Rice et al. (1971) studied 652 children, half of whom were preschoolers, in 253 families in which one parent was mentally ill. A major stress for children was the hospitalization of the mother. When the father was hospitalized, there was little disruption in living arrangements, but when mothers were hospitalized, 42 per cent of the children were separated from their homes. In more than half of the families, relatives provided substitute child care, albeit with varying degrees of willingness and adequacy. Thirty-five per cent of families did not have a child care plan either for the duration of the first hospitalization or for subsequent admissions.

Investigators who have studied the children of the mentally ill (Rutter 1966, Rodnick and Goldstein 1974, Garmezy 1980) have pleaded for greater awareness of children's needs in community program development. Rice et al. (1971) have suggested that mental hospitals should routinely identify patients who have children at home so that the children's needs can be met while the parent is hospitalized. They advocate that home is the best place for children regardless of the hazards involved and that every effort should be made to help sick mothers raise their own children. Toward this end, day-care and homemaker services are recommended along with the extension of psychiatric services into the home. Psychosocial interventions focused on developing parenting skills in sick mothers and fathers and on alternative living arrangements for the children of schizophrenics will undoubtedly emerge in the wake of deinstitutionalization (Pavenstadt and Bernard 1971, Gruenbaum et al. 1975).

7. Fostering Social Competence

Schizophrenic patients have much difficulty with job performance, interpersonal relationships, self-care, community survival skills, and enjoyment of leisure time—the negative symptoms of this disorder and the markers of chronicity (DSM III 1980). The disability resulting from these symptoms accounts for perhaps 70 per cent of the disorder's annual cost in the United States (Gunderson and Mosher 1975). Studies of schizophrenics have focused primarily on its positive symptoms, such as hallucinations and delusions, which are the target behavior of neuroleptic drugs. Follow-up studies of mixed groups of acute and chronic schizophrenics have shown that degree of social deterioration is weakly related to persistence of symptoms (Strauss and Carpenter 1974, Schwartz et al. 1975).

Outcome studies of schizophrenia have shown that premorbid social behavior is a critical predictor of the patient's social adjustment after the psychotic phase (Strauss and Carpenter 1974), and prognostic studies have shown the same thing. Poor premorbid social adjustment is associated with a narrow range of outcomes, usually poor, and good premorbid social adjustment is associated with a wider range of outcomes, both good and poor (Gittelman-Klein and Klein 1969). For institutionalized chronic schizophrenics, brain abnormalities, detected with computer-axial tomography (CAT scans), are associated with poor premorbid social histories and poor response to psychotropic medication (Weinberger et al. 1980a, 1980b).

Environment has also been implicated as a cause of social decline among schizophrenics. The "social breakdown syndrome" (Gruenberg 1967) has been attributed to bad social environments, such as the back wards of mental hospitals and back alleys of the community (Stanton and Schwartz 1954, Goffman 1961). How such environmental factors as interpersonal stress and the quality of the social support system contribute to social decline has not yet been established. However, long stays in mental hospitals have been associated with social decline (Honigfeld and Gillis 1967, Herz et al. 1977) and with decreased likelihood of discharge (Dunham and Weinberg 1960, Wing and Brown 1970, Anthony and Buell 1973). One assumption of the deinstitutionalization movement was that treatment of patients in the community would help them to maintain active lives. It is now widely recognized that community treatment has not eliminated the social sequelae of schizophrenia.

Interest in social competence—which encompasses social behavior outside of traditional roles in areas such as social interaction, self-care, and daily activities (Paul and Lentz 1977), which are of particular significance to severely disabled schizophrenics who do not have the usual role of worker, homemaker, spouse, or parent—has paralleled the recognition that performance in social roles and relationships is an axis of behavior distinct from psychiatric symptoms (DSM III 1980) and only partly influenced by them. Defining and measuring social adjustment have dealt primarily with the patient's performance and subjective feelings in everyday roles (Weissman 1975, Paykel et al. 1978, Weissman et al. 1978).

The social isolation of many schizophrenic patients, the result of their inability to participate in social networks, has challenged clinicians to devise new therapies that improve performance in instrumental roles and develop and maintain appropriate social behaviors. Interventions that affect symptoms do not always affect patient adjustment, although connections have not been studied in detail. It is likely that all psychotherapies have their greatest effect on the patient's social life, but this effect cannot be evaluated for months or years (Hogarty et al. 1974b, Linn et al. 1979). How much time is required to bring about a desired change is an open question (Mosher and Keith 1979).

Equivocal findings from studies of insight-oriented therapy with schizophrenics (Rogers et al. 1967, May 1968, Grinspoon et al. 1972, Karon and Vandenbos 1972) have stimulated the development of therapies geared to problems in living rather than to personality changes. These therapies have a behavioral, or social-learning, perspective and use techniques such as shaping, positive and negative reinforcement, prompting, modeling, and behavior rehearsal. One therapy, the token economy, has been used primarily with inpatients to improve instrumental role behavior. Others work with outpatients and focus heavily on people and events in the patient's natural environment.

Lamb (1976) contends that the chronic patient's difficulty in adjusting to the community is in large part due to a lack of such essential skills as managing money and using public transportation. Moreover, many lack the fundamentals of meal planning, shopping, personal hygiene, sex education, and use of leisure time. In short, they have not developed the basic social amenities that make the difference between a life of isolation and having friends, or that permit even a minimally independent existence either in an institution or in the community. Although many investigators concur with this assessment, there are many different opinions on what to do about it.

Teaching Coping Skills in the Community

According to (Glasscote et al. (1971a), Ludwig (1971), and Lamb (1976), the most effective way to teach coping skills is to adopt a formal educational model with classes and a curriculum. Educational programs have been set up in connection with other formal mental health programs, such as day centers and aftercare programs. A possible liability of incorporating training in community coping skills into the mental health care delivery system is that this could foster unnecessary dependence on the system (Lamb 1976). An alternative is to base such a program in a public facility, such as a library or recreation hall. Lamb made his coping skills education project for discharged mental patients part of the adult education program at a local high school. The course, entitled "Personal Growth Education," was given by a teacher with experience in dealing with the emotionally handicapped. Lamb also describes "friendship" centers and drop-in social centers, staffed by volunteers and sponsored by the local mental health association, where discharged patients can socialize and engage in leisure activities.

Another effort to help patients reach out beyond the aftercare clinic is a companion program in which patients have prolonged one-to-one contact and "a warm, supportive relationship with a stable, well-adjusted member of the community" (Lamb 1976, p. 127). Companions are volunteers from the community who make a six-month commitment to spend from four to ten hours per week with a patient. Volunteers are given a three-week orientation but are not required to have any professional training. San Jose State University's Community of Communities program, in which college students earn three credits for working with patients on a day-to-day basis, is an example of another program designed to help patients interact with members of the community.

Training in Community Living

Stein and Test (1978) have carried the idea of patient involvement in the community a step further by developing a treatment that teaches coping skills as part of a 24-hour outpatient alternative to hospitalization. Staff of the Training in Community Living (TCL) program visit patients' homes and neighborhoods to assist them in daily activities. Some help patients find a job or get placed in a sheltered workshop. Daily contact with patients and with their employers facilitates on-the-job problem-solving. Patients are also encouraged to become involved in social and community activities. Contact with the patient is daily or even hourly in the beginning, but then it gradually declines as the patient progresses. Even when contact between staff and patient is relatively sparse, the relationship is maintained so that staff can intervene at the first indication of regression.

This social skills component of the TCL program was tested along with other facets of the program. Sixty-five chronic patients suffering from functional psychoses and deemed in need of in-patient care were randomly assigned to the TCL program, and 65 control subjects were assigned to a standard public psychiatric ward and routine aftercare. Assessment of social functioning one year after discharge revealed that, although there were no differences in the numbers of TCL and control patients in the labor force, TCL patients spent significantly less time unemployed and significantly more time in sheltered employment. Further, TCL subjects earned more money than control subjects because significantly more TCL subjects in competitive jobs worked full-time.

Scales to measure leisure time activities, social relationships, and quality of life revealed no significant differences in TCL and control subjects except that TCL subjects had more contact with friends than control subjects. Unfortunately, areas such as self-care and participation in community and daily activities were not assessed.

Major Role Therapy

Major Role Therapy (MRT) was developed by Hogarty et al. (1974b) while they were studying drugs and sociotherapy in aftercare treatment of schizophrenics. It focused on the interpersonal, social, and rehabilitative needs of patients and their families, and its goal was to resolve problems that affected the patient's performance as homemaker or wage earner. MRT aimed to improve the quality of patients' interpersonal relationships and their ability to care for themselves and to provide counseling on financial matters. It was administered by social workers with MSW degrees who were graduates of a Rankian school and had an average of nearly seven years of work experience. In one experiment, 360 subjects with a hospital diagnosis of schizophrenia (confirmed by a hospital psychiatrist) were randomly assigned to one of four conditions: MRT and placebo, placebo alone, MRT plus drugs, and drugs alone. An interaction between MRT and drugs was noted at the eighteen- and twenty-four-month follow-ups. Among drug-treated patients, those who received MRT adjusted better and enjoyed better interpersonal relationships, as assessed with patient self-reports and ratings from physicians and social workers. Effects of sociotherapy were not apparent until after eighteen months of treatment.

Social Learning

Paul and Lentz (1977) have devised a "token-economy" treatment geared to helping minimally functioning hospitalized schizophrenics achieve greater self-sufficiency. Extending the concepts and techniques of social influence and learning from the laboratory to the clinical situation and drawing heavily on the work of Krasner and Ullmann (1965), Ullmann and Krasner (1975), Atthowe and Krasner (1968), and Ayllon and Azrin (1965, 1968), the social-learning therapy devised by Paul and Lentz is based on two principles of learning: the law of effect and the law of association and contingency.

The law of effect says that the frequency of behavior depends on the effects it produces. Positive consequences reinforce behavior and increase its frequency. Negative consequences weaken behavior and decrease its frequency. Systematic manipulation of consequences can bring about a change in behavior.

The law of association and contingency says that objects, actions, or environmental changes that occur spontaneously come to be associated with each other, function in a similar way, or share the same meaning. New reinforcers can be created by pairing existing reinforcers several times with another stimulus event. *Shaping* uses positive consequences to move a person closer and closer to the target behavior until only that behavior is reinforced. *Chaining* is used when a particular target behavior consists of a sequence of separate but linked acts. Reinforcement is initially applied only to the first or last act, then to a combination of that act and the next in the series, and so on, until the total behavior is rewarded.

Social learning is not dependent upon spontaneous behavior. Shaping and chaining can be speeded up through prompting. In *prompting*, the behavior may be modeled for the subject or he or she may be assisted in performing the act or given instructions describing it. Verbal instructions, concrete specifications, and social reinforcers are most efficient after patients have themselves become verbal.

In Paul and Lentz's program, all material goods, services, and privileges are purchased with plastic tokens, which patients earn through appropriate behavior and lose through fines for inappropriate behavior. The tokens can be used to purchase other reinforcers. Their utility as reinforcers does not wane easily. Because the tokens are paid immediately after appropriate behavior, patients are more likely to associate the behavior with the reward. Obviously, the success of the token economy depends on ensuring that no patient misses earned tokens or receives unearned ones.

Moreover, no patient is allowed to receive "free" any material goods or privileges for which there is a token charge.

Once patients begin responding to social stimuli, tokens and other tangible reinforcers become less crucial to learning but can still support performance. Patients in the program are gradually removed from the token economy as they progress to greater responsibility and privileges.

In Paul and Lentz's social-learning unit, each patient is assigned a daily schedule, which at the beginning includes six hours of classes and activities, three hours of informal interaction, two hours for meals, and one to two hours for small and large group meetings. As patients advance, scheduled activities and classes give way to individual assignments and more informal interaction. Tokens are disbursed immediately for punctual attendance at classes and scheduled activities, and at their end as a reward for participation. Tokens are also disbursed for cleanliness and personal appearance, maintenance of bed and belongings, and appropriate mealtime behavior. As patients improve, the criteria for receiving a token gradually shift upward.

The token economy is designed so that residents performing at minimal levels do not receive many rewards. As patients advance in their level of performance, they gradually earn more tokens, thereby gaining access to more reinforcers in all areas. As patients advance, they eventually buy themselves out of the token system by purchasing a credit card that gives them free access to all reinforcers as long as they meet the requirements expected of them. Staff in a token economy are instructed to always reinforce desirable behavior immediately, never reinforce undesirable behavior, clearly specify the behavior being rewarded, and pair allocation of tokens with verbal compliments or praise: "You did a really good job smoothing the sheets and putting things away this morning, George. Here is your token for keeping your room in order" (Paul and Lentz 1977, p. 78).

Tokens have implications for day-to-day life on the ward. For example, patients sleep in one of four types of rooms: six-bed dormitories having no draperies, chairs, or tables; two- and four-bed units having draperies but no other accessories; and single rooms having draperies, chairs, and bedside tables. The six-bed units are free, but rooms with more privacy and accessories are available only by weekly token rental. In addition to having more privacy and accessories, patients in rented rooms are awakened later than those sleeping in the free dormitories. Patients also use tokens to purchase television time and use of the classroom-lounge.

Paul and Lentz tested their social-learning program on forty schizophrenic patients with an average of seventeen years of psychiatric hospitalization prior to the study. All patients had bleak prospects and had been rejected for community placement during aggressive deinstitutionalization efforts in the four Illinois state hospitals from which they were chosen. They were of low socioeconomic status and were in the process range on the process-reactive continuum.

These forty patients were compared with control groups matched on a number of clinical and functional characteristics and randomly assigned to milieu therapy and traditional hospital treatment. After 120 weeks of treatment, thirty-six of the social-learning patients were released to board-and-care homes and three others were able to live alone. Although milieu therapy patients did not fare so well, twenty-two of thirty-one of them were discharged, two to independent living. In contrast, of twenty-nine patients given traditional hospital treatment, only thirteen were released, none to independent living.

Improvements in a patient's level of functioning as a result of social-learning therapy is illustrated by this case from Paul and Lentz (1977):

> Jess, a 48-year-old, single ex-farmer, had been hospitalized continuously for about six years. He was typical of many long-term institutional residents. In the hospital, Jess was usually sitting or sleeping unless otherwise directed, and he frequently refused to perform even simple self-care tasks. While his bizarre behavior was relatively infrequent, he was reported to be "rather mute," never initiating a conversation or attempting to be friendly and always avoiding other people.
>
> Upon his transfer to the social-learning program, Jess sat alone for hours neither speaking nor responding, with no interest in activities. He was found staring blankly or with his eyes closed on half of the hourly observational checks. He never engaged in normal interactions or participated in activities or meetings, never

cleaned his living area appropriately, failed to eat properly at meals, and rarely presented an acceptable appearance.

Eighteen weeks into the program, Jess was far less frequently found with eyes closed or staring blankly and was interacting with others more often. His self-care increased significantly, his meal behavior was normal almost half the time, his appearance was normal virtually all the time, and his personal cleanliness was excellent. He appeared for all scheduled classes and meetings and performed appropriately in those situations 83 per cent of the time. Jess continued to show steady improvement, eventually achieved release, and became independent of the mental health care system after completing the declining-contact aftercare phase of the program. When the study ended, Jess had been employed and self-supporting for over three years, with no indication of need for future services.

Social-Skills Training

Another social-learning program, commonly referred to as assertiveness training, social effectiveness training, or social-skills training, has been used with both inpatient and outpatient groups. Wallace et al. (1980) have defined the context of social-skills training as an interpersonal one consisting of the patient and at least one other person. Elements of social-skills training include:

1. The patient's feelings and attitudes and his or her perception of a social interaction
2. The patient's behavior, particularly nonverbal communication gestures such as eye contact and posture
3. The outcome of the interaction as reflected in the achievement of the patient's goals
4. The outcome of the interaction as reflected in the attitudes, feelings, behavior, and goals of the other participants

Definitions of social skills, although varied, emphasize that they involve the "ability to maximize the rate of positive reinforcement and to minimize the strength of punishments from others" (Libet and Lewinsohn 1973). Liberman et al. (1975, p. 1) see in social skills "the ability to express feelings or to communicate interests and desires to others."

All such definitions imply that the objective of social-skills training is to increase the patient's ability to cope. Training is done in "sessions", that is, in a setting where communication is structured (as opposed to "interaction", which implies a natural communication interchange between people) in which the patient is first asked to act out an interpersonal situation with either the trainer or a fellow patient. The trainer reviews the patient's performance, reinforces the correct behaviors, and instructs the patient to try other behaviors that will presumably result in a more skilled social performance. The cycle is repeated until the performance comes up to the standards set by the trainer. Sessions may be videotaped for review (Liberman et al. 1975). Modeling and coaching may also be used to demonstrate and prompt the more effective behaviors. Training is usually conducted in groups, although individual sessions are not uncommon.

Homework assignments are frequently used to extend the effects of training beyond the session and require patients to practice their newly acquired social skills in the real world (Liberman et al. 1975, Goldstein et al. 1976, Falloon et al. 1977, Finch and Wallace 1977). Homework may be carried out by the patient alone or with another patient. On occasion, the trainer accompanies the patient on the homework assignment.

Because training time is limited, only a certain number of interpersonal situations can be covered in a social-skills program. The usual method of determining problem areas is a self-report by the patient that a particular situation has been troublesome or has caused anxiety (Liberman et al. 1975, Finch and Wallace 1977). Although selecting problems this way maximizes the relevance of the program for each patient, it does not consider problems and social inadequacies outside the patient's awareness.

In other instances, significant others have been queried for an inventory of the patient's problems (Field and Test 1975, Matson and Stephens 1978). Other workers in the field, such as Hersen and Bellack (1976), Hersen et al. (1972), and Goldsmith and McFall (1975), have made a priori decisions to deal with problematic situations common to most psychiatric patients.

Studies on the efficacy of social-skills training for schizophrenic patients must assess the many dimensions of social functioning influenced by this interaction. Included are topographical features of social skills, such as eye contact, voice volume, posture, and use of hand gestures. Inasmuch as training is designed to influence the patient's internal state, studies dealing with this aspect of training have assessed self-reputed anxiety or discomfort in social situations (Goldsmith and McFall 1975, Falloon et al. 1977), difficulty in meeting and talking with people, future ability to perform in interpersonal situations, feelings of self-worth, and skill and comfort in interpersonal situations (Goldsmith and McFall). The ultimate determination of efficacy is the patient's behavior in social situations. One approach to evaluating social-skills training is to give the patient a "test." For example, Goldsmith and McFall (1975) and Liberman et al. (1978) asked patients to complete four tasks (such as a luncheon invitation) with a male stranger. In another instance, successful completion of homework assignments was used as a measure of efficacy (Liberman et al. 1978).

Studies of the use of social-skills training with chronic psychiatric patients have demonstrated that this approach can effect change. However, patient samples have been small, and diagnostic and prognostic variables have not been well controlled. In addition, other forms of therapy, such as medication, have not been controlled. Lastly, "social-skills" training does not refer to one well-defined set of procedures, reducing comparability across studies and perhaps accounting for contradictory findings. Single-subject studies have shown that social behaviors change as soon as training is begun (Fredericksen et al. 1976, Bellack et al. 1976, Hersen and Bellack 1976). Changes do not occur in every patient, however, and those that do occur are not easily carried over to new situations (Wallace et al. 1980).

Liberman et al. (1978) used the successful completion of homework assignments to evaluate the effects of thirty hours per week for ten weeks of training with three schizophrenics. The assignments were interaction with members of the nursing staff, with parents, and with social and vocational contacts in the community, and assignment completion was the dependent variable. For two weeks, patients were rated on all three types of interaction. Then training was begun. The investigators found that completion of homework assignments did not change until training was begun.

Wallace et al. reported a study in progress in which there was a deliberate attempt to specify a social-skills training intervention package. The training package is currently being used in a ten-week program in which therapy is conducted three to six hours daily, five days per week. Twenty-eight patients diagnosed as schizophrenics using the Present State Examination have been randomly assigned to either social-skills training or an equally intensive "control" therapy. Patients are being followed up for a two-year period.

Employment

The schizophrenic patient who maintains gainful employment is very likely to be considered successfully adjusted regardless of symptom level or number of rehospitalization episodes. In fact, such patients are rare. Anthony et al. (1972) conducted a literature survey of employment among schizophrenics, defining employment outcome as the percentage of patients who either worked full-time throughout the follow-up period or were employed at the follow-up date. On the basis of available data, Anthony concluded than 20 to 30 per cent of discharged patients were employed full-time, regardless of the duration of the follow-up period. The data also suggested that, in the six months following discharge, from 30 to 50 per cent of the patients worked at least part-time.

Subsequent studies on rates of employment among schizophrenics suggest that Anthony's 20 to 30 per cent rate may be too high. Wolkon et al. (1971) found an employment rate of only 18 per cent one to two years after discharge. Lamb and Goertzel's (1972) five-year follow-up study of discharged state hospital patients revealed that only about 15 per cent were partially or fully self-supporting or functioning in a homemaking role. In addition, Hume and Anthony (1975) found an employment rate of 12 per cent for a sample of state hospital patients one year after release. Caton (1981) found evidence of decline in social functioning among 119 lower-class chronic schizophrenics in New York City. Although 89 per cent had once held a job, only 27 per cent worked during a one-year study period, with 12 per cent working full-time for pay at some point in the study but only one person working full-time for pay continuously throughout the year.

Buell and Anthony (1976) reviewed studies that investigated the relationship between employment and demographic factors, such as sex, race, age, educational level, marital status, number and length of previous hospitalizations, employment history, and occupational level. They found that the best predictor of employment success is previous employment history (Olshansky et al. 1960, Hall et al. 1966, Lorei 1967, Green et al. 1968, Anthony and Buell 1973, Lorei and Gurel 1973, Buell and Anthony 1976). In addition, employment is more related to ratings of social effectiveness and work skills than to ratings of psychiatric symptoms. Job motivation, ability to get along well and work with others, and preference for group rather than solitary activities correlate well with employment.

The meager success rate when schizophrenics seek employment on their own has stimulated various private and public vocational rehabilitation efforts. In some cases, programs are exclusively for the mentally ill. In others, released mental patients are given services along with the mentally retarded and those suffering from physical disabilities. There is at present no evidence that disability mix has any relation to rehabilitation outcome.

The elements included in comprehensive vocational rehabilitation are prevocational assessment, job training, sheltered work, and transitional employment. In many cases, standard tests are used to aid in assessment.

Anthony et al. (1972, 1978) outlined a procedure for making a *rehabilitation diagnosis* distinct from a psychiatric diagnosis. In exploring a patient's strengths and deficits, the focus is on determining ability to function in a specific work environment. For example, an assessment of how well the patient would do working in a post office would compare the job-qualifying skills of the patient with the functions of an actual postal employee (Anthony et al. 1978). The desired outcome of rehabilitation diagnosis is a treatment plan that will work. Rehabilitation as presently practiced is designed to either improve the patient's skills or else adapt the environment to the patient's present level of functioning. If a patient is to be placed initially in a sheltered workshop, certain skills, such as those needed for job interviewing, would not be required. It is important to note that Anthony has broadened the definition of "rehabilitation assessment" to encompass household, social interaction, and community coping skills in addition to work skills.

Industrial Therapy

Black (1970) used the term "industrial therapy" to describe all rehabilitation and resocialization programs for mental patients in which activities of the workplace are utilized. Included in industrial therapy are a number of programs in which a real work situation is simulated, such as rehabilitation workshops. These workshops vary in content and organization, and few have been carefully evaluated. One that has been studied is the Maudsley Rehabilitation Workshop in London, established in 1967 and described by Stevens (1973). This workshop is run on industrial lines and was established as an adjunct to a day hospital program. The sheltered work program, a small, nonprofit business, contracts for work and assumes responsibility for delivery of the product. Patients are paid for the labor they contribute but are not obligated to work full-time.

Patients are evaluated at the day hospital and prepared for the workshop there. When they are capable of working thirty hours per week, they are transferred to the workshop, which provides clerical, secretarial, graphic, data-processing, and industrial training. The program is designed for thirty-five people at a time, and attendees work thirty-eight hours per week. Psychiatric care is given after working hours. About 35 per cent of program graduates go on to competitive employment, and another 45 per cent settle into sheltered work or domestic life. The remaining 15 per cent drop out, are discharged, or transfer out of the program.

In *transitional employment* programs, employment is in real-life, competitive situations. Fountain House in New York City has pioneered such a program, in which entry-level jobs with various local companies are held by former patients. Fountain House guarantees an employee to the company for a designated

period of time and places patients in the job temporarily for
learning purposes only. Thus, patients rotate through the jobs
and "graduate" to competitive employment.

Outcome of Employment Programs

There is a paucity of data on the effects of work rehabilitation,
sheltered work, and transitional employment on employment
outcome. Watson and Maddigan (1972) studied the effects of a
paid sheltered work program on chronic and short-term inpatients in a VA hospital. Ninety-one patients were randomly
assigned to the program, which consisted of low-skill jobs fur-
nished by local industries. A control group of forty-two patients
took part in traditional hospital programs consisting of manual
arts, industrial therapy, or occupational therapy. Subjects were
then split into high-chronicity and low-chronicity groups. There
were no differences in release date or in number of days spent in
the community for the high-chronicity subjects in both groups.
However, low-chronicity patients in the paid work program were
released earlier than control patients and spent significantly more
time in the community.

Employment in the community was not evaluated in this study.
Indeed, there is limited information on how sheltered work
programs affect outpatients. Similarly, there is little understanding of how effective a transitional employment program is in
preparing schizophrenic patients for the competitive job market.

Of the three types of work programs, work rehabilitation has
been studied most extensively. Originally developed for inpatients, early studies demonstrated the value of work rehabilitation
in preparing severely disabled patients for life in the community
(Early 1966). The study by Wing et al. found that twenty-four of
forty-five long-stay, chronic schizophrenics were employed one
year after discharge from an industrial rehabilitation unit.

Stevens (1973) evaluated a combined day hospital and rehabilitation workshop in England. Patients were chronic schizophrenics
who were seriously impaired (approximately one third were actively delusional), lacked drive and initiative, and had been unemployed for at least one year prior to the work rehabilitation
program. Following an eighteen-month trial, rehabilitation had

no significant effect on competitive employment or social impairment.

Subsequent follow-up studies on psychiatric rehabilitation have found that, in cases where outcome had led to successful employment, patients have tended to be young (Wing et al. 1972) and less chronic. Moreover, previous occupational stability was associated with stable resettlement at work (Watts and Bennett 1977, Strauss and Carpenter 1974). Future studies of the effects of work programs on labor force participation should control for age, level of chronicity, and work history. A patient's previous work record is a good predictor of employment after a rehabilitation program.

8. Housing Alternatives

Alternative housing must be part of any comprehensive system of community management of schizophrenia because many chronic schizophrenics cannot live independently or with their families. Housing needs were emphasized in a government report on the status of the chronic mental patient (Report to the President 1978) in response to numerous accounts of released patients living in welfare hotels or public shelters or on the streets (New York State Department of Social Services 1980, Baxter and Hopper 1981). Community residence programs have proliferated since World War II, but the shortage of community residences is still severe. Budson (1978) has estimated that 5000 community residences are needed in the United States, but only 289 existed in 1974.

The most rapidly expanding segment of community residential care is the large, multi-bed, proprietary adult home, a business enterprise requiring substantial capital investment and attention to costs and profits (Emerson et al. 1981). Segal and Aviram (1978) report that in California, 72 per cent of community residences, serving 82 per cent of the sheltered-care population in the state, fall into this category. Many such facilities are staffed by untrained people without a therapeutic orientation. Reports of inadequate care and supervision and even exploitation of patients have not been uncommon (Van Putten and Spar 1979).

The needs of the chronically mentally ill for housing, both transitional and long-term, are increasingly coming under the purview of mental health care. A 1975 amendment to the Community Mental Health Centers Act (U.S. Congress 1975) included the community residence as one of the essential services of a community mental health center. As mental health professionals enter this new area of service responsibility, it is useful to review what is known about community residence programs both from an operational perspective and in terms of their effect on patients.

Types of Community Residence Programs

Segal and Aviram (1978) use the term "sheltered care" to describe a residential setting that provides supervised living and include in it foster-family care, halfway houses, and board-and-care homes. In *foster-family care*, the patient lives with a family to which she or he has no kin ties. The head of household serves as a sponsor for the patient, who has a private bedroom but shares meals and common rooms with the family. Frequently, the patient is asked to participate in social and leisure family activities. In some cases, the patient does domestic chores and some income-yielding work that supplements direct payments to sponsors from public or private agencies (Srole 1977).

Halfway houses are transitional residences located off the grounds of the mental hospital. Their goal is to smooth the transition from the protected environment of the hospital to the demands of community life (Reik 1953, Raush and Raush 1968, Glasscote et al. 1971b). In contrast to other types of community residences, halfway houses have closer ties to mental health professionals and a more therapeutic orientation (Landy and Greenblatt 1965, Rothwell and Doniger 1966, Raush and Raush 1968, Glasscote et al. 1971b). The best halfway houses are small enough (not more than thirty residents) for people to get to know one another and provide mutual support. Supervision is provided by live-in houseparents, who often attempt to create a family-like atmosphere (Budson 1978). Halfway houses are open settings in which residents typically work outside the home during the day. Residents share meals and household chores. Halfway houses usually have rules governing curfews, use of alcohol and drugs, and sexual behavior. Psychiatric and other medical and support services are obtained from outside programs not affiliated with the houses. The first halfway houses were founded as private, nonprofit corporations, but now sponsorship by public agencies is common. In most cases, residents' fees make up only part of a house's funding base. Length of stay is varied, ranging from three months to well over a year. Although houses were halfway initially conceived as transitional, some authors (Glasscote et al. 1971a, 1971b; Budson 1978) have advocated expanding their function to include long-term sheltered care or a permanent substitute for hospitalization.

Community lodges are similar to halfway houses but tend to be long-term rather than transitional. In the community lodge program developed by Fairweather et al. (1969), patients made their communal living arrangement economically self-sustaining and free of intervention by mental health professionals.

Satellite housing or *supervised apartments* are the terms used to describe sponsorship of independent community housing by treatment of rehabilitative agencies on behalf of discharged patients (Richmond 1969). Housing is leased by the sponsoring agency or jointly with the patients. Patients occupy the dwelling, usually in groups of two to five, without live-in staff. Supervision is available from the sponsoring agency. Lamb (1981a) has pointed out that satellite housing comes closest to a genuine natural community living arrangement.

Board-and-care homes are distinguished by their large size (typically fifty beds or more) and by the fact that they are strictly a business venture. They provide a shared room, three meals a day, and supervision of medication by a physician under contract to the operator (Lamb 1981a). Staff are usually nonprofessional, and care is custodial rather than therapeutic.

Foster-Family Care

Placement of the mentally ill in families other than their own is one of the oldest forms of community care and can be traced to thirteenth-century Geel, Belgium, and the shrine of St. Dymphna (Chapter 1). As the idea of foster-family care spread to other European countries in the mid-1800's, the number of patients per home grew larger. Linn (1981) reports that placement of one to four patients with a family was typical. However, in Germany, some large villas were converted into family-care homes for as many as thirty patients.

Family care was introduced into the United States by Dorothea Dix in 1809. However, the first U.S. family-care system, in Massachusetts, was not established until 1885. Family-care programs remained small, despite a resurgence of interest in the 1930's, when Pollock (1936) touted the advantages of a foster-family care system along the lines of Geel for "custodial" cases over long-term state hospital treatment. Foster-family care has not achieved widespread acceptance in connection with state mental hospitals. The largest U.S. program of foster-family care is sponsored by the Veterans' Administration. Initiated in 1951, it has reached approximately 60 000 veterans.

Geel foster-family care has survived to the present day and was studied extensively by Srole (1977). In 1971, when Srole was in the midst of his study of the Geel colony, there were 1200 patients in foster care in that community of 30 000. No more than two patients are placed in a single home, thus preventing foster care from becoming a major source of a family's income. Geel foster homes are places of residence, not of treatment. A backup inpatient facility provides crisis intervention when necessary, and hospital staff monitor medication. Home visits by staff are not uncommon, but there is little direct psychiatric treatment.

Pierloot and Demarsin (1981) studied seventy-eight patients in foster-family care in Geel. They found that most were unmarried and between 40 and 60 years old. Twenty-eight were mentally retarded, and forty-one carried a diagnosis of chronic schizophrenia. Only 58 per cent had any contact with their natural families.

Srole studied sixty-four patients transferred from a Belgian mental hospital to Geel families for from six months to seven years after placement. The majority of patients were middle-aged females carrying a diagnosis of chronic schizophrenia or mental retardation. Outcomes at follow-up, based on information from the staff of the mental health service network serving Geel residents, revealed that only five required rehospitalization because of a deteriorated psychiatric condition. The vast majority (forty-nine) were considered relatively well integrated into foster-family life. Five sevenths of the patients who remained in foster care had a positive relationship with their foster mother, undoubtedly a critical factor in the success of a foster-family program.

Foster-family care has not been compared with other types of community living arrangements. Studies to date contrast foster care with long-term hospitalization. Murphy et al. (1976) studied 106 primarily single, middle-aged male chronic schizophrenics in fifty-eight different foster homes in three Canadian provinces. The foster homes were quite varied, ranging in size from four patients to thirty and operated in most cases by nonprofessionals. An eighteen-month follow-up compared the foster-home patients with twenty-eight control patients who remained in the hospital for administrative reasons. Both foster-home and hospitalized patients experienced a substantial decline in symptoms, but there were no differences in social functioning.

In another comparison between foster-family care and continued hospitalization (Linn et al. 1977), 572 psychiatric inpatients, 71 per cent of whom carried a diagnosis of schizophrenia, at five VA hospitals were studied. Before discharge, the 210 patients randomly assigned to foster care were prepared for placement with an average of forty-four days of individual casework or a combination of casework and group therapy. Following baseline assessments, patients were evaluated at placement and four months and one year after placement. Baseline assessments revealed that those selected for foster-home placement showed greater community adjustment potential on the Discharge Readiness Inventory. At four months, two thirds of those placed were still in foster care. Although 20 per cent were readmitted to hospital at some time during the follow-up period, 88 per cent were living in the community at the end of one year. Foster-home patients showed significant improvement in social adjustment four months after placement. At the end of one year, the rehospitalization rate for foster-care patients was 38 per cent. Patients diagnosed as suffering from chronic brain syndrome had the highest failure rate in foster care. Once placed, schizophrenics did as well as nonschizophrenics.

Keskiner and Zaleman (1974) developed, in two small Missouri towns, a foster community model patterned after the Geel colony. Patients in the program, selected from a state hospital, began their orientation by learning social and daily living skills while still in the hospital. Because of low community participation and because some patients could not tolerate the intimacy of family living, the study was conducted both on patients living in foster-care homes and on several patients living together in their own apartment under the supervision of community volunteers. A controlled study of this program has not been done.

Advocates of foster-family placement assert that social adaptation is easier for foster-care patients than for patients who live with kin. This point is hard to prove because patients typically seek foster-family placement only after natural family supports have been lost. Dynamic aspects of the foster-family environment, such as level of interpersonal stress and degree of patient isolation, deserved as much attention in studies of foster families as in studies of patients residing with kin. Moreover, including foster-family members in treatment might benefit the patient's adjustment (Chapter 6).

Halfway Houses

Halfway houses in the United States have their roots in British hostels of the nineteenth century and are a post-World War II phenomenon. Before 1954, the only three halfway houses in the country were all located in rural settings and were guided by the philosophy that a return to a simpler, rural life was preferred. Rutland Corner House in Boston, which grew out of a shelter for distressed women set up in the 1870's, was the first modern urban halfway house. Since its establishment in 1954, halfway houses for the mentally ill have mushroomed across the country. Raush and Raush (1968) located 40 in the mid-1960's, and by 1970 there were 128 in 90 cities (Glasscote et al. 1971b). An NIMH survey in 1973 (Ozarin and Witkin 1975) uncovered 209 halfway houses. There are undoubtedly countless others that have arisen since passage of a 1975 amendment to the Community Mental Health Centers Act (Title III, Public Law 94-63) that mandates transitional halfway house programs.

Many of the first halfway houses had no close ties to mental hospitals and psychiatric outpatient programs. Raush and Raush (1968) found that, although two thirds of halfway houses are supervised on a day-to-day basis by nonprofessionals, a mental health professional is involved in the administration of most.

A minority (19 per cent) of halfway houses provide shelter only (Glasscote et al. 1971b). The more therapeutic orientation of halfway houses is reflected in the findings from Glasscote's survey that 37 per cent provide vocational services and 23 per cent provide counseling.

The profile of halfway houses emerging from the Glasscote study is that they are relatively small (an average of 22 residents, although the range was from 4 to 200) and that the average length of stay is four to six months. Fewer than half (47 per cent) limit clientele to the mentally ill. The majority serve the mentally ill along with alcoholics (27 per cent), mental defectives (25 per cent), drug addicts (11 per cent), former convicts (11 per cent), and the physically handicapped (8 per cent).

Patients in halfway houses have widely varying clinical and social characteristics. However, halfway houses, more than other types of community residence, serve a younger, less chronically disturbed population. Segal and Aviram (1978) rated patients on level of distress and symptoms in halfway houses, foster-family care, and board-and-care homes and found that the patients accepted in halfway houses are generally more verbal and have greater insight into their problem.

Although halfway houses have existed in the United States for over a quarter century, studies comparing their efficacy with that of other types of community residences are lacking. Moreover, comparisons of halfway houses with different programs or treatment philosophies have not been done. Rog and Raush (1975) studied former residents of thirty-six halfway houses and found that 55.2 per cent were employed or in school, 58.2 per cent were living independently in the community, and only 20.5 per cent were rehospitalized.

Other uncontrolled studies of patients admitted to halfway houses (Landy and Greenblatt 1965), Budson et al. 1978) indicate that patients selected for admission are able to move on to more independent living arrangements. Studies have been skewed, however, to facilities serving young and middle- and upper-class patients. For example, in Budson et al.'s study of seventy-five former residents of Berkeley House (former McLean Hospital patients), 90 per cent were between the ages of 17 and 24 and were from the middle or upper classes.

The Community Lodge

Fairweather et al. (1969) initiated a novel community residence program in Palo Alto, California, in which thirty-three patients with a history of multiple psychiatric hospitalizations were trained to live and work together as a "small society" in a community setting without staff in residence. Patients were selected for the program during a hospitalization episode and were prepared for community and group living while still inpatients. During the preparation phase, the importance of employment, money management, group decision-making, and peer social support was emphasized in a social environment in which members took responsibility for each other's welfare.

Staff helped the patients first to find a suitable house and then to maintain it independently. An experienced psychologist became the lodge coordinator. This role, which Fairweather has likened to that of a teacher, was to "push, cajole, shape, and urge the group of ex-patients towards ultimate autonomy (1980, p. 19). The coordinator visited the lodge daily to supervise medication, provide job counseling, and deal with interpersonal problems. Lodge members established a janitorial and gardening business that eventually enabled them to be self-supporting. A community physician was contracted to provide medical care and treated patients in his private office, consistent with efforts to make relationships with the community as natural as possible. The level of involvement of the lodge coordinator was reduced as the group became more self-sufficient. After four years, the role of lodge coordinator was turned over to a layperson. Thus, the lodge society gradually became autonomous and separate from the mental health service system.

The lodge program was compared with routine outpatient care and other residence programs. All patients completed the same small-group hospital treatment program before random assignment. The lodge program reduced recidivism, evidenced by the fact that lodge residents spent about 98 per cent of their time in the community during the first year, in contrast to less than 30 per cent for controls. During the second year, median time in the community was about 95 per cent for lodge members and 30 per cent for controls. Moreover, lodge members spent significantly more time in gainful employment than controls. During the first year, the median time in gainful employment was more than 50 per cent for lodge members but minimal in the control group.

Lodge programs have been established in many other settings, albeit with many adaptations (Fairweather 1980). An Alaskan group set up a house-cleaning business (Daggett 1971), and in

Williamsburg, Virginia, a group of women who live together have formed a corporation in which they work at different jobs rather than conduct a single business (Shean and Zeidberg 1971). It is notable that the inpatient phase has been dropped from most new lodge programs and some, such as Cleveland's Panta Rhei, include group living in apartments.

Satellite Housing

The need for permanent housing after release from a halfway house has stimulated the development of satellite housing. The Fountain House social rehabilitation center in New York City is credited with the innovation of using apartments for patient housing. In a typical satellite-housing program, the sponsoring organization locates an apartment and may at first pay rent and utilities. Apartment leases are eventually taken over by patients, who remain as long as they are willing and able to meet their contractural obligations. In the satellite-housing program developed by the El Camino halfway house in San Mateo, California, from two to four residents who have lived together in the halfway house are placed together in an apartment (Richmond 1969). Similar satellite housing programs have developed from the Woodley House in Washington, D.C. (Kresky et al. 1976) and Brooklyn's Boerum Hill. In some programs, patients are referred directly from the hospital or an outpatient clinic to an apartment in the community (Sandall et al. 1975), avoiding halfway houses. Another modification of the satellite-housing concept is Goldmeier et al.'s (1978) program providing for temporary (type A) and long-term (type B) housing. In the first instance, the agency holds the lease and in the latter the lease is held by residents. In a program in Topeka (Bowen and Fry 1971), patients move into rented houses directly after discharge from hospital.

Board-and-Care Homes

Board-and-care homes have rapidly taken over the custodial function of the state hospital. Lamb and Goertzel (1977) report that, in California, 50 per cent of long-term patients with a psychotic diagnosis and under age 65 live in such settings. The homes usually have more than fifty beds (some running into the hundreds), have no affiliation with a mental health facility, and are run as a private business. A typical fee of $14 per day in New York State purchases a shared room, three meals a day, housekeeping services, and medication supervision.

As with halfway houses, the mentally ill live with other disabled groups, such as the mentally retarded or frail elderly. However, unlike halfway houses, board-and-care homes are not therapeutically oriented. Segal and Aviram (1978) found that approximately 50 per cent of the California board-and-care homes they studied had a curfew and 82 per cent had a system for dispensing medication. Although there were some organized activities, these were usually voluntary. There were no curfews or bedchecks, but meal hours were fixed and no alcohol was allowed. Operators typically play a parental role; in half of the board-and-care homes studied by Segal and Aviram the operator controlled the patient's spending money. Similarly, Lamb (1979b) found that a patient's personal funds were managed by staff in the California board-and-care home he studied.

The typical sheltered-care resident in Segal and Aviram's study was between 50 and 65 years of age, white, Protestant, unemployed, and on Supplemental Security Income. Most were leading a fairly settled life in a facility not far from their hometown.

In Lamb's (1981) study, the median age of residents was 39 years and there were twice as many men as women. Most (86 per cent) were on Supplemental Security Income and had a median of eighteen months of prior hospitalization. Although length of stay in the home ranged from four days to fifteen years, a median stay was thirty-two months. Forty-two per cent lived in the home for at least five years. Most (92 per cent) were being treated with major tranquilizers, but 63 per cent had no contact with a mental health professional other than the psychiatrist who visited the facility for medication management.

In a clinical interview, Lamb (1979b) determined that 32 per cent of residents of one home had been hospitalized within the past year. Ninety per cent either never tried to live alone (27 per cent) or failed in an attempt to (62 per cent). Although 55 per cent had had some contact with family in the previous three months, 45 per cent were isolated from kin.

Issues in Community Residential Care

Facility Size

Size is an important determinant of the location of a facility in the community. In some states, such as California and Wisconsin, small facilities (one to six beds) can qualify as single-family units under state zoning laws. In Segal and Aviram's (1978) California study of sheltered care, more than half of the small facilities were in residential areas. Although regulations vary from state to state, intermediate-size facilities (seven to fifty) are considered group living and as such can be located in residential areas. Large facilities (more than fifty beds) are usually considered business operations and located in commercial districts.

Segal and Aviram reported that larger homes were associated with entrepreneurs' coming into the sheltered-care "industry." About 9 per cent of the sheltered-care facilities in their study served one fifth of the population. They also noted that community residences operated as businesses evoked a more negative reaction from patients than facilities run under other auspices. Of facilities run as businesses, 37 per cent were viewed favorably by residents, in contrast to 62 per cent of other types of facilities.

Although it is often asserted that larger facilities are more institution-like, there is limited evidence that size alone has a critical impact on a patient's well-being. In one of the only studies of the relationship between the characteristics of the community residence and patient outcome, Linn et al. (1980) found that patients in larger homes showed a decline in social functioning. Although these workers invoke the "wisdom of Geel" by advocating that the size of family-care homes be limited to no more than two patients per home, the issue of optimal size deserves further study.

Operator Characteristics

The relative independence of sheltered care from the formal mental health care delivery system has produced a cadre of facility operators with little or no professional training. Although it has been suggested that foster families be screened for psychopathology and alcoholism (Milosak and Basic 1981), Baxter (1980) reported that in Geel, a family's psychiatric history is not a consideration in the selection of foster homes. The tradition of foster families is transmitted from generation to generation, as evidenced by the fact that 75 per cent of the foster families in Srole's (1977) study had relatives who took in "boarders." Families are given no formal training. Rather, they are expected to rely on intuitive under-standing and skill acquired through their own life experience and observation of friends and relatives who have taken in boarders in the past.

Srole noted that the economic motive was strong among Geel foster families. Segal and Aviram (1978) found that many of the sheltered-care operators in their study had backgrounds as hospital attendants or vocational nurses. Owing to the fact that 75 per cent of the facilities in the Segal and Aviram sample were owned and operated by the same person, the board-and-care business is a vehicle for upward mobility. For 75 per cent of the operators, most of whom were married women over 50 and half of whom were black, this type of work was a step up from their previous occu-pation. Fifty-eight per cent derived only part of their income from this activity.

In Beatty and Seeley's (1980) study of operators in thirty-nine foster homes, the typical operator was a woman who had gained caretaking skills as a result of raising a family. Such women had had little formal education and no previous work experience. How well the typical sheltered-care staff can form relationships bene-ficial to patients is an area in need of research and assessment.

Therapeutic Orientation

Many community residences provide shelter only. A patient is expected to make independent arrangements for psychiatric treat-ment. The exception is the larger board-and-care home, where medication maintenance is provided. In contrast, social therapy is built into Fairweather's et al's (1969) lodge program and some halfway houses. A patient's daily activities are highly structured, and there is every expectation that the patient will engage in competitive employment or sheltered work or otherwise make productive use of time.

Edelson (1976) has noted that a key factor in residential treatment is the extent to which the resident is "enveloped" by a housing facility, meaning the extent to which the facility limits the number of choices the resident is free to make alone. *High-envelopment* facilities, exemplified by hospitals and nursing homes, are often locked and have intensive round-the-clock supervision for severely disabled patients. *Midrange-envelopment* facilities include open residences with some programmed social activities. Those settings most like natural living arrangements are termed *low-envelopment* environments.

Community residences have also been classified by the activities of typical residents. *High-expectation* environments encourage as much participation as possible in activities involving society at large. Budson (1978) defines "high expectation" as a situation in which residents are required to attend school or work. An *intermediate-expectation* environment is when residents are actively engaged in a day hospital program, an ex-patient social club, or a sheltered workshop. A *low-expectation* environment leaves patients to their own devices for meaningful use of time. There is virtually no attempt to involve patients in work and social activities. Because no alternative for social and cultural stimulation is offered, television is often the primary link with the outside world in low-expectation settings.

There have been few studies of how the characteristics of a sheltered-care facility affect a patient's well-being. Linn et al. (1980) found that the presence of young children in foster-family homes was associated with improved adjustment in patients. Noting that there is an air of normality when there are children at play, these workers speculated that the spontaneity of children in social relations may benefit patients.

Linn et al. also found that more sponsor-initiated activity in the home was associated with improvements for all patients but those diagnosed as schizophrenic. For schizophrenics, a highly stimulating environment was associated with deterioration in functioning. In addition, intense supervision produced the same outcome: deterioration in schizophrenics but improvement in nonschizophrenics.

Hyperarousal has been associated with deterioration in chronic schizophrenic patients (Venables and Wing 1962). Brown et al. (1972) warned that overly active efforts to rehabilitate long-term schizophrenics may lead to sudden relapse. Likewise, May (1976) concluded that high stimulus input and role diffusion are disastrous to patients who have deficiencies in perception, attention, and information-processing. Clearly, the degree of stimulation and arousal in different living settings is in need of careful assessment. Lamb and Goertzel (1972) studied a high-expectation community program that included a day-treatment center and vocational rehabilitation services as well as a halfway house. The patients' level of social and vocational functioning was improved, although the high-expectation setting was no more effective than a low-pressure setting in keeping patients out of the hospital.

Resident Characteristics

Budson (1978, 1981) maintains that there are two kinds of patients likely to benefit from halfway house: chronic long-term patients who have been in the hospital so long that they have lost contact with family and friends and young, isolated adults who have suffered from a chronic psychotic illness for a number of years and have experienced severe social isolation during late adolescence and young adulthood. After a brief period of hospitalization, this second type of patient either cannot return home because of parental rejection or because the home atmosphere places the patient in a situation in which she or he is likely to regress to a dependent, nonfunctioning position.

Glasscote et al. (1971b) and White (1981) have pointed out that, in the selection of patients for community residences, behavior is more relevant than diagnosis. Patients who display behavior that is dangerous or disturbing to themselves or others are greater risks in a community residential setting, particularly if the residence staff is unskilled or unprepared to deal with such problems. Violent patients are excluded from some community residence programs (Keskiner and Zaleman 1974). Moreover, when residents display behavior that is intolerable to the community at large, the very existence of the community residence can be threatened. Alcoholism, drug addiction, violence, and sex deviation are the most common characteristics for exclusion from halfway houses (Raush and Raush 1968, Glasscote et al. 1971b), particularly if they are current.

Among those accepted into community residences, there are

specific clinical characteristics that can cause management problems. White (1981) lists seven types of difficult patients: the paranoid patient, the medication-refusing patient, the entitled patient, the assaultive patient, the medically ill patient, the patient over- or underinvolved with family, the suicidal patient, and the community provocateur.

Although staff are not always professionally trained, they need to know how to handle psychiatric emergencies, such as what to do in case of overdose and how to control an assaultive patient. Staff should be aware of regulations and procedures governing restraint and of emergency use of medication. A strong therapeutic alliance between residents and staff can ameliorate or forestall many difficult clinical situations. For example, patients are less likely to be assaultive to staff members with whom they have a positive and trusting relationship. Moreover, a strong therapeutic alliance with a patient refusing medication may result in improved compliance.

Patients who are frequently assaultive can be a management problem in a community residence because of the lack of a seclusion room or of sufficient staff. In fact, admission of violent patients is probably contraindicated. Patients who are only infrequently assaultive can be managed more easily when the circumstances associated with previous assault episodes are known and can be avoided. A firm, calm, business-like approach to a problem can preserve the patient's sense of dignity and self-respect by giving her or him a choice in the treatment plan, such as going to the hospital or taking additional medication. Early intervention and early recognition of symptoms of decompensation, before the onset of psychosis, are important in managing patients with a history of violence.

Segal and Aviram (1978) found that complaints from the "outside" world, more likely to be lodged against patients rehospitalized in the past year, cause facility operators to seek help from mental health professionals. Illness-related behavior is most likely to receive complaints, especially when it touches on the outside world. However, frequency of service use is related more strongly to the characteristics of the area and of the facility's residents. Operators who use professional services more frequently are treatment-oriented and have a larger, "more professional" facility. Social workers were selected 42 per cent of the time to deal with problems in the Segal and Aviram study, general practitioners 20 per cent, and psychiatrists 15 per cent. Seventy-five per cent of operators sought help for suicide attempts, refusal to take medication, sexual acting out, or disorganization in the patient. In smaller, family-like homes, operators were more likely to seek help if the patient did not pay rent or misbehaved sexually.

Resident Mix

Patients in community residences have an opportunity to live with nonpatients. A 1979 study of adult-home residents in New York State revealed that only 29 per cent were former mental patients, sharing their fate with a variety of other disability groups, such as the frail elderly, the mentally retarded, and the mildly medically ill. The deliberate mixing of patients with those having no known history of psychiatric problems provides role models for patients to follow in social and work adjustment (Doniger et al. 1963, Bennett 1964, Gumruku 1968). Nonpatient residents live with the mentally ill at San Francisco's Conrad House (Gumruku). In addition, Harvard and Radcliffe undergraduates have lived with the mentally ill at Welmet, a halfway house in Cambridge, Massachusetts (Kantor and Greenblatt 1962). At halfway houses in a YMCA (Baganz et al. 1971) and in a mid-Manhattan hotel, former patients live with residents who have no known psychiatric history. Doniger et al. concluded from their experience at Woodley House that halfway houses should board two or three healthy people.

It is unfortunately not known how mixing the mentally ill with nonpatients influences the social adjustment of the former both within the community residence and in the community at large.

Community Reaction

From their inception in the United States, community residences have been vulnerable to rejection by the community. In Raush and Raush's (1968) study of halfway houses, seventeen of forty had some trouble with the community at the beginning of the project. As these authors point out, "People may favor the idea of a halfway house, but, like a fire department, no one wants it next door" (p. 52).

Segal and Aviram (1978) noted that community reaction to residences seems to be based on a stereotyped fear of the mentally ill, on a perceived threat to the community by the patients (in terms of norm-violating behavior), and on concern about declining property values.

The fear expressed by community members toward the mentally ill is largely the result of the stereotyped notion that mental disorder is characterized by unpredictable and irrational behavior (Starr 1955, Cumming and Cumming 1957). Although studies in California and New York reported high arrest and conviction rates for murder among discharged patients (California State Department of Health 1973, Sosowsky 1974, Zitrin et al. 1976), even the highest crime rate reported indicates that only 31 of 10 000 former patients represent a real threat to others (California State Department of Health). There is weak evidence that the average mental patient is an unusually and predominantly dangerous person. More crimes are committed by younger patients (age 20 to 29) than older ones (Sosowsky). However, in the younger group, the crime rate for former mental patients was 5.3 times that of the general population, but in the older group, it was 9 times that of the general population.

Evidence regarding the actual impact of sheltered-care facilities on property values is scarce but indicates little, if any, effect (Dear 1977). Neighborhoods likely to attract a heavy concentration of sheltered-care homes are often on the decline. The homes may, in fact, revitalize the area. Using data from a county assessor's office, Garr (1973) found a steady increase over five years in property values in an area with many sheltered-care facilities.

Hazelton et al. (1975) conducted a survey in Santa Clara County, California, and found that the social distance desired by the general public between themselves and the mentally ill is smaller than one would imagine. Eighty-three per cent of the general public were willing to have a formerly hospitalized patient live in a supervised facility on their block, and 78 per cent were willing to have the ex-patient as a next-door neighbor. However, people were unfamiliar with treatment of mental illness and uninformed about the location and nature of treatment facilities.

In a study of public reaction to treatment facilities in Toronto, Dear and Taylor (1979) again found a low public awareness of existing mental health facilities. Only 36 per cent of respondents who lived within one quarter mile of a mental health facility were aware of its existence.

It is notable that only 13 per cent of the 1091 respondents in the Dear and Taylor study were opposed to having a mental health facility located near them. Twelve per cent rated a location within seven to twelve blocks undesirable to some degree, 22 per cent revealed that a location within two to six blocks was undesirable, and 37 per cent said the location of a facility within one block would be undesirable.

In a telephone survey of New York City residents by Rabkin et al. (1983), ninety subjects who lived within one block of a psychiatric facility (either small residence, outpatient clinic, or SRO hotel) were queried along with a control group of ninety respondents not residing close to such a facility. All respondents were middle-aged, white-collar, and well educated and had lived at the same address for an average of nine years. Attitudes toward mental illness were not related to proximity to such facilities. A key finding was that three fourths of those living within one block of selected facilities were unaware of their presence. Ninety per cent of respondents were unprepared to oppose the establishment of a mental health facility on their block, and the majority were not concerned about the effect of patients on their personal safety, property values, or the reputation of their neighborhood.

Location of Community Residences

Negative community reaction toward residences for the mentally ill can be accounted for in part by the high concentration of facilities in a given area because this results in high visibility of former patients. For example, Sheffer (1980) cites that a forty-four-block area in Manhattan has approximately 7000 to 10 000 former mental patients.

Overconcentration of the mentally ill has prompted Long Beach, New York, to pass an ordinance preventing persons requiring continuous psychiatric or medical services from registering in local hotels. In addition, there are innumerable ways in which board-and-care homes have been discouraged, both informally and legally.

Raush and Raush (1968) state that a community residence cannot avoid public confrontation in a small town or in a well-established, stable, residential community. Indeed, locating a community residence in such a setting requires that confrontation be planned for. Quite different, however, are transitional neighborhoods in large cities. Woodley House in Washington, D.C., was located in a "busy, mind your own business" neighborhood (Rothwell and Doniger 1966) in which apartments, hotels, boarding houses, stores, and private homes are mixed in a middle-class section of the city. Facilities located in such settings do not depend on the immediate neighborhood for work or social opportunities. Because such neighborhoods are anonymous, the house can more easily maintain its own anonymity and protection from too many social pressures. Meenach (1964) recommends neighborhoods zoned for business in or near a residential area, within walking distance of shops and churches, near public transportation, on well-lighted streets, with police patrols, and near food markets. Rural homes are more apt to be self-contained in terms of both work and social activities.

Segal and Aviram (1978) have confirmed that the closer a facility is to community resources and medical and social services, the greater the social integration of its residents. Integration is difficult in middle-class neighborhoods of single-family homes because of their distance form these services. Facilities in downtown areas are more likely to be closer to community resources and therefore enhance social integration. In addition to the distance factor, middle-class areas tend to be characterized by stabler family networks, and socialization between these networks and disaffiliated individuals is difficult. Moreover, facilities situated close to community resources and medical and social services are more likely to rely on these programs than to develop their own internally oriented ones.

There are different philosophies for setting up community residences. Rothwell and Doniger (1966), in setting up Woodley House, moved in quietly, without informing the neighborhood of what they were doing, warning that the trouble with asking permission of too many people is that you might not get it. An opposing view, expressed by Levy (1980), contends that it is absurd to keep a low profile and assume that "sneaking" a facility into the neighborhood will work. Stickney (1980) advocates deliberate, cooperative planning at all levels of government and among the various human services systems in order to avoid overconcentration in certain areas. Assessing community attitudes, involving local leaders and public officials early on, educating the public, organizing support in local mental health groups and political and civic organizations, and establishing a community advisory board can help to ensure the life of a new program.

There is no agreement on optimal patient density, but local zoning policies are designed to prevent overconcentration. The patient density at Geel is 40 patients per 1000 general population (Srole 1977). A community residential-care program of this density is feasible if instituted slowly and with thorough community preparation and participation. Greater patient density in foster-family care is more cost-efficient.

Some states, such as Wisconsin (Cupaiuolo 1980), license community residences with up to eight persons with social, physical, or mental disabilities to locate in a single-family-use zone without the need for a variance. Larger facilities (up to forty-six residents) can locate in other zones without applying for a variance. Overconcentration is controlled by granting municipalities the right to prohibit community residences from locating within 1500 feet of one another. Density is monitored by allowing a municipality to prohibit additional community residences once the number of persons being served exceeds 1 per cent of the population. Thoughtfully designed zoning policies can greatly facilitate the integration of patients into the community.

9. Research and Quality of Care

> The quality of the life lived by the patient and his relatives is the final criterion by which services must be judged. A good hospital is better than a poor hospital or a poor family environment. A good family environment is better than a poor hospital or a poor hostel. The same may be said of daytime environments—open employment, enclaves in ordinary commercial business, rehabilitation or sheltered workshops, or protected day centers. Universal denunciation of any one type of setting is likely to be harmful since it is clearly not based on rational principles of assessment, treatment, or care.
>
> (WING 1978, P. 254)

People are an essential ingredient in any social institution, whether asylum, kinship system, or community program. As Wing (1978) and others (Wing and Brown 1970, Bennett 1978) have pointed out, both harmful and constructive relationships can be found in all types of social institutions. Deinstitutionalization has shown that merely changing the locus of care from the hospital to the community does not guarantee improved quality of life for chronic schizophrenic patients.

The deinstitutionalization era has witnessed innovations in the clinical care and treatment of schizophrenia that use both inpatient and outpatient settings. A general conclusion from this work is that the chronic schizophrenic patient needs long-term, individually tailored care from the mental health delivery system that includes the following:

1. Drug therapy, carefully monitored for both efficacy and side effects

2. Crisis intervention to stabilize episodes of psychosis, carried out on an inpatient basis if the patient is violent, suicidal, or otherwise unmanageable in a community setting
3. Extended full or partial hospitalization and/or outpatient care to implement specific psychosocial therapies
4. Housing alternatives or humane custodial care if the patient is unable to live independently or with family

Still at issue is the length of time that specific interventions should be in effect for optimal results (Gudeman et al. 1983), the combination of elements of care required for specific clinical and social characteristics, and when in the course of schizophrenia certain treatment goals are most appropriate (Gudeman et al. 1983, Wing 1982). While it is generally agreed that aggressive efforts at social and vocational rehabilitation should be abandoned at some point in favor of custodial efforts to help the patient gain satisfaction from simple everyday activities, (Lamb 1981b), there are few guidelines for the transition from active to custodial treatment.

Despite impressive advances, development of effective technologies is still a top priority as the delivery of mental health services becomes established on a firmer scientific basis. Methods to ensure that the best treatments and management methods known are routinely available to patients in large public mental health delivery systems are essential.

The Staff and Quality of Care

The diagnosis and treatment skills of mental health professionals and the way they interact with their patients define quality of care. The long history of inadequate treatment in public mental institutions stems largely from the difficulties of recruiting and holding competent staff. Many professionals prefer the private sector. Hollingshead and Redlich's (1958) classic study showed that lower-class patients were less likely to be treated by well-trained psychiatrists. Two decades later, concern that psychiatrists are insufficiently involved in the care and treatment of public psychiatric patients, particularly those suffering from chronic schizophrenia, was expressed in policy statements on the status of mental care in the United States (Report to the President 1978, Talbott 1978a). Indeed, the persistent shortage of psychiatrists on the staffs of state mental hospitals and community mental health centers (Langsley and Robinowitz 1979, Pardes et al. 1979) indicates a lack of commitment to public psychiatric programs.

The disadvantages of a career in public psychiatry are numerous: lower pay than in a private practice, more patients per staff member with fewer opportunities to provide either intensive treatment or continuity of care, burdensome paperwork mandated by administrators and third-party payors, excessive legal constraints, and vulnerability to scapegoating by the media and politicians (Nielsen et al. 1981). The political and social approval of working with the poor so apparent in the 1960's and 1970's has eroded (Eichler 1982). Also, even the most dedicated mental health professionals in the public sector are susceptible to "burnout."

Burnout: Scourge of the Dedicated

Lamb (1979a) observed that deinstitutionalization has increased services for the chronically mentally ill in the absence of any underlying conceptual framework for their care. Consequently, staff do not have realistic notions of what can and cannot be accomplished with such patients, who have varying needs and capabilities. It is not uncommon for staff to enter the field with optimism, only to lose interest and become frustrated when patients do not improve to the degree anticipated.

Pines and Maslach (1978) point out that intensive and intimate work with people over an extended time often arouses strong emotions that can be quite stressful. Because personal resources are a vital asset in human services work, protracted stress—including long hours and low financial and other rewards—can have a devastating effect on job performance. Although there has been little systematic study of the characteristics of mental health professionals who work with chronic schizophrenic patients and of how they respond to stress at work, a syndrome having behavioral and emotional symptoms and known as "burnout" has been identified (Freudenberger 1974, Maslach 1976). This condition is generally thought to affect disproportionately high numbers of hard-working, dedicated "samaritans" (Maslach).

Its symptoms include exhaustion, fatigue, gastrointestinal disturbances, insomnia, depression, irritability, anxiety, cynicism, and a lack of curiosity (Freudenberger). Staff who have burned out are less likely to engage in meaningful relationships with patients. Decreased productivity, increased time lost from work, and job turnover are believed to be consequences of burnout.

In a study of this syndrome, Thompson (1980) queried live-in houseparents in small, free-standing group homes for emotionally disturbed adolescents. Questionnaires, which included a self-impression measure of the subject's feelings when first becoming a houseparent and (if applicable) when leaving the position, were sent to 146 current and former houseparents. The response rate was only 32 per cent, but findings revealed higher burnout scores for those with no power in deciding which adolescents were accepted as residents. Minimal burnout was found among houseparents with good support from friends and with time away from the home.

Pines and Maslach (1978) studied burnout among psychiatrists, psychologists, nurses, social workers, attendants, and volunteers at a variety of mental health institutions in the San Francisco area. Staff were interviewed concerning their social and professional backgrounds, the characteristics of their jobs, their attitudes and feelings about mental health work, and self-perceptions. Job dissatisfaction correlated well with larger patient-to-staff ratios, higher percentages of schizophrenics in the patient population, and longer work hours. Staff who were very satisfied with their jobs treated smaller percentages of schizophrenics, worked fewer hours a day, were less involved in administrative work, had good working relationships with other staff members, and felt they had some input into the institution's policies. Staff who had worked in the mental health field for a long time were more dissatisfied and more likely to have a custodial rather than humanistic view of mental illness.

Controlling Burnout

The critical need for a committed and capable cadre of mental health professionals involved in the long-term care and treatment of the chronic schizophrenic patient demands that burnout be controlled. Measures to prevent it should be built into administrative practices and educational programs. Pines and Maslach suggest that reasonable patient-to-staff ratios; shorter work hours; greater sharing of the patient load among staff, particularly when patients are chronic schizophrenics; and management of intrastaff conflict can help to prevent burnout. Because peer-group support and good leadership are important contributors to job satisfaction, service programs must reward outstanding performers (Wise and Berlin 1981).

The most promising antidote to burnout, however, is an atmosphere of vitality and creativity. The clinical research discussed in this volume has breathed new life into psychiatry in the public sector. This body of knowledge delineates the new skills that must be acquired by psychiatrists, clinical psychologists, nurses, social workers, and rehabilitation counselors.

Quality of Research

The development of innovative psychosocial treatments for schizophrenia has accelerated over the past decade as clinicians have attempted to help patients and their families cope better with this difficult illness. The knowledge acquired through treatment focused on the patient's family, social, and vocational life now complements the body of research on control of florid symptoms. Antipsychotic drugs have proven efficacious in controlling positive symptoms, and there is mounting evidence that drug efficacy is enhanced by psychosocial therapies (Goldstein and Kopeikin 1981, Falloon et al. 1982). When free of psychotic symptoms, patients can pursue social activities, but drug therapy alone is not sufficient to help them cope with the social consequences of schizophrenia. Family therapies, the teaching of social and coping skills, and vocational assessment and rehabilitation hold promise in assisting patients to lead more useful and meaningful lives.

Because these treatments focus on such important issues, they deserve to be studied carefully. The most distinguished treatment studies have set standards for research of this type, and today techniques such as random assignment to treatment and control groups have become commonplace. These studies suggest that the following issues deserve attention whenever psychosocial treatment studies are designed.

Level of Chronicity

The goals of psychosocial treatments for first-episode patients in adolescence or young adulthood are quite different from the goals for long-term chronic patients in midlife or senescence (Bachrach 1982). Aggressive efforts to help a patient approximate his or her preillness level of social functioning have a greater chance of success after an initial acute episode or in the prechronic phase. Therefore, the acute-chronic dimension deserves attention in program planning (Mosher and Keith 1979).

The effects of long-term, intensive inpatient care versus brief hospitalization for young patients require careful study. Further work is needed to determine the efficacy of nonbiological therapies for young patients who have been ill for only a short while. The some is true of social intervention therapies for chronic patients who have reached midlife unable to gain satisfaction from productive work or personal relationships.

Control of Neuroleptic Medication

May (1976) has emphasized the importance of controlling for neuroleptic medication in isolating the effect of a psychosocial treatment intervention for schizophrenia. This recommendation can be implemented either by tailoring the drug and its dosage to each subject (Linn et al. 1979) or by prescribing a standard dosage of a specific drug to all subjects in a treatment group. The latter approach was used by Goldstein and Kopeikin (1981) in his study of family therapy. Injecting the drug helps to guarantee compliance.

Research Diagnostic Procedures

Recent developments in clinical assessment and diagnosis should be applied in selecting subjects for intervention studies. Standardized diagnostic interviews, such as the Schedule for Affective Disorder and Schizophrenia (Endicott and Spitzer 1978), should be used routinely and administered by trained raters. In addition, schizophrenics should be distinguished from nonschizophrenics when analyzing treatment effects (May and Van Putten 1974).

Premorbid Social Competence

Premorbid social competence is an important predictor of social functioning outcome in schizophrenia. The value of routinely assessing premorbid social functioning is illustrated by Goldstein and Kopeikin's (1981) study of family therapy, which found differences in treatment effect for good and poor premorbids.

Describing and Measuring Treatment Intervention

The most innovative psychosocial treatment researchers have devised detailed protocols to both describe and standardize their interactions with study subjects (Wallace et al. 1980). Although difficult to accomplish, such procedures facilitate assessment of treatment efficacy and promote the systematic replication of the intervention with new therapists and subjects.

To give a clear statement of treatment interventions, the context, intensity, and duration of treatment should be described. It is notable that the new interventions for families of schizophrenics, although sharing a common theoretical base, vary considerably in context, some including only the nuclear family with or without the patient and others consisting of multiple family groupings. Moreover, duration is from six weeks (Goldstein and Kopeikin 1981) to two years (Falloon et al. 1981).

Psychotherapy research has emphasized the importance of considering the training and experience of the therapists when evaluating treatment efficacy (May 1974). In some programs, research staff conduct the intervention on both subjects and controls, whereas in others controls are treated by another staff. It is important to explore the attitudes of staff about an intervention, their level of commitment to it, and their experiences using it.

Outcome Measures

Measures of outcome should be standardized across studies as much as possible, using a common battery of research instruments to measure mental status, social adjustment, use of hospital and community services, and life satisfaction (Schulberg and Bromet 1981). A common set of research instruments facilitates the comparison of findings from one study to another. Special instruments may be required to measure behavior targeted by a specific intervention, such as intrafamilial stress or social interaction skills.

Short-Term and Long-Term Follow-up

Baseline measurement of all dependent variables permits careful study of the effects of treatment while it is in progress. Assessment of outcome at termination and at follow-up several months or even years later is critical in evaluating the long-term effects of psychosocial therapies. Evidence from studies of psychosocial treatment of schizophrenic populations, such as Stein and Test's (1980) Training in Community Living Program and Paul and Lentz's (1977) investigation of social learning, indicates that advances made tend to diminish once intervention is withdrawn. May (1974) has underscored the practical problems of conducting long-term follow-up, such as loss of subjects and of the ability to control for subsequent treatment. Nevertheless, if follow-up procedures, such as obtaining addresses and telephone numbers of key relatives and periodic telephone or mail contact with the patient, are built into the study design, long-term follow-up will be easier.

Experiments at Multiple Sites

Most treatment research projects have been carried out in a single location. Although it is administratively more complex to organize research at more than one site, the scientific advantages of so doing are obvious. The study of ten day-treatment programs reported by Linn et al. (1979) produced findings that could not possibly have emerged from the study of a single program.

Conducting experimental programs at multiple sites enhances understanding of how they can be adapted to new settings, countering the arguments of Suchman (1967), Mechanic (1978), and Bachrach (1980) that such "model programs" are merely hypotheses and cannot be generalized.

Relationship Between Research Quality and Care Quality

Rigorously designed, controlled trials of psychosocial interventions produce findings of greater value to mental health care systems. For example, a thorough decription of an experimental intervention and of the activities of staff involved can help identify either any "Hawthorne effect" or the extent to which positive results are attributable to "exceptionally devoted persons" (Rossi 1978, Bachrach 1980).

Model programs are important in developing programming principles for mental health care. A major difference between model programs and mental health systems is that systems contain many program elements tailored to the needs of different patients. The fact that model programs are targeted to patients in specific age, sex, social class, or symptom groups is instructive in determining how models can be translated into service systems.

The contention of mental health professionals that public mental health care is fragmented and that programs are unresponsive to the needs of seriously disabled patients has been made so often in the last decade that it is in danger of being accepted as absolutely true. Another lament by workers in the field is that the results of experimental programs have not been adequately applied to service systems.

There have been few attempts to disseminate findings from successful experiments, but a notable exception to this is the effort of Fairweather and his colleagues (1969, 1978, 1980) to establish lodge societies at mental hospitals across the United States. In their study of various ways of getting hospitals to set up a lodge program (Fairweather et al. 1980), they randomly assigned 148 state and VA hospitals who had agreed to participate in the study to one of three groups: a group who would be asked to learn about the program only through a brochure, a group who would be asked to learn about the program through a one-day workshop put on by members of the Fairweather team, and a group who would be asked to learn about the program through a demonstration ward set up in their own hospital.

In the brochure group, only 65 per cent actually did read the brochure and, of that 65 per cent, only 5 per cent attempted to set up their own lodge program. In the one-day workshop group, 68 per cent agreed to attend the workshop and, of this 68 per cent, only 12 per cent then established their own lodge. Much better results emerged, however, with the demonstration ward group. Only twelve of the hospitals in this group (14 per cent) agreed to have the ward set up in their hospital but, of those twelve, nine (75 per cent) went on to establish their own program.

Fairweather and his group have influenced the development of more than seventy lodge programs in the United States and elsewhere (Ch. 8). Their experiences in adapting the program to many different client groups provide valuable information on the processes involved in translating model programs into service systems.

In summary, the new treatment programs developed during the deinstitutionalization era have shown that the seriously mentally ill can be helped to live satisfying and productive lives in the community. The debate over where the mentally ill should live and be treated has given way to greater flexibility in using hospital and community based programs, as both are necessary. Research which would enable identification of the most effective treatment and support programs for specific patients should continue. Bringing high quality programs to large public mental health care systems so that benefits from recent advances reach more than a few is a new challenge for the coming years.

References

Alivisatos, G., and G. Lyketsos (1964). A preliminary report of research concerning the attitude of the families of hospitalized mental patients, *Int. J. Social Psychiat.* **10**:37.

Amdur, M. (1979). Medical compliance in outpatient psychiatry, *Comp. Psychiat.* **20**:339.

Anderson, C., G. Hogarty, and D. Reiss (1980). Family treatment of adult schizophrenic patients: A psycho-educational approach, *Schizophrenia Bull.* **6**:490.

Anderson, C. M., G. Hogarty, and D. J. Reiss (1981). The psycho-educational family treatment of schizophrenia, in *New Developments in Interventions with Families of Schizophrenics, New Directions for Mental Health Services* (M. J. Goldstein, ed.). San Francisco: Jossey-Bass, vol. 12, p. 79.

Anthony, W. A. (1977). Psychological rehabilitation: A concept in need of a method, *Am. Psychologist* **32**:658.

Anthony, W. A., and G. J. Buell (1973). Psychiatric aftercare clinic effectiveness as a function of patient demographic characteristics, *J. Consult. Clin. Psychol.* **41**:116.

Anthony, W. A., G. J. Buell, S. Sharratt, and M. E. Althoff (1972). Efficacy of psychiatric rehabilitation. *Psychol. Bull.* **78**:447.

Anthony, W. A., M. R. Cohen, and R. Vitalo (1978). The measurement of rehabilitation outcome. *Schizophrenia Bull.* **4**:365.

Arnhoff, F. N. (1975). Social consequences of a policy toward mental illness. *Science* **188**:1277.

Asnis, G., M. A. Leopold, R. C. DuVoisin, and A. H. Schwartz (1977). A survey of tardive dyskinesia in psychiatric outpatients. *Am. J. Psychiat.* **134**:1367.

Astrachan, B. M., L. Brauer, M. Harrow, and C. C. Schwartz (1974). Symptomatic outcome in schizophrenia. *Arch. Gen. Psychiat.* **31**:155.

Atthowe, J. M., and L. Krasner (1968). A preliminary report on the application of contingent reinforcement procedures (token economy) on a "chronic" psychiatric ward. *J. Abnorm. Psychol.* **73**:37.

Ayllon, T., and N. H. Azrin (1965). The measurement and reinforcement of behavior of psychotics. *J. Exp. Analysis Behavior* **8**:357.

Ayllon, T., and N. H. Azrin (1968). *The Token Economy: A Motivational System for Therapy and Rehabilitation.* New York: Appleton-Century-Crofts.

Bachrach, L. L. (1976). *Deinstitutionalization: An Analytical Review and Sociological Perspective.* Rockville, Md.: U.S. Dept. of HEW.

Bachrach, L. L. (1980). Overview: Model programs for chronic mental patients. *Am. J. Psychiat.* **137**:1023.

Bachrach, L. L. (1981). The effects of deinstitutionalization on general hospital psychiatry. *Hospital Community Psychiat.* **32**:786.

Bachrach, L. L. (1982). Young adult chronic patients: An analytical review of the literature. *Hospital Community Psychiat.* **33**:189.

Baekeland, F., and L. Lundwall (1975). Dropping out of treatment: A critical review. *Psychol. Bull.* **82**:738.

Baganz, P. C., A. E. Smith, R. Goldstein, and N. K. Pou (1971). The YMCA as a halfway facility. *Hospital Community Psychiat.* **22**:156.

Bahr, H. M. (ed.) (1973). *Skid Row: An Introduction to Disaffiliation.* New York: Oxford University Press.

Baker, A. A., M. Morison, J. A. Game, and J. G. Thorpe (1961). Admitting schizophrenic mothers with their babies. *Lancet* **2**:237.

Baker, F., J. Intagliata, and R. Kirshstein (1980). *Case Management Evaluation Phase One: Final Report.* Buffalo: Tefco Services.

Baldessarini, R. J., and D. Tarsey (1978). Tardive dyskinesia, in *Psychopharmacology: A Generation of Progress* (M. A. Lytton, A. DiMascio, and K. F. Killam, eds.). New York: Raven, p. 993.

Barrett, W. W., R. B. Ellsworth, L. D. Clark, and J. Enniss (1957). Study of the differential behavioral effects of reserpine, chlorpromazine and a combination of these drugs in chronic schizophrenia. *Dis. Nerv. Sys.* **18**:209.

Barrow, S. (1980). Project reachout, in *New York City Community Support System Monitoring and Evaluation Project*, Reports 4–6, Sept. 1980, Jan. 1981, June 1981.

Barrow, S., L. Gutwirth, and C. C. Schwartz (1979). Aftercare compliance of chronic patients. Paper presented at Annual Meeting of American Psychiatric Association, Chicago, May 1979.

Bass, R., and C. Windle (1973). A preliminary attempt to measure continuity of care in a community mental health center. *Community Mental Health J.* **9**:53.

Bassuk, E., and S. Gerson (1978). Deinstitutionalization and mental health services. *Sci. Am.* **238** (February):46.

Baxter, E. (1980). Geel, Belgium: A radical model for the intergration of deviancy, in *Proceedings in Overcoming Public Opposition to Community Care for the Mentally Ill* (R. C. Baron, I. D. Rutman, and B. Klaczynska, eds.). Philadelphia: Horizon House, p. 67.

Baxter, E., and K. Hopper (1981). *Private Lives/Public Spaces: Mentally Disabled Adults on the Streets of New York City*, Interim Report #2. New York: Community Services Society Institute for Social Welfare Research.

Beard, J. H. (1978). The rehabilitation services of Fountain House, in *Alternatives to Mental Hospital Treatment* (L. I. Stein and M. A. Test, eds.). New York: Plenum, p. 201.

Beatty, L. S., and M. Seeley (1980). Characteristics of operators of adult foster homes. *Hospital Community Psychiat.* **31**:771.

Beck, T. R. (1811). An inaugural dissertation on insanity.

Becker, A., and H. C. Schulberg (1976). Phasing out state hospitals: A psychiatric dilemma. *N. Engl. J. Med.* **294**:255.

Bellack, A. S., M. Hersen, and S. M. Turner (1976). Generalization effects of social skills training with chronic schizophrenics: An experimental approach. *Behavior Res. Ther.* **14**:391.

Bennett, C. L. (1966). The Dutchess County project, in *Evaluating the Effectiveness of Community Mental Health Services* (E. M. Gruenberg, ed.). New York: *Milbank Memorial Fund*, p. 79.

Bennett, D. (1978). The Camberwell District psychiatric services, 1964–1974: The provision of alternatives to mental hospital care, in *Alternatives to Mental Hospital Treatment* (L. I. Stein, and M. A. Test, eds.). New York: Plenum, p. 265.

Bennett, W. A. (1964). Students, patients share halfway house. *Rehab. Rec.* **5**:21.

Berkowitz, R., L. Kuipers, R. Eberlein-Fries, and J. Leff (1981). Lowering expressed emotion in relatives of schizophrenics, in *New Developments in Interventions with Families of Schizophrenics, New Directions for Mental Health Services* (M. J. Goldstein, ed.). San Francisco: Jossey-Bass, vol. 12, p. 27.

Birky, H. J., J. E. Chambliss, and R. Wasden (1971). A comparison of residents discharged from a token economy and two traditional psychiatry programs. *Behavior Ther.* **2**:46.

Black, B. J. (1970). *Principles of Industrial Therapy for the Mentally Ill*. New York: Grune and Stratton.

Blackwell, B. (1972). The drug defaulter. *Clin. Pharmacol. Therapeutics* **13**:841.

Blackwell, B. (1979). Treatment adherence: A contemporary overview. *Psychosomatics* **20**:27.

Bleuler, M. (1974). The offspring of schizophrenics. *Schizophrenia Bull.* **8**:93.

Blumenthal, R., D. Kreisman, and P. A. O'Connor (1982). Return to the family and its consequences for rehospitalization among recently discharged mental patients. *Psychological Med.* **12**:141.

Bockoven, J. L. (1963). *Moral Treatment in American Psychiatry*. New York: Springer.

Bolton (Arthur) Associates (1976). Report to the California State Legislature.

Borus, J. F. (1981). Deinstitutionalization of the chronically mentally ill. *N. Engl. J. Med.* **303**:339.

Bowen, W. T., and T. J. Fry (1971). Group living in the community for chronic patients. *Hospital Community Psychiat.* **22**:205.

Braun, P., G. Kochansky, R. Shapiro, S. Greenberg, J. E. Gudeman, S. Johnson, and M. F. Shore (1981). Overview: Deinstitutionalization of psychiatric patients, a critical review of outcome studies. *Am. J. Psychiat.* **138**:736.

Brill, H., and R. E. Patten (1959). Analysis of population reduction in New York State mental hospitals during the first four years of large-scale therapy with psychotropic drugs. *Am. J. Psychiat.* **116**:495.

Brooks, G. W. (1960). Rehabilitation of hospitalized chronic schizophrenic patients, in *Chronic Schizophrenia* (L. Appleby, J. M. Scher, and J. Cummings, eds.). Glencoe, Ill.: Free Press.

Brown, G. W. (1959). Experiences of discharged chronic schizophrenic mental hospital patients in various types of living groups. *Millbank Memorial Fund Quarterly* **37**:105.

Brown, G. W., J. L. T. Birley, and J. K. Wing (1972). Influence of family life on the course of schizophrenic disorders: A replication. *Br. J. Psychiat.* **121**:241.

Brown, G., M. Bone, B. Dalison, and J. Wing (1966). *Schizophrenia and Social Care*. London: Oxford University Press.

Brown, G., G. M. Carstairs, and G. Topping (1958). Post-hospital adjustment of chronic mental patients. *Lancet* **2**:685.

Brown, G. W., E. M. Monck, G. M. Carstairs, and J. K. Wing (1962). Influence of family life on the course of schizophrenic illness. *Br. J. Preventive Social Med.* **16**:55.

Budson, R. D. (1978). *The Psychiatric Halfway House*. Pittsburgh: University of Pittsburgh Press.

Budson, R. D. (1981). Challenging themes in community residential care systems, in *Issues in Community Residential Care, New Directions for Mental Health Services* (R. D. Budson, ed.). San Francisco: Jossey-Bass, vol. 11, p. 105.

Budson, R. D., M. C. Grob, and J. E. Singer (1978). A follow-up study of Berkeley House, a psychiatric halfway house, in *The Psychiatric Halfway House* (R. D. Budson, ed.). Pittsburgh: University of Pittsburgh Press, p. 191.

Buell, G. J., and W. A. Anthony (1976). The relationship between patient demographic characteristics and psychiatric rehabilitation outcome. *Community Mental Health J.* 11:208.

Caffey, E. M., C. R. Galbrecht, and C. J. Klett (1971). Brief hospitalization and aftercare in the treatment of schizophrenia. *Arch. Gen. Psychiat.* 24:81.

California State Dept. of Health (1973). Special Study on Community Care in Santa Clara County. Sacramento, Dec. 30.

Caplan, G. (1964). *Principles of Preventive Psychiatry.* New York: Basic Books.

Caplan, R. B. (1969). *Psychiatry and the Community in Nineteenth-Century America.* New York: Basic Books.

Carling, P. J. (1981). Nursing homes and chronic mental patients: A second opinion. *Schizophrenia Bull.* 7:574.

Caton, C. L. M. (1981). The new chronic patient and the system of community care. *Hospital Community Psychiat.* 32:475.

Caton, C. L. M. (1982). Effect of length of inpatient treatment for chronic schizophrenia. *Am. J. Psychiat.* 139:856.

Caton, C. L. M., and J. Goldstein (1983). Housing change of chronic mental patients: A consequence of the revolving door. New York: New York State Psychiatric Institute.

Caton, C. L. M., J. Goldstein, O. Serrano, and R. Bender (1983). Discharge planning for the chronic mental patient: Process and outcome. *Hospital Community Psychiatr.*, in press.

Caudill, W. (1958). *The Psychiatric Hospital as a Small Society.* Cambridge, Mass.: Harvard University Press.

Chafetz, L., and R. A. Terry (1981). Homelessness and transiency among the chronic mentally ill. Paper delivered at Annual Meeting of American Orthopsychiatric Association, New York, March 30.

Clark, M. L., H. R. Ramsey, R. E. Ragland, D. K. Rahal, E. A. Serafetinides, and J. D. Costeloe (1970). Chlorpromazine in chronic schizophrenia: Behavioral dose-response relationships. *Psychopharmacologia* 18:260.

Clausen, J., and M. R. Yarrow (eds.) (1955). The impact of mental illness on the family. *J. Social Issues* 11:4.

Crane, G. E. (1973). Persistent dyskinesia. *Br. J. Psychiat.* 122:395.

Criteria Committee, New York Heart Association (1964). *Diseases of the Heart and Blood Vessels: Nomenclature and Criteria for Diagnosis*, 6th ed. Boston: Little Brown.

Cumming, E., and J. Cumming (1957). *Closed Ranks: An Experiment in Mental Health Education*. Cambridge, Mass.: Harvard University Press.

Cumming, J. (1968). Screening of admissions. Memo 68-27. Albany: New York State Department of Mental Hygiene.

Cumming, J. H., and E. Cumming (1962). *Ego and Milieu: Theory and Practice of Environmental Therapy*. New York: Atherton.

Cupaiuolo, A. A. (1980). Zoning issues in the planning of community residences, in *Proceedings in Overcoming Public Opposition to Community Care for the Mentally Ill* (R. C. Baron, I. D. Rutman, and B. Klaczynska, eds.). Philadelphia: Horizon House, p. 355.

Daggett, S. R. (1971). The lodge program: A peer group treatment program for rehabilitation of the chronic mental patient. *Rehab. Rec.* 12:31.

Dain, N. (1976). From colonial America to bicentennial America: Two centuries of vicissitudes in the institutional care of mental patients. *Bull. N.Y. Acad. Med.* 52:1179.

Davis, J. M. (1975). Overview of maintenance therapy in psychiatry. I. Schizophrenia. *Am. J. Psychiat.* 132:1237.

Davis, A., S. Dinitz, and B. Pasamanick (1974). Schizophrenics in the new custodial community: Five years after the experiment. Columbus: Ohio State University Press.

Dear, M. (1977). Impact of mental health facilities on property values. *Community Mental Health J.* 13:150.

Dear, M., and S. M. Taylor (1979). Community attitudes toward neighborhood public facilities: A study of mental health services in metro Toronto. Hamilton, Ont.: Dept. of Geography, McMaster University.

Dept. HHS Steering Committee on the Chronically Mentally Ill (1980). *Toward a National Plan for the Chronically Mentally Ill*. Washington, D.C.: U.S. Dept. HHS, December.

Detre, T., D. R. Kessler, and J. Sayers (1961). A socio-adaptive approach to treatment of acutely disturbed psychiatric inpatients. *Proc. 3rd World Cong. Psychiat.* 1:501.

Deutsch, A. (1937). *The Mentally Ill in America: A History of Their Care and Treatment from Colonial Times*. New York: Columbia University Press.

Deutsch, A. (1948). *The Shame of the States*. New York: Harcourt Brace.

Diagnostic and Statistical Manual of Mental Disorders, 2nd ed. (1968). Washington, D.C.: American Psychiatric Association.

Diagnostic and Statistical Manual of Mental Disorders, 3rd ed. (1980). Washington, D.C.: American Psychiatric Association, p. 188.

Dorwart, R. A. (1980). Deinstitutionalization: Who is left behind? *Hospital Community Psychiat.* 31:336.

Doniger, J., N. D. Rothwell, and R. Cohen (1963). Case study of a halfway house. *Mental Hos.* 14:191.

Dunham, H. W., and S. K. Weinberg (1960). *The Culture of the State Mental Hospital.* Detroit: Wayne State University Press.

Dunham, M. L., and G. L. Pierce (1982). Beyond deinstitutionalization: A commitment law in evolution. *Hospital Community Psychiat.* 33:216.

Earle, P. (1887). *The Curability of Insanity: A Series of Studies.* Philadelphia: Lippincott.

Early, D. F. (1966). The industrial therapy organization (Bristol): A development of work in hospital. *Lancet* 2:754.

Edelson, M. D. (1976). Alternative living arrangements, in *Community Survival for Long-Term Patients* (H. R. Lamb, ed.). San Francisco: Jossey-Bass, vol. 11, p. 33.

Eichler, S. (1982). Why young psychiatrists choose not to work with chronic patients. *Hospital Community Psychiat.* 33:1023.

Ellsworth, R. B. (1964). The psychiatric aide as rehabilitation therapist. *Rehab. Counseling Bull.* 7:81.

Ellsworth, R. B., B. T. Mead, and W. H. Clayton (1958). The rehabilitation and disposition of chronically hospitalized schizophrenic patients. *Mental Hyg.* 42:343.

Ellsworth, R. B., and H. A. Stokes (1963). Staff attitudes and patient release. *Psychiatric Stud. Projects* 7:1.

Emerson, R. M., E. B. Rochford, and L. L. Shaw (1981). Economics and enterprise in board and care homes for the mentally ill, *Am. Behavioral Scientist*, 24:771.

Endicott, J., J. Cohen, J. Nee, J. L. Fleiss, and M. I. Herz (1979). Brief vs. standard hospitalization: For whom? *Arch. Gen. Psychiat.* 36:706.

Endicott, J., M. I. Herz, and M. Gibbon (1978). Brief versus standard hospitalization: The differential costs. *Am. J. Psychiat.* 135:707.

Endicott, J., and R. L. Spitzer (1978). A diagnostic interview: The schedule for affective disorders and schizophrenia. *Arch. Gen. Psychiat.* 35:837.

Fairweather, G. (1978). The development, evaluation, and diffusion of rehabilitative programs: A social change process, in *Alternatives to Mental Hospital Treatment* (L. I. Stein, and M. A. Test, eds.). New York: Plenum, p. 295.

Fairweather, G. W. (1980). The Fairweather lodge: A twenty-five year retrospective, in *New Directions for Mental Health Services*, (G. W. Fairweather, ed.). San Francisco: Jossey-Bass, vol. 7, p. 3.

Fairweather, G. W., D. H. Sanders, H. Maynard, and D. L. Cressler (1969). *Community Life for the Mentally Ill: An Alternative to Institutional Care*. New York: Aldine.

Fakhruddin, A. K. M., A. Manjooran, N. P. V. Nair, and A. Neufeldt (1972). A five-year outcome of discharged chronic psychiatric patients. *Can. Psychiatr. Assoc. J.* **17**:433.

Falloon, I. R. H., J. L. Boyd, C. W. McGill, J. Razani, H. B. Moss, and A. M. Gilderman (1982). Family management in the prevention of exacerbation of schizophrenia: A controlled study. *N. Engl. J. Med.* **306**:1437.

Falloon, I. R. H., J. L. Boyd, C. W. McGill, J. S. Strang, and H. B. Moss (1981). Family management training in the community care of schizophrenics, in *New Developments in Interventions with Families of Schizophrenics, New Directions for Mental Health Services* (M. J. Goldstein, ed.). San Francisco: Jossey-Bass, vol. 12, p. 61.

Falloon, I. R. H., P. Lindley, R. McDonald, and I. M. Marks (1977). Social skills training of outpatient groups: A controlled study of rehearsal and homework. *Br. J. Psychiat.* **131**:599.

Feighner, J. P., E. Robins, S. B. Guze, R. A. Woodruff, G. Winokur, and R. Munoz (1972). Diagnostic criteria for use in psychiatric research. *Arch. Gen. Psychiat.* **26**:57.

Field, G. D., and M. A. Test (1975). Group assertive training for severely disturbed patients. *J. Behavior Ther. Exp. Psychiat.* **6**:129.

Finch, B. E., and C. J. Wallace (1977). Successful interpersonal skills training with schizophrenic inpatients. *J. Consult. Clin. Psychol.* **45**:885.

Fox, R. R., and D. V. Potter (1973). Using inpatient staff for aftercare of severely disturbed chronic patients. *Hospital Community Psychiat.* **24**:482.

Fredericksen, L. W., J. O. Jenkins, D. W. Foy, and R. M. Eisler (1976). Social skills training to modify abusive verbal outbursts in adults. *J. App. Behavior Analysis* **9**:117.

Freeman, H. (1961). Attitudes toward mental illness among relatives of former patients. *Am. Sociological Rev.* **26**:59.

Freeman, H. E., and O. G. Simmons (1963). *The Mental Patient Comes Home*. New York: Wiley.

Freudenberger, H. J. (1974). Staff burn-out. *J. Social Issues* **30**:159.

Fullerton, D. T., J. J. Cayner, and T. McLaughlin-Reidel (1978). Results of a token economy. *Arch. Gen. Psychiat.* **35**:1451.

Galioni, E. G., F. H. Adams, and F. F. Tallman (1953). Intensive treatment of back-ward patients: A controlled pilot study. *Am. J. Psychiat.* **109**:576.

Gallant, D. M., M. P. Bishop, and R. Guerrero-Figueroa (1968). Molindone: A controlled evaluation in chronic schizophrenic patients. *Curr. Therapeutic Res.* **10**:441.

Garmezy, N. (1974). Children at risk: The search for antecedents of schizophrenia. *Schizophrenia Bull.* **8**:14.

Garmezy, N. (1980). The current status of research with children at risk for schizophrenia and other forms of psychopathology, in *Risk Factor Research in the Major Mental Disorders* (D. A. Regier and G. Allen, eds.). Rockville, Md.: U.S. Dept. HHS, NIMH, p. 23.

Garr, D. (1973). Mental health and the community: San Jose, a preliminary assessment. Unpublished paper, San Jose State University, San Jose, Calif.

General Accounting Office (1977). *Returning the Mentally Disabled to the Community: Government Needs To Do More.* Washington, D.C.: GAO.

Gericke, O. L. (1965). Practical use of operant conditioning procedures in a mental hospital. *Psychiatric Stud. Projects* **3**:1.

Gittleman-Klein, R., and D. F. Klein (1969). Premorbid asocial adjustment and prognosis in schizophrenia. *J. Psychiatric Res.* **7**:35.

Glasscote, R. M., E. Cuming, I. D. Rutman, J. N. Sussex, and S. M. Glassman (1971a). Rehabilitating the mentally ill in the community: A study of psychosocial rehabilitation centers. Washington, D.C.: Joint Information Services, APA and NAMH.

Glasscote, R. M., J. E. Gudeman, and J. R. Elpers (1971b). Halfway houses for the mentally ill: A study of programs and problems. Washington, D.C.: Joint Information Services, APA and NAMH.

Glick, I. D., and W. A. Hargreaves (1979). Hospitals in the 1980's: Service, training and research. *Hospital Community Psychiat.* **30**:125.

Glick, I. D., W. A. Hargreaves, J. Drues, J. A. Showstack, and J. J. Katzow (1977). Short vs. long hospitalization: VII. Two-year follow-up results for nonschizophrenics: A prospective controlled study. *Arch. Gen Psychiat.* **34**:314.

Glick, I. D., W. A. Hargreaves, M. Raskin, and S. J. Kutner (1975). Short versus long hospitalization: A prospective controlled study: II. Results for schizophrenic patients. *Am. J. Psychiat.* **132**:385.

Goffman, E. (1961). *Asylums.* Garden City, N.Y.: Doubleday.

Goldberg, S. C., N. R. Schooler, G. E. Hogarty, and M. Roper (1977). Prediction of relapse in schizophrenic outpatients treated with drugs and sociotherapy. *Arch. Gen. Psychiat.* **34**:171.

Goldman, H. H., A. A. Gattozzi, and C. A. Taube (1981). Defining and counting the chronically mentally ill. *Hospital Community Psychiat.* 32:21.

Goldman, H. H., D. Regier, and C. Taube (1980). The present and future role of the state mental hospital. Paper presented at Annual Meeting of American Psychiatric Association. San Francisco, May.

Goldmeier, J., F. V. Mannino, and M. F. Shore (eds.) (1978). *New Directions in Mental Health Care: Cooperative Apartments.* Adlephi, Md.: HEW Monograph ADM 78-685, NIMH.

Goldstein, J. B., and R. M. McFall (1975). Development and evaluation of an interpersonal skill training program for psychiatric patients. *J. Abnorm. Psychol.* 84:51.

Goldstein, A. P., R. P. Sprafkin, and N. J. Gershaw (1976). *Skill Training for Community Living: Applying Structured Learning Therapy.* New York: Pergamon.

Goldstein, J., and C. L. M. Caton (1983). Effect of the social environment on chronic mental patients. *Psychological Med.* 13:193.

Goldstein, M. J., and H. S. Kopeikin (1981). Short- and long-term effects of combining drug and family therapy, in *New Developments in Intervention with Families of Schizophrenics, New Directions for Mental Health Services.* San Francisco: Jossey-Bass, vol. 12, p. 5.

Goplerud, E. N. (1979). Unexpected consequences of deinstitutionalization of the mentally disabled elderly. *Am. J. Community Psychol.* 7:315.

Gordon, H. L., A. Low, K. E. Hohman, and C. Groth (1960). The problem of overweight in hospitalized psychotic patients. *Psychiat. Q.* 34:69.

Gottesman, I. I. (1978). Schizophrenia and genetics: Where are we? Are you sure? in *The Nature of Schizophrenia: New Approaches to Research and Treatment* (L. C. Wynne, R. L. Cromwell, and S. Mathysse, eds.). New York: Wiley, p. 59.

Grad, J., and P. Sainsbury (1963). Mental illness and the family. *Lancet* 1:544.

Green, H. J., R. W. Miskimins, and E. C. Keil (1968). Selection of psychiatric patients for vocational rehabilitation. *Rehab. Counseling Bull.* 11:297.

Greenblatt, M. (1978). The third revolution in psychiatry, in *Psychopharmacology: A Generation of Progress* (M. A. Lipton, A. DiMascio, and K. F. Killam, eds.). New York: Raven, p. 1179.

Greenblatt, M., and E. Glazier (1975). The phasing out of mental hospitals in the United States. *Am. J. Psychiat.* 132:1135.

Grinspoon, I., J. R. Ewalt, and R. I. Shader (1967). Long-term treatment of chronic schizophrenia: A preliminary report. *Int. J. Psychiat.* 4:116.

Grinspoon, L., J. R. Ewalt, and R. I. Shader (1968). Psychotherapy and pharmacotherapy in chronic schizophrenia. *Am. J. Psychiat.* **124**: 1645.

Grinspoon, L., J. R. Ewalt, and R. I. Shader (1972). *Schizophrenia: Pharmacotherapy and Psychotherapy.* Baltimore: Williams and Wilkins.

Grinspoon, L., and R. I. Shader (1975). Psychotherapy and drugs in schizophrenia, in *Drugs in Combination with Other Therapies* (M. Greenblatt, ed.). New York: Grune and Stratton, p. 49.

Grob, G. (1966). *The State and the Mentally Ill: A History of Worchester State Hospital in Massachusetts, 1830-1920.* Chapel Hill: University of North Carolina Press.

Grob, G. N. (1973). *Mental Institutions in America: Social Policy to 1875.* New York: Free Press.

Group for the Advancement of Psychiatry (1978). *The Chronic Mental Patient in the Community.* New York: GAP.

Gruenbaum, H., J. L. Weiss, B. J. Cohler, C. R. Hartman, and D. H. Gallant (1975). *Mentally Ill Mothers and Their Children.* Chicago: University of Chicago Press.

Gruenberg, E. M. (1967). The social breakdown syndrome: Some origins. *Am. J. Psychiat.* **123**:12.

Gruenberg, E. M. (1982). Social breakdown in young adults: Keeping crisis from becoming chronic, in *The Young Adult Chronic Patient, New Directions for Mental Health Services* (B. Pepper and H. Ryglewicz, eds.). San Francisco: Jossey-Bass, vol. 14, p. 43.

Gudeman, J. E., M. F. Shore, and B. Dickey (1983). Day hospitalization and an inn instead of inpatient care for psychiatric patients. *N. Engl. J. Med.* **308**:749.

Gumruku, P. (1968). The efficacy of a psychiatric halfway house: A three-year study of a therapeutic residence. *Sociological Q.* **9**:374.

Gunderson, J., and L. Mosher (1975). The cost of schizophrenia. *Am. J. Psychiat.* **132**:901.

Guy, W., M. Gross, G. E. Hogarty, and H. Dennis (1969). A controlled evaluation of day hospital effectiveness. *Arch. Gen. Psychiat.* **20**:329.

Hall, J. C., K. Smith, and A. Shimkunas (1966). Employment problems of schizophrenic patients. *Am. J. Psychiat.* **123**:536.

Hamilton, S. W. (1944). The history of American mental hospitals, in *One Hundred Years of American Psychiatry* (J. K. Hall et al., eds.). New York: Columbia University Press, p. 73.

Hargreaves, W. A., I. D. Glick, J. Drues, J. A. Showstack, and E. Feigenbaum (1977). Short vs. long hospitalization: A prospective controlled study: VI. Two-year follow-up results for schizophrenics. *Arch. Gen. Psychiat.* **34**:305.

Hatfield, A. B. (1979). The family as partner in the treatment of mental illness. *Hospital Community Psychiatr.* **36**:338.

Haynes, R. B. (1979). Determinants of compliance: The disease and the mechanisms of treatment, in *Compliance in Health Care* (R. Haynes, D. W. Taylor, and D. Sackett, eds.). Baltimore: Johns Hopkins University Press, p. 49.

Hazelton, N., D. Mandell, and S. Stern (1975). *A Survey and Education Plan Around the Issue of Community Care for the Mentally Ill: The Santa Clara County Experience.* Sacramento: California State Dept. of Health, July.

Heap, R. F., W. E. Boblitt, C. H. Moore, and J. E. Hord (1970). Behavior-milieu therapy with chronic neuropsychiatric patients. *J. Abnorm. Psychol.* **76**:349.

Henry, G. W. (1941). Mental hospitals, in *A History of Medical Psychology* (G. Zilboorg, ed.). New York: Norton, p. 558.

Hersen, M., and A. S. Bellack (1976). Social skills training for chronic psychiatric patients: Rationale, research findings, and future directions. *Comp. Psychiat.* **17**:559.

Hersen, M., R. M. Eisler, B. S. Smith, and W. S. Agras (1972). A token reinforcement ward for young psychiatric patients. *Am. J. Psychiat.* **129**:228.

Herz, M. I., J. Endicott, and M. Gibbon (1979). Brief hospitalization: Two-year follow-up. *Arch. Gen. Psychiat.* **36**:701.

Herz, M., J. Endicott, and R. L. Spitzer (1971). Day versus inpatient hospitalization: A controlled study. *Am. J. Psychiat.* **127**:1371.

Herz, M. I., J. Endicott, and R. L. Spitzer (1977). Brief hospitalization: A two-year follow-up. *Am. J. Psychiat.* **134**:502.

Hirsch, S. R., and J. P. Leff (1975). *Abnormalities in Parents of Schizophrenics. Institute of Psychiatry, Maudsley Monograph No. 22.* London: Oxford University Press.

Hoenig, J., and M. Hamilton (1969). *The Desegregation of the Mentally Ill.* London: Routledge and Kegan Paul.

Hofmeister, J. F., A. F. Scheckenbach, and S. H. Clayton (1979). A behavioral program for the treatment of chronic patients. *Am. J. Psychiat.* **136**:394.

Hogarty, G. (1968). Hospital differences in the release of discharge-ready chronic schizophrenics. *Arch. Gen. Psychiat.* **18**:362.

Hogarty, G. (1972). Discharge readiness inventory. *Arch. Gen. Psychiat.* **26**:419.

Hogarty, G. E., and S. C. Goldberg (1973). Drugs and sociotherapy in the aftercare of schizophrenic patients: One-year relapse rates. *Arch. Gen. Psychiat.* **28**:54.

Hogarty, G. E., S. C. Goldberg, and N. R. Schooler (1974a). Drugs and sociotherapy in the aftercare of schizophrenic patients: III. Adjustment of nonrelapsed patients. *Arch. Gen. Psychiat.* 31:609.

Hogarty, G. E., S. C. Goldberg, N. R. Schooler, and R. P. Ulrich (1974b). Drugs and sociotherapy in the aftercare of schizophrenic patients: II. Two-year relapse rates. *Arch. Gen. Psychiat.* 31:603.

Hogarty, G. E., and R. P. Ulrich (1977). Temporal effects of drug and placebo in delaying relapse in schizophrenic outpatients. *Arch. Gen. Psychiat.* 34:297.

Hollingshead, A. B., and F. C. Redlich (1958). *Social Class and Mental Illness.* New York: Wiley.

Hollingsworth, R., and J. P. Fareyt (1975). Community adjustment of released token-economy patients. *J. Behavior Ther. Exp. Psychiat.* 6:271.

Honigfeld, G., and R. Gillis (1967). The role of institutionalization in the natural history of schizophrenia. *Dis. Nerv. Sys.* 28:660.

Hopper, K., E. Baxeter, and S. Cox (1982). Not making it crazy: The young homeless patients in New York City, in *The Young Adult Chronic Patient, New Directions for Mental Health Services* (B. Pepper and H. Ryglewicz, eds.). San Francisco: Jossey-Bass, vol. 14, p. 33.

Hume, K., and W. A. Anthony (1975). *Rehabilitation Outcome,* unpublished manuscript. Boston University.

Isaacs, D. M., and H. T. G. LaFave (1964). An evaluation-incentive system for chronic psychotics. *Psychiatric Q.* 38:33.

Jasnau, K. F. (1967). Individualized vs. mass transfer of nonpsychotic geriatric patients from mental hospitals to nursing homes with special reference to the death rate. *J. Am. Geriat. Soc.* 15:280.

Jeste, D. V., S. G. Potkin, S. Sinha, S. Feder, and R. J. Wyatt (1979). Tardive dyskinesia: Reversible and persistent. *Arch. Gen. Psychiat.* 36:585.

Jones, M. S. (1953). *The Therapeutic Community: A New Treatment Method in Psychiatry.* New York: Basic.

Kantor, D., and M. Greenblatt (1962). Wellmet: Halfway to community rehabilitation. *Mental Hos.* 13:146.

Karon, B. P., and G. R. Vandenbos (1972). The consequences of psychotherapy for schizophrenic patients. *Psychotherapy: Theory Res. Prac.* 9:111.

Keskiner, A., and M. Zaleman (1974). Returning to community life: The foster community model. *Dis. Nerv. Sys.* 35:419.

Kirk, S. A., and M. E. Therrien (1975). Community mental health myths and the fate of former hospitalized patients. *Psychiatry* 38:209.

Klein, D. F. (1982). Psychopharmacology: Special considerations, in *The Young Adult Chronic Patient, New Directions for Mental Health Services* (B. Pepper and H. Ryglewicz, eds.). San Francisco: Jossey-Bass, vol. 14, p. 51.

Klein, D. F., and J. M. Davis (1969). *Diagnosis and Drug Treatment of Psychiatric Disorders.* Baltimore: Williams and Wilkins.

Klerman, G. L. (1977). Better but not well: Social and ethical issues in the deinstitutionalization of the mentally ill. *Schizophrenia Bull.* 3:617.

Kramer, M. (1975). Population Changes and Schizophrenia, 1970–1985. Paper presented at the 2nd Rochester International Conference on Schizophrenia, Rochester, N.Y., May.

Kramer, M. (1977). *Psychiatric Services and the Changing Institutional Scene 1950–1985.* Rockville, Md.: DHEW, NIMH.

Krasner, L., and L. P. Ulmann (eds.) (1965). *Research in Behavior Modification.* New York: Holt Rinehart and Winston.

Kreisman, D. E., and V. D. Joy (1974). Family response to the mental illness of a relative: A review of the literature. *Schizophrenia Bull.* 10:34.

Kreisman, D. E., S. J. Simmens, and V. D. Joy (1979). Rejecting the patient: Preliminary validation of a self-report scale. *Schizophrenia Bull.* 5:220.

Kresky, M., E. M. Maeda, and N. D. Rothwell (1976). The apartment living program: A community living option for halfway house residents. *Hospital Community Psychiat.* 27:153.

Kringlen, E. (1978). Adult offspring of two psychotic parents, with special reference to schizophrenia, in *The Nature of Schizophrenia: New Approaches to Research and Treatment* (L. C. Wynne, R. L. Cromwell, and S. Mathysse, eds.). New York: Wiley, p. 9.

Kris, E. B. (1961). Prevention of rehospitalization through relapse control in a day hospital, in *Mental Patients in Transition* (M. Greenblatt, ed.). Springfield, Ill.: Charles C Thomas, p. 155.

Kuldau, J. M., and S. J. Dirks (1977). Controlled evaluation of a hospital-originated community transitional system. *Arch. Gen. Psychiat.* 34:1331.

Labreche, G., R. J. Turner, and L. J. Zabo (1969). Social class and participation in outpatient care of schizophrenics. *Community Mental Health J.* 5:394.

Lamb, H. R. (1976). *Community Survival for Long-term Patients.* San Francisco: Jossey-Bass.

Lamb, H. R. (1979a). Staff burnout in work with long-term patients. *Hospital Community Psychiat.* 30:396.

Lamb, H. R. (1979b). The new asylums in the community. *Arch. Gen. Psychiat.* 36:129.

Lamb, H. R. (1980a). Board-and-care home wanderers. *Arch. Gen. Psychiat.* 37:135.

Lamb, H. R. (1980b). Therapist-case managers: More than brokers of services. *Hospital Community Psychiat.* 31:762.

Lamb, H. R. (1981a). Maximizing the potential of board-and-care homes, in *Issues in Community Residential Care, New Directions for Mental Health Services* (R. D. Budson, ed.). San Francisco: Jossey-Bass, vol. 11, p. 19.

Lamb, H. R. (1981b). What did we really expect from deinstitutionalization? *Hospital Community Psychiat.* 12:105.

Lamb, H. R., and V. Goertzel (1971). Discharged mental patients: Are they really in the community? *Arch. Gen. Psychiat.* 24:29.

Lamb, H. R., and V. Goertzel (1972). High expectations of long-term ex-state hospital patients. *Am. J. Psychiat.* 129:471.

Lamb, H. R., and V. Goertzel (1977). The long-term patient in the era of community treatment. *Arch. Gen. Psychiat.* 34:679.

Lamb, H. R., and R. W. Grant (1982). The mentally ill in an urban county jail. *Arch. Gen. Psychiat.* 39:17.

Landy, D., and M. Greenblatt (1965). *Halfway House: A Socio-Cultural and Clinical Study of Rutland Corner House, a Transitional After-care Residence for Former Psychiatric Patients.* Washington, D.C.: Dept. HEW, Vocational Rehabilitation Administration.

Langsley, D. G., and C. B. Robinowitz (1979). Psychiatric manpower: An overview. *Hospital Community Psychiat.* 30:749.

Laska, E., E. Varga, J. Wanderling, G. Simpson, G. W. Logemann, and B. K. Shah (1973). Patterns of psychotropic drug use for schizophrenia. *Dis. Nerv. Sys.* 34:294.

Leff, J., L. Kuipers, R. Berkowitz, R. Eberlein-Vries, and D. Sturgeon (1982). A controlled trial of social intervention in the families of schizophrenic patients. *Br. J. Psychiat.* 141:121.

Letemendia, F. J., A. D. Harris, and J. A. Willems (1967). Effects on chronic patients of administrative changes. *Br. J. Psychiat.* 113:959.

Levy, P. R. (1980). Coexistence implies reciprocity, in *The Community Imperative: Proceedings in Overcoming Public Opposition to Community Care for the Mentally Ill* (R. C. Baron, I. D. Rutman, and B. Klaczynska, eds.). Philadelphia: Horizon House, p. 323.

Liberman, R. P., L. W. King, W. J. DeRisi, and M. McCann (1975). *Personal Effectiveness.* Champaign, Ill.: Research Press.

Liberman, R. P., F. Lillie, I. R. H. Falloon, C. E. Vaughn, E. Harpin, J. Leff, W. Hutchinson, P. Ryan, and M. Stoute (1978). Social skills training for schizophrenic patients and their families. Unpublished manuscript, Clinical Research Center, Camarillo, Calif.

Libet, J. M., and P. M. Lewinsohn (1973). The concept of social skills with special reference to the behavior of depressed persons. *J. Consult. Clin. Psychol.* **40**:304.

Lidz, T. (1978). Egocentric cognitive regression and the family setting of schizophrenic disorders, in *The Nature of Schizophrenia: New Approaches to Research and Treatment* (L. C. Wynne, R. L. Cromwell, and S. Mathysse, eds.). New York: Wiley, p. 526.

Lidz, T., A. Cornelison, D. Terry, and S. Fleck (1958). Intrafamilial environment of the schizophrenic patient: III. The transmission of irrationality. *Arch. Neurol. Psychiat.* **79**:305.

Lidz, T., S. Fleck, and A. Cornelison (1965). *Schizophrenia and the Family*. New York: International Universities Press.

Lindemann, E. (1944). Symptomatology and management of acute grief. *Am. J. Psychiat.* **101**:141.

Linn, M. W. (1981). Can foster care survive? in *Issues in Community Residential Care, New Directions in Mental Health Services* (R. D. Budson, ed.). San Francisco: Jossey-Bass, vol. 11, p. 35.

Linn, M. W., E. M. Caffey, C. J. Klett, and G. Hogarty (1977). Hospital vs. community (foster) care for psychiatric patients. *Arch. Gen. Psychiat.* **34**:78.

Linn, M. W., E. M. Caffey, J. Klett, and G. E. Hogarty (1979). Day treatment and psychotropic drugs in the aftercare of schizophrenic patients. *Arch. Gen. Psychiat.* **36**:1055.

Linn, M. W., J. Klett, and E. M. Caffey (1980). Foster home characteristics and psychiatric patient outcome. *Arch. Gen. Psychiat.* **37**:129.

Lloyd, K. E., and L. Abel (1970). Performance on a token economy psychiatric ward: A two-year summary. *Behavior Res. Ther.* **8**:1.

Lorei, T. W. (1967). Prediction of community stay and employment for released psychiatric patients. *J. Consult. Psychol.* **31**:349.

Lorei, T. W., and L. Gurel (1973). Demographic characteristics as predictors of post-hospital employment and readmission. *J. Consult. Clin. Psychol.* **40**:426.

Lourie, H. V. (1978). Case management, in *The Chronic Mental Patient* (J. A. Talbott, ed.). Washington, D.C.: APA.

Ludwig, A. M. (1971). *Treating the Treatment Failures: The Challenge of Chronic Schizophrenia*. New York: Grune and Stratton.

Main, T. F. (1957). The ailment. *Br. J. Med. Psychol.* **30**:129.

Markson, E., and J. H. Cumming (1975). The post-transfer fate of relocated mental patients in New York. *Gerontologist* **15**:104.

Martin, M. A. (1950). A practical treatment program for a mental hospital "back" ward. *Am. J. Psychiat.* **10**:758.

Maslach, C. (1976). Burned out. *Hum. Behavior* **3**:16.

Matson, J. L., and R. M. Stephens (1978). Increasing appropriate behavior of explosive chronic psychiatric patients with a social-skills training package. *Behavior Modif.* **2**:61.

Maxmen, J. S., and G. J. Tucker (1973). The admission process. *J. Nerv. Mental Dis.* **156**:327.

Maxmen, J. S., G. J. Tucker, and L. E. Bow (1974). *Rational Hospital Psychiatry: The Reactive Environment.* New York: Brunner/Mazel.

May, P. R. A. (1968). *Treatment of Schizophrenia.* New York: Science House.

May, P. R. A. (1974). Psychotherapy research in schizophrenics: Another view of present reality. *Schizophrenia Bull.* **9**:126.

May, P. R. A. (1975). Adopting new models for continuity of care: What are the needs? *Hospital Community Psychiat.* **26**:599.

May, P. R. A. (1976). When, what, and why? Psychopharmacology and other treatments in schizophrenia. *Comp. Psychiat.* **17**:688.

May, P. R. A., A. H. Tuma, and W. J. Dixon (1976). Schizophrenia: A follow-up study of results of treatment. I. Design and other problems. *Arch. Gen. Psychiat.* **33**:474.

May, P. R. A., and T. Van Putten (1974). Treatment of schizophrenia. II. A proposed rating scale of design and outcome for use in literature surveys. *Comp. Psychiat.* **15**:267.

McClellan, T. A., and G. Cowan (1970). Use of antipsychotic and antidepressant drugs by chronically ill patients. *Am. J. Psychiat.* **126**: 1771.

McGreadie, R. B., and I. M. MacDonald (1977). High-dosage haloperidol in chronic schizophrenia. *Br. J. Psychiat.* **131**:310.

McReynolds, W. T., and J. Coleman (1972). Token economy: Patient and staff changes. *Behavior Res. Ther.* **10**:29.

Mechanic, D. (1978). Alternatives to mental hospital treatment: A sociological perspective, in *Alternatives to Mental Hospital Treatment* (L. I. Stein and M. A. Test, eds.). New York: Plenum, p. 309.

Mednick, S. A., A. Schulsinger, and F. Schulsinger (1975). Schizophrenia in children of schizophrenic mothers, in *Childhood Personality and Psychopathology: Current Topics* (A. Donis, ed.). New York: Wiley, p. 221.

Meenach, L. (1964). The stepping stone: A report of residential rehabilitation houses for the mentally ill. Frankfort, Ky.: VRA Grant RD 366-60, State Dept. of Education, Bureau of Rehabilitation Services.

Meltzoff, J., and R. Blumenthal (1966). *The Day Treatment Center: Principles, Application, and Evaluation.* Springfield, Ill.: Charles C Thomas.

Mesnikoff, A. (1982). Street people on the upper West Side, in *The Homeless and Single Room Occupants: Three Studies Illuminating the*

Situation in New York City. New York: Community Council of Greater New York, p. 10.

Michaux, M. H., M. R. Chelst, S. A. Foster, R. J. Pruim, and E. M. Dasinger (1973). Post-release adjustment of day and full-time psychiatric patients. *Arch. Gen. Psychiat.* **29**:647.

Miller, D. H. (1954). The rehabilitation of chronic open-ward neuropsychiatric patients. *Psychiatry* **17**:347.

Miller, D. H., and J. Clancy (1952). An approach to the social rehabilitation of chronic psychotic patients. *Psychiatry* **15**:435.

Milosak, A., and M. Basic (1981). Prolonged hospital treatment of patients in families other than their own. *Int. J. Social Psychiat.* **27**:129.

Minkoff, K. (1978). A map of chronic mental patients, in *The Chronic Mental Patient* (J. A. Talbott, ed.). Washington, D.C.: APA.

Minuchin, S. (1974). Structural family therapy, in *American Handbook of Psychiatry* (S. Arieti, ed.). New York: Basic Books, vol. 2, p. 178.

Morrissey, J. R., H. H. Goldman, and L. V. Klerman (1980). *The Enduring Asylum: Cycles of Institutional Reform at Worcester State Hospital.* New York: Grune and Stratton.

Mosher, L. B., and S. J. Keith (1979). Research on the psychosocial treatment of schizophrenia: A summary report. *Am. J. Psychiat.* **136**:623.

Mosher, L. B., and S. J. Keith (1980). Psychosocial treatment: Individual, group, family and community support approaches. *Schizophrenia Bull.* **6**:10.

Mosher, L. B., A. Z. Menn, and S. M. Matthews (1975). Soteria: Evaluation of home-based treatment for schizophrenia. *Am. J. Orthopsychiat.* **45**:455.

Muller, C., and C. L. M. Caton (1983). Economic costs of schizophrenia: A post-discharge study. *Medical Care* **21**:92.

Muller, J. B. (1981). Alabama Community Support Project evaluation of the implementation and initial outcomes of a model case manager system. *Community Support Service J.* **6**:1.

Murphy, H. B. M., F. Englesmann, and F. Tcheng-Laroche (1976). The influences of foster home care on psychiatric patients. *Arch. Gen. Psychiat.* **33**:179.

Myers, J. K., and L. C. Bean (1968). A decade later: A follow-up of social class and mental illness. New York: Wiley.

Myers, J. K., and B. H. Roberts (1959). *Family and Class Dynamics in Mental Illness.* New York: Wiley.

Myers, K., and D. H. Clark (1972). Results in a therapeutic community. *Br. J. Psychiat.* **120**:51.

New York City Asylum for the Insane Annual Report (1875). Wards Island, N.Y.

New York State Department of Social Services (1980). *Survey of the Needs and Problems of Single-Room-Occupancy Hotel Residents in the Upper West Side of Manhattan*. New York: N.Y. State Dept. SS, May.

New York State Welfare Research (1979). *Survey of the Needs and Problems of Adult Home Residents in New York State*. Albany: NYS Welfare Research Institute.

New York Times (1974). Where can mental patients go? *The Week in Review*, Feb. 24.

New York Times (1981). Mayor defends city's handling of its homeless. Nov. 20, p. B1.

Nielsen, A. C., J. A. Talbott, L. I. Stein, H. R. Lamb, D. N. Osser, and W. M. Glazer (1981). Encouraging psychiatrists to work with chronic patients: Opportunities and limitations of residency education. *Hospital Community Psychiat.* **32**:767.

O'Brian, J. (1979). Teaching psychiatric inpatients about their medications. *Psychiatric Nursing* **17** (October):30.

Olshansky, S., S. Grob, and M. Ekdahl (1960). Survey of employment experiences of patients discharged from three state mental hospitals during period 1951–1953. *Mental Hyg.* **44**:510.

Ozarin, L. D., and M. J. Witkin (1975). Halfway houses for the mentally ill and alcoholics: A 1973 survey. *Hospital Community Psychiat.* **26**:101.

Pardes, H., P. Sirovatka, and J. W. Jenkins (1979). Psychiatry in public service: Challenge of the eighties. *Hospital Community Psychiat.* **30**:756.

Pasamanick, B., F. R. Scarpitti, and S. Dinitz (1967). *Schizophrenics in the Community: An Experimental Study in the Prevention of Hospitalization*. New York: Appleton-Century-Crofts.

Paul, G. L., and R. J. Lentz (1977). Psychosocial treatment of chronic mental patients: Milieu versus social learning programs. Cambridge, Mass.: Harvard University Press.

Pavenstedt, E., and V. W. Bernard (eds.) (1971). *Crisis of Family Disorganization: Programs to Soften Their Impact on Children*. New York: Behavioral Publications.

Paykel, E. S., M. M. Weissman, and B. A. Prusoff (1978). Social maladjustment and severity of depression. *Comp. Psychiat.* **19**:121.

Pepper, B., M. C. Kirshner, and H. Ryglewicz (1981). The young adult chronic patient: Overview of a population. *Hospital Community Psychiat.* **32**:463.

Pepper, B., H. Ryglewicz, and M. C. Kirshner (1982). The uninstitu-
tionalized generation: A new breed of psychiatric patient, in *The
Young Adult Chronic Patient, New Directions for Mental Health
Services* (B. Pepper and H. Ryglewicz, eds.). San Francisco: Jossey-
Bass, vol. 14, p. 3.

Pierloot, R. A., and M. Demarsin (1981). Family care versus hospital stay
for chronic psychiatric patients. *Int. J. Social Psychiat.* **27**:217.

Pines, A., and C. Maslach (1978). Characteristics of staff burnout in mental
health settings. *Hospital Community Psychiat.* **29**:233.

Pinsker, H. (1966). Fallacies in hospital community therapy, in *Current
Psychiatric Therapies* (J. Masserman, ed.). New York: Grune and
Stratton, vol. 6, p. 344.

Pollock, H. M. (1936). *Family Care of Mental Patients.* Utica, N.Y.:
Utica State Hospital.

Prevost, J., and A. Arnold (1978). *Five-Year Plan for Community Placement and Support.* Albany: State of New York Office of Mental
Health.

Quitkin, F., A. Rifkin, and D. F. Klein (1975). Very high dosage vs.
standard dosage fluphenazine in schizophrenia. *Arch. Gen. Psychiat.*
32:1276.

Rabkin, J. (1972). Opinions about mental illness: A review of the
literature. *Psychol. Bull.* **77**:153.

Rabkin, J. G., G. Muhlin, and P. W. Cohen (1983). *What the Neighbors
Think: Community Attitudes Toward Local Psychiatric Facilities.*
New York: New York State Psychiatric Institute.

Rachlin, S., A. Pam, and J. Milton (1975). Civil liberties versus involuntary hospitalization. *Am. J. Psychiat.* **132**:189.

Raush, H. L., and C. L. Raush (1968). *The Halfway House Movement:
A Search for Sanity.* New York: Appleton-Century-Crofts.

Rashkis, H. A., and E. R. Smarr (1957). Drug and milieu effects with
chronic schizophrenics. *Arch. Neurol. Psychiat.* **78**:89.

Redick, R. W. (1974). *Patterns in Use of Nursing Homes by the Aged
Mentally Ill.* Washington, D.C.: NIMH, Statistical Note 107, June.

Reik, L. E. (1953). The halfway house: The role of laymen's organizations
in the rehabilitation of the mentally ill. *Mental Hyg.* **37**:615.

Reilly, E., W. Wilson, and H. McClinton (1967). Clinical characteristics
and medication history of schizophrenics readmitted to the hospital.
Int. J. Neuropsychiat. **3**:85.

Renton, G. A. (1968). A follow-up of schizophrenic patients in Edinburgh.
Acta Psychiat. Scand. **39**:548.

*Report to the President from the President's Commission on Mental
Health* (1978). Washington, D.C.: vol. 1.

Rice, E. P., M. C. Ekdahl, and L. Miller (1971). *Children of Mentally Ill Parents: Problems in Child Care.* New York: Behavioral Publications.

Richards, A. D. (1964). Attitudes and Drug Acceptance. *Br. J. Psychiat.* **110**:46.

Richmond, C. (1969). Expanding the concepts of the halfway house: A satellite housing program. *Int. J. Social Psychiat.* **16**:96.

Rifkin, A., F. Quitkin, and D. F. Klein (1975). Akinesia, a poorly recognized drug-induced extrapyramidal behavioral disorder. *Arch. Gen. Psychiat.* **32**:672.

Rodnick, E. H., and M. J. Goldstein (1974). Premorbid adjustment and recovery of mothering function in acute schizophrenic women. *J. Abnorm. Psychol.* **83**:623.

Rodnick, E. H., M. J. Goldstein, J. M. Lewis, and J. A. Deane (1983). Parental communication style, affect, and role as precursors of offspring schizophrenia spectrum disorders, in *Children at Risk: A Longitudinal Perspective* (N. F. Watt, E. J. Anthony, L. C. Wynne, and J. Rolf, eds.), in preparation.

Rog, D. J., and H. L. Raush (1975). The psychiatric halfway house: How is it measuring up? *Community Mental Health J.* **11**:155.

Rogers, C. R., E. G. Gendin, D. J. Kiesler, and C. B. Truax (1967). *The Therapeutic Relationship and Its Impact.* Madison: University of Wisconsin Press.

Rose, C. L. (1959). Relatives' attitudes and mental hospitalization. *Mental Hyg.* **43**:194.

Rosen, B., A. Katzoff, C. Carrillo, and D. F. Klein (1976). Clinical effectiveness of "short" vs. "long" psychiatric hospitalization. *Arch. Gen. Psychiat.* **33**:1316.

Rosenhann, D. L. (1973). On being sane in insane places. *Science* **179**:250.

Rossi, P. H. (1978). Issues in the evaluation of human services delivery. *Evaluation Q.* **2**:573.

Rothman, D. J. (1971). *The Discovery of the Asylum.* Boston: Little Brown.

Rothman, T. (1970). Comparing therapeutic results of community care in early schizophrenics, in *Changing Patterns in Psychiatric Care* (T. Rothman, ed.). Los Angeles: Rush Research Foundation.

Rothwell, N. D., and J. M. Doniger (1966). *The Psychiatric Halfway House: A Case Study.* Springfield, Ill.: Charles C Thomas.

Rush, B. (1962). *Medical Inquiries and Observations upon the Diseases of the Mind.* New York: Hafner (orig. published Philadelphia: Kimber Richardson, 1812).

Rutter, M. (1966). *Children of Sick Parents: An Environmental and Psychiatric Study.* London: Oxford University Press.

Rybolt, G. A. (1975). Token reinforcement therapy with chronic psychiatric patients: A three-year evaluation. *J. Behavior Ther. Exp. Psychiat.* 6:188.

Sampson, H., S. Messinger, and R. Towne (1962). Family processes and becoming a mental patient. *Am. J. Sociol.* 68:88.

Sanders, R., R. S. Smith, and B. S. Weinman (1967). *Chronic Psychosis and Recovery.* San Francisco: Jossey-Bass.

Sandhall, H., T. T. Hawley, and G. C. Gordon (1975). The St. Louis community homes program: Graduated support for long-term care. *Am. J. Psychiat.* 132:617.

Schaefer, H. H., and P. L. Martin (1966). Behavioral therapy for "apathy" of hospitalized schizophrenics. *Psychological Reports* 19:1147.

Scherl, D. J., and L. B. Macht (1979). Deinstitutionalization in the absence of consensus. *Hospital Community Psychiat.* 30:599.

Schulberg, H. C., and E. Bromet (1981). Strategies for evaluating the outcome of community services for the chronically mentally ill. *Am. J. Psychiat.* 138:930.

Schwartz, C. C., J. K. Myers, and B. M. Astrachan (1974). Psychiatric labeling and the rehabilitation of the mental patient. *Arch. Gen. Psychiat.* 31:329.

Schwartz, C. C., J. K. Myers, and B. M. Astrachan (1975). Concordance of multiple assessments of the outcome of schizophrenia: On defining the dependent variable in outcome studies. *Arch. Gen. Psychiat.* 32:1221.

Schwartz, S. R., and S. M. Goldfinger (1981). The new chronic patient: Clinical characteristics of an emerging subgroup. *Hospital Community Psychiat.* 32:470.

Segal, S. P., and U. Aviram (1978). *The Mentally Ill in Community-based Sheltered Care: A Study of Community Care and Social Integration.* New York: Wiley.

Segal, S. P., and J. Baumohl (1980). Engaging the disengaged: Proposals on madness and vagrancy. *Social Work* 25:358.

Segal, S. P., J. Baumohl, and E. Johnson (1977). Falling through the cracks: Mental disorder and social margin in a young vagrant population. *Social Problems* 24:387.

Serban, G., and C. Gidynski (1974). Schizophrenic patients in community: Legal misinterpretations of "right to treatment." *N.Y. State J. Med.* 74:1977.

Serban, G., and A. Thomas (1974). Attitudes and behaviors of acute and chronic schizophrenic patients regarding ambulatory treatment. *Am. J. Psychiat.* 131:991.

Shadish, W. R. Jr., and R. R. Bootzin (1981). Nursing homes and chronic mental patients. *Schizophrenia Bull.* 7:488.

Shean, G. D., and Z. Zeidberg (1971). Token reinforcement therapy: A comparison of matched groups. *J. Behavior Ther. Exp. Psychiat.* 2:95.

Sheehan, S. (1981). The patient: I. Creedmoor Psychiatric Center. II. Disappearing incidents. III. Is there no place on earth for me? IV. The air is too still. *The New Yorker,* May 25, June 1, June 8, June 15.

Sheets, J. L., J. A. Prevost, and J. Reilman (1982). The young adult chronic patient: Three hypothesized subgroups, in *The Young Adult Chronic Patient, New Directions for Mental Health Services* (B. Pepper and H. Ryglewicz, eds.). San Francisco: Jossey-Bass, vol. 14, p. 15.

Sheffer, E. (1980). The siting of residential facilities: The Upper West Side's point of view, in *Proceedings in Overcoming Public Opposition to Community Care for the Mentally Ill* (R. C. Baron, I. D. Rutman, and B. Klaczynska, eds.). Philadelphia: Horizon House.

Shenoy, R., B. W. Shires, and M. S. White (1981). Using a schiz-anon group in the treatment of chronic ambulatory schizophrenia. *Hospital Community Psychiat.* 32:421.

Singer, M. T., L. C. Wynne, and M. L. Toohey (1978). Communication disorders and the families of schizophrenics, in *The Nature of Schizophrenia: New Approaches to Research and Treatment* (L. C. Wynne, R. L. Cromwell, and S. Mathysse, eds.). New York: Wiley, p. 499.

Singh, M. M., L. V. De Dios, and N. S. Kline (1970). Weight as a correlate of clinical response to psychotropic drugs. *Psychosomatics* 11:562.

Small, J. G., J. J. Kellams, V. Milstein, and J. Moore (1975). A placebo-controlled study of lithium combined with neuroleptics in chronic schizophrenic patients. *Am. J. Psychiat.* 132:1315.

Snyder, K. S., and R. P. Liberman (1981). Family assessment and intervention with schizophrenics at risk for relapse, in *New Developments in Interventions with Families of Schizophrenics, New Directions for Mental Health Services* (M. J. Goldstein, ed.). San Francisco: Jossey-Bass, vol. 12, p. 49.

Snyder, S. H. (1974). *Madness and the Brain.* New York: McGraw-Hill, ch. 2.

Sobel, D. E. (1961). Children of schizophrenic patients: Preliminary observations on early development. *Am. J. Psychiat.* 118:512.

Sommer, R. (1958). Letter writing in a mental hospital. *Am. J. Psychiat.* 115:514.

Sommer, R. (1959). Visitors to mental hospitals, a fertile field for research. *Mental Hyg.* **43**:8.

Sosowsky, L. (1974). Putting state mental hospitals out of business: The community approach to treating mental illness in San Mateo County. Unpublished paper, University of California Graduate School of Public Policy, Berkeley.

Spadoni, A. J., and J. A. Smith (1969). Milieu therapy in schizophrenia: A negative result. *Arch. Gen. Psychiat.* **20**:547.

Spitzer, R. L., J. Endicott, and E. Robins (1975). Clinical criteria for psychiatric diagnosis and DSM III. *Am. J. Psychiat.* **132**:1187.

Spitzer, R. L., and J. L. Fleiss (1974). A reanalysis of the reliability of psychiatric diagnosis. *Br. J. Psychiat.* **125**:341.

Srole, L. (1977). Geel, Belgium: The natural therapeutic community 1475–1975, in *New Trends of Psychiatry in the Community* (G. Serban, ed.). Cambridge, Mass.: Ballinger, p. 111.

Stanton, A. H., and M. S. Schwartz (1954). *The Mental Hospital: A Study of Institutional Participation in Psychiatric Illness and Treatment.* New York: Basic Books.

Starr, S. (1955). The public's ideas about mental illness. Paper presented at Annual Meeting of National Association for Mental Health, Indianapolis, November.

Steadman, H. J., and S. A. Ribner (1980). Changing perceptions of the mental health needs of inmates in local jails. *Am. J. Psychiat.* **137**: 1115.

Steffy, R. A., D. Torney, J. Hart, M. Craw, and N. Martlett (1966). An application of learning techniques to the management and rehabilitation of severely regressed chronically ill patients: Preliminary findings. Paper presented at meeting of Ontario Psychiatric Association, Ottawa, February.

Stein, L. I., and M. A. Test (eds.) (1978). *Alternative to Mental Hospital Treatment.* New York: Plenum.

Stein, L. I., and M. A. Test (1980). Alternatives to mental hospital treatment: I. Conceptual model, treatment program, and clinical evaluation. *Arch. Gen. Psychiat.* **37**:392.

Stevens, B. C. (1973). Evaluation of rehabilitation for psychotic patients in the community. *Acta. Psychiat. Scand.* **49**:169.

Stickney, P. (1980). Siting residential facilities strategies for gaining community acceptance, in *Proceedings in Overcoming Public Opposition to Community Care for the Mentally Ill* (R. C. Baron, I. D. Rutman, and B. Klaczynska, eds.). Philadelphia: Horizon House, p. 331.

Stoffelmayr, B. E., G. E. Faulkner, and W. S. Mitchell (1973). *The*

Rehabilitation of Chronic Hospitalized Patients: A Comparative Study of Operant Conditioning Methods and Social Therapy Techniques. Final report to the Scottish Home and Health Department, Edinburgh, August.

Strauss, J. S. (1975). A comprehensive approach to psychiatric diagnosis. *Am. J. Psychiat.* **132**:1193.

Strauss, J. S., and W. T. Carpenter (1974). The prediction of outcome in schizophrenia: II. Relationship between prediction and outcome variables. *Arch. Gen. Psychiat.* **31**:37.

Suchman, E. A. (1967). *Evaluative Research.* New York: Russell Sage Foundation.

Sussex, J. N. (1963). Factors influencing the emotional impact on children of an acutely psychotic mother in the home. *South. Med. J.* **56**:1245.

Sussex, J. N., F. Gassman, and S. C. Raffel (1963). Adjustment of children with psychotic mothers in the home. *Am. J. Orthopsychiat.* **33**: 849.

Swank, G. E., and D. Winer (1976). Occurrence of psychiatric disorder in a county jail population. *Am. J. Psychiat.* **133**:1331.

Swanson, R., and S. Spitzer (1970). Stigma and the psychiatric patient career. *J. Health Social Behavior* **11**:44.

Szasz, T. S. (1960). The myths of mental illness. *Am. Psychol.* **15**:113.

Talbott, J. A. (ed.) (1978a). *The Chronic Mental Patient: Problems, Solutions, and Recommendations for a Public Policy.* Washington, D.C.: APA.

Talbott, J. A. (1978b). *The Death of the Asylum.* New York: Grune and Stratton.

Talbott, J. A. (1979). Deinstitutionalization: Avoiding the disasters of the past. *Hospital Community Psychiat.* **30**:621.

Talbott, J. A. (ed.) (1980). *State Mental Hospitals: Problems and Potentials.* New York: Human Sciences Press.

Talovic, S. A., S. A. Mednick, F. Schulsinger, and I. B. H. Falloon (1983). Schizophrenia in high-risk subjects: Prognostic maternal characteristics, in *Children at Risk: A Longitudinal Perspective* (N. F. Watt, E. J. Anthony, L. C. Wynne, and J. Rolf, eds.), in preparation.

Thompson, J. W. (1980). "Burnout" in group home houseparents. *Am. J. Psychiat.* **137**:710.

Tsuang, M. T. (1978). Suicide in schizophrenics, manics, depressives, and surgical controls. *Arch. Gen. Psychiat.* **35**:133.

Turner, J. E. C., and W. J. Tenboor (1978). The NIMH Community Support Program: Pilot approach to needed social reform. *Schizophrenia Bull.* **4**:319.

Ullmann, L. P., and L. Gurel (1964). Size, staffing and psychiatric effectiveness. *Arch. Gen. Psychiat.* 11:360.

Ullmann, L. P., and L. Krasner (1975). *A Psychological Approach to Abnormal Behavior*, 2nd ed. Englewood Cliffs, N.J.: Prentice-Hall.

U.S. Congress (1975). Amendment to Community Mental Health Centers Act, Title III, Public Law 94-63.

Van Putten, T. (1978). Drug refusal in schizophrenia: Causes and prescribing hints. *Hospital Community Psychiat.* 29:110.

Van Putten, T. (1973). Milieu therapy: Contraindications? *Arch. Gen. Psychiat.* 29:640.

Van Putten, T. (1974). Why do schizophrenic patients refuse to take their drugs? *Arch. Gen. Psychiat.* 31:67.

Van Putten, T., and J. E. Spar (1979). The board-and-care home: Does it deserve a bad press? *Hospital Community Psychiat.* 30:461.

Vaughn, C. E., and J. P. Leff (1976). The influence of family and social factors on the course of psychiatric illness: A comparison of schizophrenic with depressed neurotic patients. *Br. J. psychiat.* 129:123.

Venables, P. H., and J. F. Wing (1962). Level of arousal and the subclassification of schizophrenia. *Arch. Gen. Psychiat.* 7:114.

Wallace, C. J., C. J. Nelson, R. P. Liberman, R. A. Attchison, D. Lukoff, J. P. Elder, and C. Ferris (1980). A review and critique of social skills and training with schizophrenic patients. *Schizophrenia Bull.* 6:42.

Ward, C. H., A. T. Beck, M. Mendelson, J. E. Mock, and J. K. Erbaugh (1962). The psychiatric nomenclature. *Arch. Gen. Psychiat.* 7:198.

Washburn, S., M. Vannicelli, R. Longabaugh, and B. J. Scheff (1976). A controlled comparison of psychiatric day treatment and inpatient hospitalization. *J. Consult. Clin. Psychol.* 44:665.

Waters, M., and J. Northover (1965). Rehabilitated long-stay schizophrenics in the community. *Br. J. Psychiat.* 111:258.

Watson, C. G., and R. F. Maddigan (1972). The effects of a paid-work program on chronic and short-term patients. *Hospital Community Psychiat.* 23:376.

Watts, F. N., and D. H. Bennett (1977). Previous occupational stability as a predictor of employment after psychiatric rehabilitation. *Psychological Med.* 7:709.

Weinberger, D. R., L. B. Bigelow, J. E. Kleinman, S. T. Klein, J. E. Rosenblatt, and R. J. Wyatt (1980a). Cerebral ventricular enlargement in chronic schizophrenia: An association with poor response to treatment. *Arch. Gen. Psychiat.* 37:11.

Weinberger, D. R., E. Cannon-Spoor, S. G. Potkin, and R. J. Wyatt (1980b). Poor premorbid adjustment and CT scan abnormalities in chronic schizophrenia. *Am. J. Psychiat.* 137:1410.

Weinman, B., and R. J. Kleiner (1978). The impact of community living and community member intervention on the adjustment of the chronic psychotic patient, in *Alternatives to Mental Hospital Treatment* (L. I. Stein and M. A. Test, eds.). New York: Plenum, p. 139.

Weisbrod, B. A., M. A. Test, and L. I. Stein (1980). Alternative to mental hospital treatment: II. Economic benefit-cost analysis. *Arch. Gen. Psychiat.* 37:400.

Weisman, G., A. Feirstein, and C. Thomas (1969). Three-day hospitalization: A model for intensive intervention. *Arch. Gen. Psychiat.* 21:620.

Weissman, M. M. (1975). An assessment of social adjustment: A review of techniques. *Arch. Gen. Psychiat.* 33:357.

Weissman, M. M., B. A. Prusoff, W. D. Thompson, P. S. Harding, and J. K. Myers (1978). Social adjustment by self-report in a community sample and in psychiatric outpatients. *J. Nerv. Mental Dis.* 166:317.

Whatley, C. (1958). Social attitudes toward discharged mental patients. *Social Problems* 6:313.

White, H. S. (1981). Managing the difficult patient in the community residence, in *Issues in Community Residential Care, New Directions in Mental Health Services* (R. D. Budson, ed.). San Francisco: Jossey-Bass, vol. 11, p. 517.

Whitely, J. S. (1970). The response of psychopaths to a therapeutic community. *Br. J. Psychiat.* 116:517.

Wilcox, D. R. C. (1965). Do psychiatric outpatients take their drugs? *Br. Med. J.* 2:790.

Wilder, J. F., G. Levin, and I. Zwerling (1966). A two-year follow-up evaluation of acute psychotic patients treated in a day hospital. *Am. J. Psychiat.* 122:1095.

Wilmer, H. A. (1958). *Social Psychiatry in Action.* Springfield, Ill.: Charles C Thomas.

Wilson, J. D., and M. D. Enoch (1967). Estimation of drug rejection by schizophrenic inpatients with analysis of clinical factors. *Br. J. Psychiat.* 113:209.

Wing, J. K. (1965). Long-stay schizophrenic patients and results of rehabilitation, in *Psychiatric Hospital Care* (H. Freeman, ed.). London: Bailliere.

Wing, J. K. (1978). Planning and evaluating services for chronically handicapped psychiatric patients in the United Kingdom, in *Alternatives to Mental Hospital Treatment* (L. I. Stein and M. A. Test, eds.). New York: Plenum, p. 227.

Wing, J. K. (ed.) (1982). Long-term community care: Experience in a London borough. *Psychol. Med.* monograph suppl. 2.

Wing, J. K., and G. W. Brown (1970). *Institutionalism and Schizo-*

phrenia: A Comparative Study of Three Mental Hospitals. Cambridge: Cambridge University Press.

Wing, J. K., J. E. Cooper, and N. Sartorius (1974). *Measurement and Classification of Psychiatric Symptoms.* Cambridge: Cambridge University Press.

Wing, J. K., E. Monck, G. W. Brown, and G. M. Carstairs (1964). Morbidity in the community of schizophrenic patients discharged from London mental hospitals in 1959. *Br. J. Psychiat.* 110:10.

Wing, L. W., J. K. Wing, B. C. Stevens, and A. Hailey (1972). An epidemiological and experimental evaluation of industrial rehabilitation of chronic psychotic patients in the community, in *Evaluating a Community Psychiatric Service: The Camberwell Register 1964–71* (J. K. Wing and A. Hailey, eds.). London: Oxford University Press, ch. 19.

Wise, T. N., and R. M. Berlin (1981). Burnout: Stresses in consultation-liaison psychiatry. *Psychosomatics* 22:744.

Wolkon, G. H., M. Karmen, and H. T. Tanaka (1971). Evaluation of social rehabilitation program for recently released psychiatric patients. *Community Mental Health J.* 7:312.

Wolpert, J., M. Dear, and R. Crawford (1974). Mental health satellite facilities in the community. Paper presented at NIMH Center for Studies of Metropolitan Problems, Seminar Series, Rockville, Md., January.

World Health Organization (1973). Report of the International Pilot Study of Schizophrenia. Geneva: WHO, vol. 1.

Wynne, L. C., I. M. Ryckoff, J. Day, and S. I. Hirsch (1958). Pseudo-mutuality in the family relations of schizophrenics. *Psychiatry* 21:205.

Yarrow, M., C. Schwartz, H. Murphy, and L. Deasy (1955a). The psychological meaning of mental illness in the family. *J. Social Issues* 11:12.

Yarrow, M., J. Clausen, and P. Robbins (1955b). The social meaning of mental illness. *J. Social Issues* 11:33.

Zitrin, A. A., S. Hardesty, E. I. Burdock, and A. K. Drossman (1976). Crime and violence among mental patients. *Am. J. Psychiat.* 133:142.

Zolik, E. S., E. M. Lantz, and R. Sommers (1968). Hospital return rates and pre-release referrals. *Arch. Gen. Psychiat.* 18:712.

Name Index

Subject Index